Economic Conditions and
Electoral Outcomes:
The United States and Western Europe

Economic Conditions and Electoral Outcomes: The United States and Western Europe

Heinz Eulau
and
Michael S. Lewis-Beck
Editors

Agathon Press, Inc.
New York

Library of Congress Cataloging-in-Publication Data

Main entry under title:

Economic conditions and electoral outcomes.

   "Originally published in Political Behavior,
volume 6, number 3 and 4, 1984 and volume 7, number 1,
1985"--Verso t.p.
   Bibliography: p.
   Includes index.
   "Papers ... originally presented at the Shambaugh
Conference on Economic Conditions and Electoral Outcomes
sponsored by the Department of Political Science of the
University of Iowa and held there in March 1984"--Pref.
   1. Elections--Europe--Congresses.   2. Elections
--United States--Congresses.   3. Europe--Economic
conditions--1945-   --Public opinion--Congresses.
4. United States--Economic conditions--1945-   --Public
opinion--Congresses.   5. Public opinion--Europe--
Congresses.   6. Public opinion--United States--
Congresses.   I. Eulau, Heinz, 1915-   . II. Lewis-
Beck, Michael S. III. Shambaugh Conference on Economic
Conditions and Electoral Outcomes (1984 : University of
Iowa)   IV. University of Iowa. Dept. of Political
Science.
JN94.A956E26 1985   320.94   85-15083
ISBN 0-87586-071-0
ISBN 0-87586-072-9 (pbk)

Printed in the United States of America

Contents

Preface

The papers in this volume were originally presented at the Shambaugh Conference on Economic Conditions and Electoral Outcomes, sponsored by the Department of Political Science of the University of Iowa and held there in March, 1984. Michael S. Lewis-Beck was the principal organizer of the conference, and Heinz Eulau served as the editor of the papers in *Political Behavior*, a journal published by Agathon Press, where they subsequently appeared. The conference was made possible by funds placed at the disposal of the Iowa Department of Political Science in memory of Professor Benjamin F. Shambaugh, who was head of the department from 1900 to 1940, and who served as president of the American Political Science Association. In recognition of the value of the Shambaugh fund for furthering scholarly exchange, any royalties which may accrue from this volume will be donated to the fund.

The Shambaugh memorial fund has permitted the Department of Political Science at Iowa to sponsor a series of lectures and conferences. Shambaugh lectures have been given by such distinguished political scientists as Karl Deutsch, Charles S. Hyneman, Dayton D. McKean, Arnold Rogow, Sheldon Wolin, and Herman Finer. Since the adoption of the conference format, Shambaugh research conferences producing significant publications have been held on the following subjects: frontiers of judicial research (1967), comparative legislative behavior research (1969), legislatures in developing countries (1971), teaching political science (1974), the role of European parliaments in managing social conflict (1977), mathematics in political science instruction (1977), the biological bases of political behavior (1980), the place of political theory in political science (1981), rural development in less-developed countries (1981), political science at the University of Iowa (1982), and, most recently, the impact of economic conditions on electoral outcomes (1984).

There is some risk in bringing together, in a single volume, a set of papers that more resembles a potpourri than a symphony; but the risk is not any greater than that involved in assembling a variety of scholars in a conference. As any veteran conference participant knows, no body of instructions to paper givers, no matter how well specified, is ever sufficient to orchestrate the multiplicity of voices that are heard, precisely because it is the purpose of a conference to allow each speaker to be heard on his or her own terms. In fact, the charm of a good scholarly conference is when it manages to steer a middle course between a Gulag Archipelago, where each person may think what he or she wishes but may not say it, and a Tower of Babel, in which each person can say what he or she wishes in some mother tongue but nobody does any thinking. On the whole, we believe that the papers here assembled are more complementary than conflictual, more concordant than discordant. To the reader who still feels that a volume like this is necessarily a grab-bag of assorted candies, we can only say that we like both the grab-bag and the candies, and that we hope most readers will do likewise.

Heinz Eulau
Michael S. Lewis-Beck

INTRODUCTION

Economic Conditions and Electoral Behavior in Transnational Perspective

Michael S. Lewis-Beck
Department of Political Science, University of Iowa

Heinz Eulau
Department of Political Science, Stanford University

Does economics influence elections? How does such influence work? Under what conditions is it more or less likely to occur? These are the basic questions addressed in the chapters of this volume. They appear to be simple questions, but answering them is difficult. And they may appear to be trivial questions to those who contend that elections in the western democracies are at best placebos that disguise the "real" dynamics of power in societies still mostly characterized by the capitalist mode of production, even if the economy is directed by government. This is an argument we do not propose to address. We do believe that free, popular elections matter, and that they make a difference precisely because, at periodic intervals, they set the limits or constraints within which capitalist as well as anticapitalist elites pursue their economic and political goals. To oppose the voice of the people to the people's manipulation by elites, it seems to us, creates an unnecessary dualism. This dualism is not useful because it cannot come to grips with the question of how and why popular electorates respond as they do to more or less elite-managed economies, and how and why elites in turn "take account of" or are "responsive to" whatever messages they may receive from the electorate.

In this brief introduction, we propose to do two things. First, we sketch the state of knowledge about the relationship between economic conditions and electoral behavior up to about early 1984 when the papers brought together here were first prepared; and we identify some problems at the frontiers of research that may have received illumination in these papers.

1

The papers here and other research on the interpenetration of economics and politics are exercises in both theory and method addressed to specialists in the field of electoral research. We hope that scholars in the broader field of comparative politics will find them of interest and possible use. We shall therefore raise, second, some questions about the continuity of cross-national and trans-national comparative research, if only to persuade those who cling to an essentially idiographic approach in comparative politics that there can surely be a "middle road" between systematic-nomothetic and descriptive-idiographic studies in the field of comparative politics.

I.

The first question, necessarily, is whether there actually exists a relationship between economic conditions and vote choice in Western democracies. An immediate response, drawing on common sense, is likely and quickly to be, "yes, obviously." A glance at recent election results from around the world – Britain in 1979, France in 1981, Germany and Italy in 1983, and the United States in 1984 – helps to convince one of the correctness of this intuition, that the electorate punishes governments for poor economic performance. This conventional wisdom was initially confirmed in two pioneering studies by Goodhart and Bhansali (1970) for Britain, and by Kramer (1971) for the United States. In the British investigation, the finding was that the level of unemployment and the rate of inflation, significantly influenced the popularity of the government as measured in national public opinion polls (Goodhart and Bhansali, 1970, p. 61). In the American study, the conclusion was that improved macroeconomic conditions, in particular rising real income, generated important vote increases for the president's party in congressional elections (Kramer, 1971, pp. 140–41). However, these positive and plausible results were soon challenged by research indicating that no relationship existed between economic circumstances and electoral outcomes.

In regard to Britain, the work of Goodhart and Bhansali was questioned by Frey and Garbers (1971) and then by Miller and Mackie (1973). Indeed, Frey and Garbers (1971, p. 320) flatly concluded that "economic variables do not have any permanent effect on the popularity lead of the government in Britain." In the United States, a study by Stigler (1973), carefully crafted and written by an economist, was especially important. Stigler took direct aim at Kramer, arguing forcefully, on grounds of theory and data, that voters did not react to changing economic conditions. Following suit, Stimson (1976) claimed that the American president's popularity was not determined by the state of the economy but rather simply followed regular cycles over time. These sophisticated and widely influential papers were the occasion for the subsequent decade's work, at least in these two countries, laying heavy emphasis on refutation of the null hypothesis. Looking at the fresh batch of studies in this volume but also elsewhere, the reader holding the conventional view should find some comfort because they all agree that the economy affects voting behavior, regardless of the Western democracy under investigation. This step forward along the path of cumulative research, while perhaps small, does allow us to move on to a set of questions with less obvious answers.

How does the economic influence work? The hypothesis dominating the literature has it that economically dissatisfied citizens tend to vote against the incumbent party (or parties). Most of the research, from either aggregate level time series or individual level survey data, is compatible with this generalization. However, for more specific hypothesis on the linking mechanisms, the time series work is not much help. Irrespective of country, there is no agreement across the time series studies on which economic variables — income, unemployment, inflation — are operating. Further, agreement is lacking as to how these variables should be measured, e.g., levels versus rates. And, these studies differ over the lag structure of the responses, e.g., $t - 1$, $t - 2$, or a distributed lag. Also, there is no consensus on the period of aggregation — monthly, quarterly, yearly.

The French case illustrates well these limitations of the aggregate time series analyses. In studying the popularity of the prime minister (quarterly data, 1961–1977), Lafay (1977) found that the statistically significant determinants were the (logged) real-salaries index lagged one quarter, the (logged) change in prices from quarter to quarter, and the (logged) number of unsatisfied employment requests lagged four quarters. By way of contrast, Lewis-Beck (1980), analyzing monthly data from 1960 to 1978, concluded that the inflation rate and the unemployment level, both measured at a lag of two months, significantly influenced the popularity of the prime minister and the president. With yet another version, Hibbs and Vasilatos (1981), looking at quarterly data from 1969 to 1978, judged economic impact on presidential popularity to derive just from the real personal disposable income growth rate. The discordant findings across these studies find parallels in the aggregate time series work on other nations. Finally, since these time series efforts utilize observations from nations rather than from individuals, they alone cannot tell us whether voters are responding to economics at all. Thus, to avoid the ecological fallacy, we must turn to data on individuals. In this endeavor, survey research has been most frequently relied upon.

Although the picture is changing, the great bulk of the survey work is on the American case (really begun by Fiorina, 1978; two European examples are Lewis-Beck, 1983; Rattinger, 1981). In this literature, largely through the influence of Kinder and Kiewiet (1979), the economic variables have come to be divided into two categories: personal (pocketbook) and collective (socio-tropic). The personal items tap how respondents evaluate their own eco-nomic circumstances, e.g., the well-known CPS-SRC question, "Would you say that you (and your family) are better off or worse off financially than you were a year ago, or about the same?" The collective items tap how respondents evaluate the economic circumstances of the nation, e.g., "Would you say that at the present time business conditions are better or worse than they were a year ago, or about the same?" With regard to findings, the consensus is that collective economic evaluations do influence the vote. For example, citizens who see the nation in an economic downturn are more likely to declare a vote against the president's party. There is little consensus, though, on the effects of personal economic evaluations. Several studies have reported that perceived individual financial hardship translates only faintly, if at all, into a vote shift. Still, many researchers are reluctant to abandon the pocketbook voter hypothesis, which seems to make such good sense. This dilemma (a good hypothesis facing resistant data) has led to more consideration of measurement issues, e.g., how are personal economic circumstances best assessed? Also, it has prompted a more thoughtful speci-fication of the conditions under which the pocketbook hypothesis might be confirmed.

Clearly, economic hard times can cause a voter to cast a ballot against the government. Nevertheless, this connection is far from automatic. Under what conditions is it more likely to occur? The most obvious relevant condi-tion is the type of election. For instance, in American presidential elections, the association between economics and the vote is decidedly greater than in legislative elections. (We would expect this to be true as well in France, although this proposition has never been tested). The U.S. president, be-cause of the powers and prestige of his office, appears more likely to be held responsible for economic events, and punished or blamed accordingly. A general implication is that, within any election, the attribution of economic responsibility can strengthen or dampen economic voting. Indeed, when such an interaction variable is taken into account, the pocketbook voter hypothesis is unambiguously sustained (see Feldman, 1982; Kinder and Me-bane, 1983). That is to say, when citizens hold government to be responsible for their personal economic hardship, they act in their self-interest by voting against the incumbent. Thus, attribution of responsibility emerges as a key condition in joining economic grievance to political preference. Further, this variable is involved in the explanation of some transnational differences in economic voting.

Economic voting is a general phenomenon in Western democracies, as this research indicates. Still, we can count on certain differences across nations, simply because of institutional variations. An important one is the degree of governmental responsibility for economic management. While all the nations under study are essentially capitalist, they exhibit considerable variation in government direction of economic activity, with Britain or Norway at one end of the continuum and the United States at the other. In the nations with more government economic involvement, one could anticipate a stronger association between economics and the vote, since their citizens would be more likely to attribute economic responsibility to government. The scanty amount of microlevel analysis available suggests this is the case. For example, the simple correlations between economic conditions and vote choice are generally stronger in French than in American surveys (Lewis-Beck, 1983).

This discussion of the relative strength of the relationship brings us to the next issue. Ignoring transnational differences, how important, generally speaking, are economic conditions in determining the vote? The aggregate time series regression models from the various countries, all with very high R-squared values, imply they are extremely important. However, one problem with these models is that they are invariably misspecified, which gives an upward bias to the economic effects. They usually contain few, if any, independent variables that are noneconomic. The individual level survey data permit better specified voting models. In particular, the surveys make it possible to control on partisan or ideological identification. When these and other control variables are applied in single-equation additive models, what can we conclude about economic influences on the vote? Basically, collective economic variables regularly exhibit statistical significance at conventional levels, while personal economic variables may or may not.

Beyond this broad conclusion, it is difficult to generalize. Little systematic attention has been paid to the importance, for the individual voter, of economic variables relative to other independent variables. However, a glance at the coefficients reported in the research literature reveals that economic issues do not exercise the impact of long-term forces such as partisan or ideological identification. Somewhat more attention has been paid to the importance, for the individual voter, of economic variables relative to other independent variables. However, a glance at the coefficients reported in the research literature reveals that economic issues do not exercise the impact of long-term forces such as partisan or ideological identification. Somewhat more attention has been given to the importance, for the national election outcome, of individual level economic votes. For instance, Kiewiet (1983, pp. 118–24) indicates, on the basis of a simulation from his probit estimates, that bad economic times could cost an incumbent American presidential candidate several percentage points in the total vote, easily enough to affect the outcome of a close race.

The foregoing outline of what we know about economic voting in Western democracies receives elaboration in these papers. They also enlighten us in areas about which little is known. These areas of comparative ignorance include the following: (1) the transnational differences in economic voting; (2) the individual mechanics linking economics and voting; (3) the importance of economic variables relative to other independent variables operating on the voter; (4) the proper place of time series and survey approaches. Productive investigation in each of these areas requires a different analytic emphasis; respectively, hypothesis formation, data gathering, causal modeling, and forecasting. Below, we look at unresolved questions within each area, and offer a strategy for their resolution.

Almost nothing is known about transnational differences in economic voting. Even hypotheses are hard to come by. Here are some possibilities for exploration:

1. The greater the country's dependency on the international economy, the less economic voting.
2. The more the government is actually involved in directing the national economy, the more economic voting.
3. The more the culture emphasizes economic individualism, the less pocketbook voting.
4. In multiparty systems, economic voting may be based on party policies as well as incumbency status. (The implication is that the dependent variable of vote choice could be usefully treated as a dimension on a left-right continuum as well as an incumbency-opposition dichotomy.)
5. As the number of incumbent parties increases, economic voting for the opposition decreases (because economic dissatisfaction might be expressed by switching to another party within the incumbent coalition).

The second area needing more work concerns the specifics of the links between economic conditions and the vote decision. A number of valuable hypotheses have already been formulated. What is scarce are the survey data, especially from Western Europe, to test them. The issues below will be brought closer to resolution after more data gathering (Lewis-Beck is currently exploring some of these questions through the analysis of American and Western European survey data):

1. Which of the economic variables – income, inflation, unemployment – have the most impact?
2. Are economic evaluations prospective or retrospective?
3. Are economic evaluations cognitive or affective?
4. What is the voter's economic memory?

5. Do voters take the economic circumstances of others important to them, e.g., fellow workers or neighbors, into account?
6. Under what conditions does the voter assign economic responsibility to elected officials?

The next area requiring more attention is assessment of the relative importance of economic variables in determining the vote. It is necessary to move from the emphasis on statistical significance in simple single-equation models to the estimation of effects in properly specified multiequation voting models. (Generally, simultaneous-equation models are becoming plentiful for the United States; Fiorina, 1981, pp. 176–90; Jackson, 1975; Markus and Converse, 1979; Page and Jones, 1979). In this way, we begin to evaluate the importance of economics compared to long-term forces such as partisan or ideological identification, and to short-term noneconomic issues. (On the anchoring role of ideological identification in Western Europe, see Inglehart and Klingemann, 1976; Lewis-Beck, 1983, 1984). This evaluation will help define the ultimate standing of economic voting in the literature on electoral politics. To the extent that it represents something more fundamental than another set of transitory issues, its importance is heightened.

The last area for resolution is the persistent gap between the time series and the survey approaches. Of the many investigators of economic voting, few have practiced both. Further, the isolated efforts to reconcile findings from the two levels have been unsuccessful. In our view, if the research focus is on how economic conditions influence the vote choice, then one should study individuals (through cross-sectional surveys, panel surveys, even experiments). What place is left to time series analysis? Forecasting. As the individual level survey analyses have now demonstrated, the relationship observed in the aggregated time series models is not entirely the product of an ecological fallacy. However, the aggregate level data are compatible with a very large number of theories about the individual vote decision. Therefore, time series analysts must necessarily be guided by the issue of which model forecasts election outcomes more accurately. This forecasting emphasis draws attention to specific features of a model:

1. The time period of the lags of the independent variables. (True forecasts are possible only if measures on the independent variables are available in advance of the election.)
2. The parsimonious inclusion of independent variables. (Given the limited number of time series observations available, independent variables must be entered judiciously, in order not to exhaust the degrees of freedom.)
3. The goodness-of-fit. (Given the forecasting goal, unusual attention

ought to be paid to measures like the R-squared and the standard error of estimate of the dependent variables.)

Recent work on aggregate time series forecasting of American presidential and congressional election outcomes suggests this is a fruitful strategy, one which could be applied in the countries under study (Lewis-Beck and Rice, 1984a,b). These models generated fairly successful forecasts of the 1984 races (Lewis-Beck, 1985a). Further, a similar modeling effort promises interesting results for the French legislative elections of 1986 (Lewis-Beck, 1985b). Hence, time series approaches, which began the whole enterprise, would seem to have a secure, albeit restricted, position in the study of economic voting.

II.

The studies reported in this volume are "single country" studies involving an implicit rather than explicit mode of comparison. From a broad methodological perspective, therefore, they would appear to be something of a throwback to the original genre of "comparative" studies that relied on inference from simple juxtaposition of two or more units (countries, states, cities, etc.) That this genre as sole mode of comparison is of highly doubtful validity has been asserted for more than twenty years now by students relying primarily on individual-level data (Eulau, 1962; Verba, 1971), and by those relying primarily on aggregate data (Lipset, 1959; Deutsch, 1961) who proposed and carried out cross-unit (cross-national, cross-state, cross-city, etc.) statistical research. This position, in turn, has not gone unchallenged and recently called forth, in a forceful yet accommodating manner, a persuasive defense by one of its methodologically most sophisticated practitioners. As Jackman (1985) points out, cross-unit and especially cross-national research faces all kinds of problems — theoretical, methodological and empirical; but these problems are not insurmountable if appropriate and adequate assumptions are made and, in particular, if it is conceded that analyses in the comparative-statistical genre require auxiliary theoretical information as well as ancillary historical and/or contextual knowledge in order to become interpretable for the purpose of comparative inference.

What, then, gives scientific warrant to the single-country analyses represented in this volume? If, as Jackman (1985, p. 179) concludes, the cross-unit (and especially the cross-national) statistical method "is only one of several methods in comparative politics, and for some substantive problems . . . is not necessarily an appropriate one," where do these trans-national "country studies" of the relationship between economic conditions and electoral behavior "fit in?" There are a number of suggestions that can be made in their defense, if "defense" is necessary.

In the first place, the empirical domain here covered is sufficiently limited so that the studies are almost invariably guided by the same or similar — at times quite explicit, at times more implicit — theoretical propositions. And this is made possible by the fact that the dependent variable, vote choice, is conceptually less ambiguous and operationally less unstable than the dependent variables one encounters in most other empirical domains of comparative politics. In other words, though measurements may differ somewhat from country to country, they are "direct" so that what is being measured has pretty much the same meaning across the several countries. Rather than having to move from concept to measurement (especially from often vague "umbrella concepts" like "political development," etc.), the voting studies can move from measurement to concept; and the concepts explicitly or implicitly defined and used (like unemployment, inflation, income, or vote) provide a common theoretical frame of reference that is *transnationally* interpretable. With conceptual equivalence relatively and reasonably assured, it would seem that, some operational differences notwithstanding, comparative inferences can be legitimately made. What we can call transnational studies, therefore, differ from the simply juxtaposed national studies in permitting more genuine comparison, even though they may not approximate as much as we would like the requirements of cross-national research.

Second, critics of the early cross-national statistical studies may well have been correct in charging that many of the operational measures used were sometimes so disparate (even if conceptual equivalence was asserted) or unreliable (especially as surrogate variables) that this mode of comparison, if not false, was premature. Indeed, who would trust the educational or demographic statistics reported from, say, countries like Afghanistan or Zaire as against those reported from Austria or Sweden, and their use in the same regression equation? In general, the data reported from the Western democracies are probably as reliable as they can be and commensurate, but as the studies reported in this volume indicate, there still remain considerable differences as to both the original units of aggregation (possibly cities, counties, provinces, census areas, etc.) and the time periods over which aggregation occurs (months, quarters, years, etc.). Cross-national research, based on the nation as the unit of comparison, can often not take account or does not take account of the mechanisms or processes of aggregation that undoubtedly shape the bottom figures. National statistics may thus disguise considerable within-unit variations and variances that are economically or politically significant, and that probably should be taken into account. The transnational studies reported here show that there are indeed differences in the reporting of the basic data and in their statistical measurement that affect both the interpretation of the data and whatever transnational inferences can be made. Put somewhat differently, there are clearly within-country variations that should be specified and, ultimately, be entered into whatever equations are estimated in both transnational and cross-national research. In this respect, then, the transnational comparisons as those made possible by the studies included in this book are both necessary and desirable complements or supplements of cross-national research.

Something should be said in this connection about transnational survey research. As we mentioned earlier, many of the problems involved in the relationship between economic conditions, voting behavior and electoral outcomes may well require for solution recourse to individual-level data obtained through polling of the electorate. Unfortunately, the survey questions asked by national polling organizations in different countries are often not commensurate. (Even within the United States, for instance, it is the exception rather than the rule when state polling organizations ask exactly the same questions.) But this is only the beginning of the difficulties in using survey data in cross-national or trans-national comparative analysis. In general, what studies have been done (the classical study is Almond and Verba, 1963) have compared the political behavior of voters *within* nations rather than the voting behavior of electorates *between* nations. In other words, at the national level, at least, survey data have not been used to close what one of us called the "micro-macro gap" (Eulau, 1971, 1977).

Last, but not least, there has been the charge that cross-national statistical studies, even if theoretically sophisticated, are insufficiently "contextual." What this translates into is, in effect, the charge that scholars doing cross-national research, and especially those whose work circles the globe's five major continents and their increasingly numerous and diverse countries, do not know what they are talking about. Again, there is an element of truth in this charge, but only an element. It is certainly not warranted to conclude from this charge that only single-country or perhaps a handful of "comparable" countries studies are scientifically viable. Whatever merits such studies may have, the desirability of large-scale cross-national research remains. In some respects, therefore, the "single-country studies" included in this volume constitute something of a "middle road." On the one hand, they can be seen as antecedent or supplemental to cross-national investigations in that they are enlightened by relatively similar measurements and theoretical points of departure. On the other hand, they are enlightened by historical-contextual knowledge that is in the possession of the investigators who are either scholars resident in the countries about which they write or non-resident ("foreign") specialists on a given country. Needless to say, the format of research papers, limited as they are in available space, does not permit these investigators to tell all they know about the historical-contextual detail behind or implicit in their analyses, though more of this enters their work than enters the work of cross-national researchers dealing with many countries. If it is correct that comparative-statistical analysis cannot do without ancillary or supportive information, it may be said that one might have more "trust" in transnational than cross-national studies, at least at this stage of research development.

Of course, this does not let either transnational or cross-national studies off the historical-contextual hook. The task ahead for both types of study is, obviously, to treat historical-developmental periods as well as contextual-environmental conditions as variables rather than constants. In this regard, perhaps, the study of comparative politics will come full circle, though at a higher plane of the research spiral: clearly, there is room for historical and contextual typologies as one finds them in the older and newer versions of what was once called "comparative government" and later "comparative politics." But there would be a difference: the older typologies (like "democracies" vs. "autocracies," or "modern" vs. "traditional" societies, etc.), even if not altogether empirically empty, came off a scholar's intuitive cuff; any new typologies of "whole" units would have to take account of the large number of theory-driven and data-supported researches that, like those reported in this volume, have been conducted in our time. There will probably always be in the social sciences a need for such comprehensive approaches to comparative analysis. The problem remains to enter indicators of historical and contextual detail into the cross-unit statistical equations; to do so without undue reliance on dummy variables whose values escape meaningful interpretation; and to do so regardless of whether the research is conducted within or between different units of analysis. And one should always keep in mind that today's research is not the end of the line in scientific endeavor but at best a prolegomenon to the research of tomorrow.

REFERENCES

Almond, Gabriel A., and Verba, Sidney (1963). *The Civic Culture: Political Attitudes and Democracy in Five Nations*. Princeton: Princeton University Press.

Deutsch, Karl W. (1961). Social mobilization and political development. *American Political Science Review* 55:493–514.

Eulau, Heinz (1962). Comparative political analysis. *Midwest Journal of Political Science* 6:397–407.

Eulau, Heinz (1971). The legislative system and after: on closing the micro-macro gap. In Oliver Walter (ed.), *Political Scientists at Work*. Belmont, CA: Duxbury Press.

Eulau, Heinz (1977). Multilevel methods in comparative politics. *American Behavioral Scientist* 21:39–62.

Feldman, Stanley (1982). Economic self-interest and political behavior. *American Journal of Political Science* 26:446–466.

Fiorina, Morris P. (1978). Economic retrospective voting in American elections. *American Journal of Political Science* 22:426–443.

Fiorina, Morris P. (1981). *Retrospective Voting in American National Elections.* New Haven: Yale University Press.

Frey, Bruno D., and Garbers, Hermann (1971). Politico-econometrics — on estimation in political economy. *Political Studies* 19:316–320.

Goodhart, C.A.E., and Bhansali, R. J. (1970). Political economy. *Political Studies* 18:43–106.

Hibbs, Douglas, A., Jr., and Vasilatos, Nicholas (1981). Economics and politics in France: economic performance and political support for Presidents Pompidou and Giscard d'Estaing. *European Journal of Political Research* 9:133–145.

Inglehart, Ronald, and Klingemann, Hans (1976). Party identification, ideological preference and the left-right dimension among western mass publics. In Ian Budge, Ivor Crewe, and Dennis Fairie (eds.), *Party Identification and Beyond.* London: Wiley.

Jackman, Robert W. (1985). Cross-national statistical research and the study of comparative politics. *American Journal of Political Science* 29:161–182.

Jackson, John (1975). Issues, party choices and presidential votes. *American Journal of Political Science* 19:161–185.

Kiewiet, D. Roderick (1983). *Macroeconomics and Micropolitics: The Electoral Effects of Economic Issues.* Chicago: University of Chicago Press.

Kinder, Donald R., and Kiewiet, D. Roderick (1979). Economic discontent and political behavior: the role of personal grievances and collective economic judgments in congressional voting. *American Journal of Political Science* 23:495–527.

Kramer, Gerald (1971). Short-term fluctuations in U.S. voting behavior, 1896–1964. *American Political Science Review* 65:131–143.

Lafay, Jean-Dominique (1977). Les consequences electorales de la conjoncture economique: essais de prevision chiffree pour Mars 1978. *Vie Et Sciences Economiques* 75:1–7.

Lewis-Beck, Michael S. (1980). Economic conditions and executive popularity: the French experience. *American Journal of Political Science* 24:306–323.

Lewis-Beck, Michael S. (1983). Economics and the French voter: a microanalysis. *Public Opinion Quarterly* 47:347–360.

Lewis-Beck, Michael S. (1984). France: the stalled electorate. In Russell J. Dalton, Scott Flanagan, and Paul Beck (eds.), *Electoral Change in Advanced Industrial Democracies: Realignment or Dealignment?* Princeton: Princeton University Press.

Lewis-Beck, Michael S. (1985a). Election forecasts in 1984: how accurate were they? *PS* 18:53–62.

Lewis-Beck, Michael S. (1985b). A forecasting model for French legislative elections (with an application to 1986). Unpublished manuscript.

Lewis-Beck, Michael S., and Rice, Tom W. (1984a). Forecasting presidential elections: a comparison of naive models. *Political Behavior* 6:9–21.

Lewis-Beck, Michael S., and Rice, Tom W. (1984b). Forecasting U.S. House elections. *Legislative Studies Quarterly* 9:475–486.

Lipset, Seymour Martin (1959). Some social requisites of democracy: economic development and political legitimacy. *American Political Science Review* 53:69–105.

Markus, Gregory, and Converse, Philip (1979). A dynamic simultaneous equation model of electoral choice. *American Political Science Review* 73:1055–1070.

Miller, W. L., and Mackie, M. (1973). The electoral cycle and the asymmetry of government and opposition popularity: an alternative model of the relationship between economic conditions and political popularity. *Political Studies* 21:263–279.

Page, Benjamin, and Jones, Calvin (1979). Reciprocal effects of policy preferences, party loyalties, and the vote. *American Political Science Review* 73:1071–1089.

Rattinger, Hans (1981). Unemployment and the 1976 election in Germany: some findings at the aggregate and the individual level of analysis. In D. A. Hibbs, Jr., and J. Fassbender (eds.), *Contemporary Political Economy*. New York: North-Holland.

Stigler, George J. (1973). General economic conditions and national elections. *American Economic Review* 63:160–167.

Stimson, James A. (1976). Public support for American presidents: a cyclical model. *Public Opinion Quarterly* 40:1–21.

Verba, Sidney (1971). Cross-national survey research: the problem of credibility. In Ivan Vallier (ed.), *Comparative Methods in Sociology*. Berkeley: University of California Press.

CHAPTER 1

Public Attitudes Toward Economic Conditions and Their Impact on Government Behavior

Friedrich Schneider

Institute of Economics, Aarhus University, Denmark *

For almost 15 years now public attitudes toward economic conditions and their impact on government behavior have been analyzed by economists and political scientists. Most of the studies deal with the behavior of two actors, the voters and the government, in representative democracies.[1] In these studies, it is assumed that voters support the party (governing or in opposition) that meets most closely their own preferences with its political actions and program, and that government tries to win the next election with the final purpose of putting its own selfish (ideological) goals into practice.

The government's behavior can be analyzed by assuming that it maximizes its own utility subject to various constraints.[2] The government's utility consists in the possibility of carrying out its ideological program. The most important constraint the government faces is a political one. A government

---

*This paper was written while the author was at GSIA, Carnegie-Mellon University.

may stay in power *only* if it is reelected. There are also important economic constraints that determine how policy instruments affect the economy, as well as the budget and legal constraints. Government is also restricted in its activity by administrative constraints, i.e., by the public administration, which resists structural changes in expenditure programs as much as possible and has an interest in continually increasing state activities.

Hence, a model of a politico-economic system emphasizes the interdependence of the economy and policy by taking into account that the electorate's vote decision depends (among other *political* issues) on economic conditions, and that the government can influence its reelection chance by changing the state of the economy. These relationships are graphed in Figure 1.

FIG. 1. Politico-economic system with two actors: voters and government.

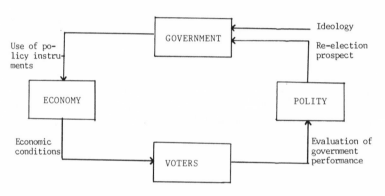

This figure shows how economic conditions (as represented by well-known macroeconomic indicators such as the rate of unemployment, the rate of inflation, and the rate of growth of real income) influence the voters' evaluation of government performance: the worse (better) the economic conditions are, the less (more) satisfied the voters are with the government, assuming that the voters held government at least partly responsible for the state of the economy.

In the political sphere, the institutional characteristics of the particular politico-economic system determine how much the government depends on the voters' wishes. Figure 1 shows, furthermore, that the government uses its policy instruments on the expenditure and revenue side in considering both its reelection prospects and its ideological goals. The lower loop shown in Figure 1, which leads from the economy to the polity, describing the voters' behavior, is termed *evaluation function*; the upper loop, which leads from the polity back to the economy, describing the government's behavior, is termed *policy function*.

The main purpose of this survey is to give a comprehensive overview on the current state of research on voters' behavior and provide some short remarks about the results of studies in which disaggregated voting behavior is analyzed. Next, this survey deals with the government's reaction in representative democracies. Furthermore, the behavior of other actors (such as the central bank and interest groups) are analyzed in this framework. Finally, in the last section, some concluding remarks are made.

VOTERS' BEHAVIOR

Most studies in the politico-economic context deal solely with voters' behavior concerning the evaluation of the government (and in some also the opposition's performance at a general election or in polls).[3] The main emphasis is on the questions of what determines the election decision of a voter and what are the main factors that are used in a voter's decision.

Voters participating in general elections evaluate the government by its past performance over the recent legislative period or even longer. The opposition parties are evaluated by looking at their party platforms and their statements over the legislative period. To undertake the evaluation of government performance, voters consider those economic and political developments for which they think government is (at least partly) responsible. As this information process is costly for voters, they will use those economic and political factors that they already know or for which they can easily get information. Economic indicators that fulfill these conditions are the rate of inflation, the rate of unemployment, the growth rate of disposable income, and the burden of taxation and government goods and services (such as transfer payments). Political factors are interior and exterior political events (such as foreign crises and domestic affairs, e.g., political scandals of politicians). On the economic side, it is rather easy to investigate empirically whether these variables have an influence on voters' decisions, but for the political factors it is difficult to find appropriate variables capturing these influences.[4]

The empirical investigation of the evaluation function began almost simultaneously in the early 1970s with the econometric estimation of popularity functions (for the United States, see Mueller, 1970, and for Great Britain, see Goodhart and Bhansali, 1970) and the econometric estimation of election functions (for the United States, see Kramer, 1971). The main emphasis in these studies is on the amount of influence exerted by a change in the economic situation on the popularity of American presidents (and of the British governing party) or on the outcome of congressional and presidental elections in the United States.

The results of vote functions are discussed first; from these the more or less direct influence of economic and political factors on the election outcome is measured. For the United States, where we have four studies of presidential elections over roughly the same time period, the empirical results are quite different: Kramer (1971) concluded that inflation and real growth of income have a significant impact. Fair (1978) found that the real per capita income or the rate of unemployment (if only one is included in the estimation question) was a significant influence; Niskanen (1979) showed that the per capita income and the rate of federal per capita tax had a significant impact. Finally, Kirchgaessner (1980) used the squared rate of inflation to explain the vote share of American presidents and found no other economic variable that was significant. One reason for these quite different results may be the long time period over which the empirical studies were done, with the consequence that structural changes (like the world economic crises of 1929–1933) may be due to the instability in the estimation results.

For Denmark and Norway, Madsen (1980) found that the inflation rate was the *only* significant influence on the vote share for the government party(ies). For Sweden, he showed that the rate of unemployment or the growth rate of real income had a significant impact. In the case of France alone, Rosa (1980) concluded, all three economic variables had a significant impact on the vote share of the left opposition parties, with the strongest influence being the inflation rate. No statistically significant influence of the economic situation on the election outcome was demonstrated by Whitely (1980) for Great Britain and by Inoguchi (1980) for Japan. A quantitatively strong and highly significant influence of the economic situation on the election outcome of the vote share of parties in the four Reichstag elections of the Weimar Republic between 1930 and 1933 was found by Frey and Weck (1983). They concluded from their estimation results that if unemployment had not risen from 14% in July 1930 to 52% of employed workers in January 1933, the Nazi party would have received 24% instead of 44% of the vote in March 1933.

A comparison of the results among all the countries may not be very useful, since the time period investigated and the type of specification and the variables included in the estimation are too different in the various studies. However, the results in the various countries show that the economic situation has a predictable influence on the election outcome, but how strong this influence is and which economic factors are crucial are difficult to tell.[5]

Because of these difficulties with vote functions, most authors concentrate their studies on the question, Which political and economic factors have an influence on the *government's popularity* and, if so, how strong and quantitatively important are they? This author knows of more than 70 studies that have been done recently on the impact of economic and political factors on government's popularity, with most of them concentrating on the United States, Great Britain, France, and Germany. As it is not possible (and may not be very useful) to survey all of them, I will focus on the main, and in probably most important, recently published results.

First let us consider the influence of the economic situation on the popularity of presidents (e.g., the popularity of presidents in France and in the United States). Lewis-Beck (1980), Hibbs (1981), and Lafay (1984) found that the rates of inflation and unemployment and the growth rate of real income have a significant and quantitatively important impact on a president's popularity in France. The same holds for the United States, as demonstrated by the studies of Frey and Schneider (1978b), Hibbs (1982a), and Schneider (1978). The interesting question now is, Which economic variable is the dominant one?

For France, the results of the studies are not the same.[6] Whereas Lewis-Beck found that the inflation rate has the strongest (in quantitative terms) impact, Hibbs and Lafay concluded that the rate of unemployment and the growth of income are the dominating economic factors on presidential popularity in France. For the United States, a more or less unique picture emerges. The rate of unemployment and/or growth rate of real income are the dominating economic factors on presidential popularity. If one compares only the influence of unemployment and inflation on presidential popularity, then up to President Nixon the elasticity of unemployment is greater than that of inflation, whereas for the popularity of Ford and Carter the opposite holds. Also the impact of the economic situation on presidential popularity has increased remarkably over time. From Kennedy to Carter the elasticities for unemployment and income almost doubled (from -0.02 to -0.36 and from 0.27 to 0.45, respectively), and for inflation the elasticity rose from -0.05 to -0.53 (according to Hibbs, 1982a, p. 456).

Next, let us consider the results of the economic condition on the popularity of governing party(ies) in four European and three Asian or Pacific states. Again a unique picture appears. In Australia (Schneider and Pommerehne, 1980), Denmark (Paldam and Schneider, 1980), West Germany (Kirchgaessner, 1976 and 1977), Great Britain (Pissarides, 1980), Japan (Inoguchi, 1980), New Zealand (Ursprung, 1983), and Sweden (Jonung and Wadensjoe, 1979), the rate of inflation and the rate of unemployment as well as the growth rate of real income have a significant impact on the popularity of the party(ies) in government. Moreover, with the exception of Japan, in these countries under study, the rate of unemployment has a quantitatively bigger effect on the government's popularity than the rate of inflation — meaning that the voters blame the government more strongly for an increase in unemployment than for one in inflation. The rate of income is quantitatively of less importance, with the exception of Japan where the estimated coefficient has almost the same size as the one on the inflation rate. When a balance of payments (or a similar) variable is included, as in the studies for Australia, Denmark, France, Great Britain, and New Zealand, it has only a significant but quantitatively less important effect in France, Great Britain, and New Zealand. From these empirical results we can conclude that even for countries with serious balance of payments difficulties (like Denmark, France, or Australia), the balance seems to be of little interest to the voter. One reason may be that voters have a difficult time understanding what balance of payments difficulties are. Another variable, the burden of taxation, which is included in three studies (i.e., studies for Australia, Denmark, and Great Britain), indicates that when the tax pressure reaches a certain level, it becomes an important factor, as well.[7]

One matter not discussed so far is whether voters evaluate the government's performance by just looking at the recent state of the economy or by looking far back into the government's previous economic performance. The empirical results are mixed: Hibbs (1981, 1982a) and Hibbs and Madsen (1981) concluded from their studies for France, West Germany, Great Britain, Sweden, and the United States that voters evaluate economic performance by comparing a president's/government's cumulative record over the past with that of the president's/government's predecessors. A similar result was reached by Chappell (1983) and Chappell and Keech (in press), who concluded that voters are *even* concerned with the future consequences of current economic policy choices and are aware of the nature of constraints imposed by economic reality. On the contrary, other researchers (Lafay, Kirchgaessner, Pissarides, and Schneider) concluded that voters are to a certain extent myopic and have only limited knowledge of the state of the economy, so that roughly only the economic events in the year of evaluation may play an important role when voters judge a president's/government's record. Hence the question of how "rational" or "myopic" voters are remain open and needs further research.

We can conclude the following from the empirical results presented so far: Most studies find a consistent relationship between the economic situation in a country and the evaluation of a president/government, which results in a statistically significant and quantitatively important impact of economic variables on a president's/government's popularity or approval rate at elections. The better (worse) the economic situation is, especially before elections, the more the government's popularity or reelection chances increase (decrease). How strong this influence is varies considerably *among countries* and *over time*.

VOTERS' BEHAVIOR – SOME RESULTS OF DISAGGREGATED STUDIES

Most research dealing with the influence of economic conditions on popularity has treated the electorate as if it were a homogenous groups. In reality, different groups of voters (different income classes, for example) can be expected to be differently affected by changes in the economy. Let us examine several studies that analyze whether or not different groups of voters also evaluate the president's performance differentially as the economy changes, exhibiting different levels of sensitivity to changes in unemployment and inflation.

Various researchers, such as Alt (1984), Alt and Chrystal (1983), Hibbs (1982b and 1982c), and Schneider (1978), have come to the conclusion that a changing economy differentially affects voters belonging to different income classes. Members of lower-income classes favor an economic situation with low unemployment, even if this means a relatively high rate of inflation. In contrast, people in upper-income brackets are mainly interested in the opposite situation, i.e., low inflation at the possible cost of high unemployment. The authors put forth the following arguments. High-income recipients are more concerned about inflation because they are more seriously affected by it (e.g., their money holding depreciate in value, there is increased uncertainty about property values). Unemployment is a less serious problem for upper-income groups because in general they enjoy higher job security. Low-income recipients are most concerned with unemployment because they are much more in danger of being dismissed and of having to incur the cost of finding a new job (search and mobility cost, costs of uncertainty). As nominal wage rates are expected to reflect inflationary movements quite closely and automatically and as the lower-income groups have little property to be concerned about, they do not attach as much importance to price stability.

These hypotheses have been empirically tested (Schneider, 1978) using monthly popularity data of the U.S. Presidents Nixon and Ford for voters belonging to six different income classes (POPP-YC1 = $0-$2,999 annual income to POPP-YC6 = $20,000 and above annual income). The estimation results for the impact of the economic variables unemployment and inflation are shown in Figure 2. The empirical estimates clearly support the theoretical hypotheses advanced. Figure 2 shows that the size of the inflation coefficient continuously rises from -1.00 to -2.60 as we move from low- to high-income groups. The opposite movement holds for the unemployment coefficient. It continuously falls from -4.44 to a value of -1.84. High-income recipients react more negatively to inflation, and low-income recipients react more negatively to unemployment. This differential evaluation corresponds well to their private interests.

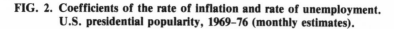

FIG. 2. Coefficients of the rate of inflation and rate of unemployment. U.S. presidential popularity, 1969–76 (monthly estimates).

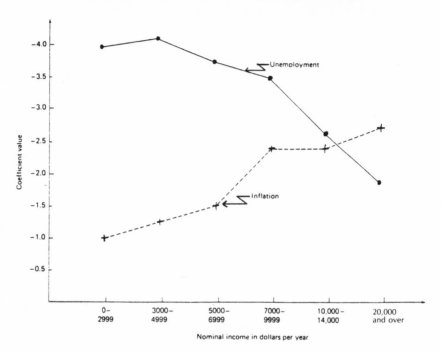

GOVERNMENT'S BEHAVIOR

In representative democracies with discontinuous elections every third to fifth year, a government can be considered to be in a special position of power similar to that of a monopolist. It has various advantages in comparison with the opposition, the most important of which is the opportunity to influence the state of the economy before elections. If not afraid of losing the next election, the government has considerable discretionary power which it can use to carry out its ideological programs. In the limiting case in which political survival is seriously threatened, government is forced to undertake a vote-maximizing policy at election time.

A good example of a vote-maximizing policy at elections is provided by Wright's (1974) cross-sectional analysis of federal government expenditures for U.S. states during the economic depression of 1933–1940. The "value" of every state to the federal government depends upon the comparison of the traditional vote share of the president's party (during this time, the Democrats) with the vote share attainable by generating income per capita in a certain state through appropriate public expenditures. A state has no "value" (in this sense) if the Democrats expect to receive a majority anyway or if it is impossible to bring the actual vote over 50% by income generation. Based on this idea, a priority index can be constructed that takes into account the case with which any state can be won. It is hypothesized that the federal government allocates public expenditures according to this priority index, i.e., not according to "needs" of the individual states, but rather to the partisan interest of the administration in power. Statistical estimation shows indeed a significant effect of this priority index on federal public expenditures – strongly confirming the idea that the administration in power wants to be reelected.

On the basis of a complete macroeconomic model of the United States, Fair (1975) has derived the vote-maximizing policy of a president. According to his estimates, the presidential vote share depends on the growth rate of real GNP only (a result that has not been found by other researchers). Moreover, voters only consider GNP in the election year, i.e., they completely discount the state of economy in previous years. Under these conditions, it turns out that it is advantageous for the president to create a marked politico-economic style. The president maximizes votes and his reelection chance if he undertakes a strongly restrictive policy in the first part of the election period and a strongly expansionary policy in the second part. It turns out, however, that most American presidents in the post–World War II period have not followed such a policy, i.e., the vote-maximizing use of instruments has weak explanatory power.

Wright's and Fair's studies tried to explain government behavior at election time or assumed that government is maximizing votes all the time. If we intend to explain actual (observed) government behavior over a whole legislative period, then we have to widen the approach and take into account that a government has considerable discretionary power between elections. Hence, the basic assumption of the studies by Frey and Schneider[8] is that government maximizes its own utility in pursuing certain ideological goals[9] subject to various constraints, of which the most important is the reelection constraint. Thus the government faces a dynamic maximization problem of when to undertake what fiscal policy action in order to maximize its utility. As the government is not able to solve this problem, we assume that it will behave in a satisfying manner and that it takes the results of popularity surveys as the best current indicator of its reelection prospects. If the current popularity is high and/or there is plenty of time until the next election, government will use its various fiscal instruments to pursue its ideological goals. Considering the ideologically motivated party programs, a left-wing government, in comparison with a right-wing government, will generally increase public sector activity, including new and/or expanded spending programs. By way of contrast, a conservative (right-wing) government will state preferences for a much smaller level of growth in current and future government activities and a strengthening of private-sphere actions.

If the reelection chances are low and/or the next election is close, the government will concentrate on securing reelection. For this purpose, *every type of government* will undertake taxing and spending policies that maximize the chance of being reelected. The concrete fiscal policy will depend on voters' evaluation of government's economic performance and their preferences for the various taxing and spending items.

Econometric estimates of government behavior as just described have been undertaken for Australia (Schneider and Pommerehne, 1980), West Germany (Frey and Schneider, 1979), Great Britain (Frey and Schneider, 1978a), and the United States (Frey and Schneider, 1978b). From the mid-1950s up to the mid-1970s, the results of these studies clearly show that the governments in all four countries undertook an *expansionary* policy when they were afraid that they would not be reelected in the forthcoming elections. They tended to increase exhaustive and transfer expenditures and decrease taxes in order to stimulate the economy and hence reduce unemployment and increase personal income – a policy that proved to be the most popular considering the results of the vote and the popularity functions discussed earlier in this paper. When governments are able to use their various fiscal instruments to pursue their ideological goals, left-wing governments have a tendency to increase the size of government by raising expenditures and taxes. Right-wing governments, on the other hand, tend to decrease the size of government by cutting expenditures and lowering the tax burden.

The results for Great Britain have been criticized by studies from Chrystal and Alt (1979, 1981, and 1983) and for the United States by Ahmad (1983). Chrystal and Alt suggested a permanent income hypothesis for the spending behavior of the British government and argued that governments plan expenditures to grow in proportion to expected levels of income. Ahmad argued in the case of the United States government that the function describing the presidential policy response has to contain both economic *and* political determinants for each policy instrument. According to Ahmad, a president *always* and *immediately* reacts to changes in economic conditions irrespective of whether he feels his reelection is in danger or not.

Against Alt and Chrystal's objections, Frey and Schneider (1981a, 1982, and 1983) argued that the authors stated no reason why the British government should desire to keep public expenditures as a stable share of national income. Against Ahmad's criticism, Schneider and Frey (1983) argued that Ahmad failed to argue convincingly why a president in the United States should have an incentive to react immediately whenever economic and political conditions change.

As it is always possible to argue about different theoretical approaches, one crucial test is how the different models work to explain reality; i.e., the politico-economic models are confronted with the competing models, using the test of the true ex post forecasts that have been undertaken for the two countries.[10] Whereas the politico-economic models for the United States by Frey and Schneider yield clearly superior forecasts over the one by Ahmad, it is an open question in the case of Great Britain whether the Chrystal and Alt model or the Frey and Schneider model leads to superior forecasts.[11]

ADDITIONAL ACTORS IN POLITICO-ECONOMIC MODELS

The politico-economic models so far discussed consider only two actors, the voters and the government, and hence leave out important other decision makers, like the central bank and interest groups (including the public bureaucracy). To overcome this shortcoming, present research moves in this direction:

1. Frey and Schneider (1981b) have demonstrated that the model use for analyzing the government behavior is also suitable for explaining central bank behavior, with the decisive constraint on the central bank being in conflict with the government. In the case of conflict, the government is for various reasons in a more powerful position, and the central bank has to yield to its politically motivated demands in order not to lose its independence. This hypothesis has been tested for West Germany, with good results. In the case of conflict over the direction of the economic policy with the government, the central bank follows, with a certain time lag, government policy. If there is no conflict with the government, the central bank pursues its own utility by employing a restrictive policy, i.e., by increasing interest rates and decreasing credits in order to combat inflation.[12]

2. In most representative democracies the existing political institutions give great power to organized interests (van Winden, 1981) and there are areas in which the influence of pressure groups on the government has been specifically studied by politometric research. Schneider and Naumann (1982) demonstrated that the position interest groups take on specific economic policy issues has a significant effect on referenda outcomes in Switzerland, *ceteris paribus.* Not surprisingly, those interest groups with large numbers of members (trade unions, farmers' union) have more impact at *this* level of the polity than those with only few members (business and banking associations).

Trade union behavior is not independent of purely political factors, as has been demonstrated by Gaertner (1977, 1978, 1981) in the case of the Federal Republic of Germany over the period 1960-1976. The rate of increase of wage rates move cyclically with elections. The trade unions, *ceteris paribus,* ask for smaller wage increases if the party in power (Social

Democrats) is ideologically close to them. On the other hand, if the government is politically right-wing, the trade unions see no reason to restrict their wage demands; they may even be particularly aggressive in order to reduce the government's reelection chance.

In general, this discussion demonstrates that there are fruitful but still preliminary efforts to include additional actors in politico-economic models. This line of research may also widen the aspect under which government and voters act, so that their roles may be modified, when *additional decision makers are fully integrated* into politico-economic models.

CONCLUDING REMARKS

The current state of research of politico-economic relations between voters and government in representative democracies leads to the following three conclusions:

1. In representative democracies there exists a consistent relationship between the economic situation and voters' evaluation of a government, which shows up in a statistically significant and quantitatively important influence of macroeconomic variables on government's popularity. The better (or worse) the economic situation is perceived by voters, the more a government's popularity increases (decreases).

2. Government behavior depends on economics and politics. The basic proposition of the politico-economic model – that governments are interested in putting their selfish goals into practice in the political contest – fares well compared with the competing proposition that governments are interested in the state of the economy as such (presumably to further the welfare of the population).

3. Governments are part of politico-economic interaction in which a *multitude of actors* is participating. In the policy functions of the politico-economic models that have been estimated, the influence of public administration and other interest groups on government lies in the incapacity of governments to change their policy instruments quickly to the value desired if they face stiff resistance from interest groups. Hence the inclusion of additional important actors is a necessary next step in order to better understand the functioning of modern democratic societies.

Acknowledgments. For helpful and most stimulating comments on earlier drafts, the author thanks Michael Lewis-Beck, Dennis Mueller, Jorgen Rasmussen, and Howard Rosenthal.

NOTES

1. Because of lack of space, voters' and government's behavior in direct democracies is not

analyzed here. For such studies, compare Pommerehne (1978), Pommerehne and Schneider (1978), Romer and Rosenthal (1979), and Schneider et al. (1981).

2. The first study analyzing government behavior in this context was done by Frey and Lau (1968). For a survey of the first studies, see Frey and Schneider (1975).

3. An extensive overview of this literature is not intended here, and only the most important results will be reported. One of the best and most recent surveys of popularity and vote functions is given by Paldam (1981).

4. In some studies, like Hibbs (1979, 1982a, 1982b), Kernell (1978), and Fair (1978), an attempt was made to consider political factors not only by dummy variables but also by such quantitative indices as the number of killed Americans in the Vietnam War or newspaper coverage of the Watergate scandal.

5. Fair (1978) and Kirchgaessner (1980) dealt extensively with problems of the specification of election functions, their stability, and their interpretation. Another test of stability, ex post facto forecasts of U.S. national election results using the Kramer equation, was done by Atesoglu and Congleton (1982). From the quite good predictive performance of the Kramer election equation, they concluded that general economic conditions have a systematic and predictable effect on national congressional elections.

6. A comprehensive survey of the popularity studies undertaken in France is by Lafay (1984).

7. Hibbs and Madsen (1981) included a tax pressure variable also for Sweden and found a significant and quantitatively important impact on the popularity of the governing party(ies).

8. Compare Frey and Schneider (1978a, 1978b) and Pommerehne and Schneider (1983).

9. When undertaking such a policy, government might only consider the preferences of its partisan voters, i.e., only a share of the whole electorate, which usually is much smaller than a majority of the electorate (needed for being reelected).

10. For West Germany, a confrontation of a "pure" econometric model developed by Krelle (1974) with a full-scale model of politico-economic interaction was undertaken by Frey and Schneider (1979). In the competing model, the policy variables, e.g., expenditures, are a function of lagged taxes and lagged GNP, without attempting to provide a theoretical rationale. Again, true ex post facto forecasts of the politico-economic model are clearly better than the one achieved by the pure econometric model.

11. A comparison of forecasts of different politico-economic models for Great Britain was done by Hibbs (1983); he found that his approach yielded to the best forecasts.

12. Similar studies of central bank behavior has been undertaken for France by Lafay and Aubin (1984) and for the United States by Laney and Willett (1983). For both countries the authors reached the conclusion that the central bank supports the government's expansionary policy for getting reelected with an appropriate monetary policy.

REFERENCES

Ahmad, Kabir V. (1983). "An Empirical Study of Politico-Economic Interaction in the United States." *Review of Economics and Statistics* 65:170–177.

Alt, James E. (1984). "Elections and Economic Outcomes in Britain." Mimeographed. St. Louis: Washington University.

Alt, James E., and Alec K. Chrystal (1983). *Political Economics.* Los Angeles: University of California Press.

Atesoglu, H., Sonmer and Roger Congleton (1982). "Economic Conditions and National Elections, Post Sample Forecasts." *The American Political Science Review* 76:873–875.

Chapell, Jr., Henry W. (1983). "Presidential Popularity and Macroeconomic

Performance: Are Voters Really So Naive?" *The Review of Economics and Statistics* 65:385–392.

Chapell, Jr., Henry W., and William R. Keech (in press). "A New View of Political Accountability for Economic Performance." *The American Political Science Review,* in press.

Chrystal, Alex K., and James Alt (1979). "Endogenous Government Behavior: Wagner's Law or Goetterdaemmerung?" In S. T. Cook and P. M. Jackson (eds.), *Current Issues in Fiscal Policy.* London: M. Robertson, pp. 224–259.

Chrystal, Alex K., and James Alt (1981). "Some Problems in Formulating and Testing a Politico-Economic Model of the United Kingdom." *Economic Journal* 91: 730–736.

Chrystal, Alex K., and James Alt (1983). "The Criteria for Choosing a Politico-Economic Model: Forecast Results for British Expenditures 1976–79." *European Journal of Political Research* 11:113–124.

Fair, Ray C. (1975). "On Controlling the Enemy to Win Elections." *Cowles Foundation Discussion Paper* 397.

Fair, Ray C. (1978). "The Effect of Economic Events on Votes for President." *The Review of Economics and Statistics* 60:159–172.

Frey, Bruno S., and Larry Lau (1968). "Towards a Mathematical Model of Government Behavior." *Zeitschrift für Nationalökonomie* 2812–355–380.

Frey, Bruno S., and Friedrich Schneider (1975). "On the Modelling of Politico-Economic Interdependence." *European Journal of Political Research* 3:339–360.

Frey, Bruno S., and Friedrich Schneider (1978). "A Politico-Economic Model of the United Kingdom." *Economic Journal* 88:243–253. (a)

Frey, Bruno S., and Friedrich Schneider (1978). "An Empirical Study of Politico-Interaction in the U.S." *Review of Economics and Statistics* 60:174–183. (b)

Frey, Bruno S., and Friedrich Schneider (1979). "An Econometric Model with an Endogenous Government Sector." *Public Choice* 34:29–43.

Frey, Bruno S., and Friedrich Schneider (1981). "A Politico-Economic Model of the U.K.: New Estimates and Predictions." *Economic Journal* 91:737–740. (a)

Frey, Bruno S., and Friedrich Schneider (1981). "Central Bank Behavior. A Positive Empirical Analysis." *Journal of Monetary Economics* 7:291–315. (b)

Frey, Bruno S., and Friedrich Schneider (1982). "Politico-Economic Models in Competition with Alternative Models: Which Predicts Better?" *European Journal of Political Research* 10:241–254.

Frey, Bruno S., and Friedrich Schneider (1983). "Do Governments Respond to Political Incentives?" *European Journal of Political Research* 11:125–126.

Frey, Bruno S., and Hannelove Weck (1983). "A Statistical Study of the Effect of the Great Depression on Elections: The Weimar Republic, 1930–1933." *Political Behavior* 5:403–420.

Gaertner, Manfred (1977). "Die Phillipskurve und staatliches Beschäftigungsziel im Zeitalter der Globalsteuerung." *Jahrbücher fur Nationalökonomie und Statistik* 192:481–503.

Gaertner, Manfred (1978). "Eine Ökonomische Analyse ideologischer und politisch-institutioneller Bestimmungsfaktoren gewerkschaftlicher Lohnpolitik." In C. C. Von Weizsaeker (ed.), *Staat und Wirtschaft.* Berlin: Duncker & Humblot, pp. 69–90.

Gaertner, Manfred (1981). "Politik und Arbeitsmarkt. Eine Übersicht über ausge-wählte Makrotheorien." *Zeitschrift für die gesamte Staatswissenschaft* 137:252–283.

Goodhart, C. A. E., and R. J. Bhansali (1970). "Political Economy." *Political Studies* 18:43–106.

Hibbs, Douglas A., Jr. (1979). "The Mass Public and Economic Performance: The Dynamics of Public Opinion Towards Unemployment and Inflation." *American Journal of Political Science* 23:705–731.

Hibbs, Douglas A., Jr. (1981). "Economics and Politics in France: Economic Per-formance and Mass Political Support for Presidents Pompidou and Giscard d'Estaing." *European Journal of Political Research* 9:133–145.

Hibbs, Douglas A., Jr. (1982). "On the Demand for Economic Outcomes: Mass Political Support in the United States, Great Britain and Germany." *The Journal of Politics* 44:426–462. (a)

Hibbs, Douglas A., Jr. (1982). "The Dynamics of Political Support for American Presidents Among Occupational and Partisan Groups." *American Journal of Political Science* 26:312–332. (b)

Hibbs, Douglas A., Jr. (1982). "Economic Outcomes and Political Support for British Governments Among Occupational Classes: A Dynamic Analysis." *The American Political Science Review* 76:259–279. (c)

Hibbs, Douglas A., Jr. (1983). "An Evaluation of Competing Time-Series Models of Voting Intentions via Ex-Post Forecasting Experiments: The Case of Great Britain." Mimeographed. Cambridge: Harvard University.

Hibbs, Douglas A., Jr., and Henrick Madsen (1981). "The Impact of Economic Performance on Electoral Support in Sweden, 1967–1968." *Scandinavian Political Studies* 4:33–50.

Inoguchi, Tanaka (1980). "Economic Conditions and Mass Support in Japan." In Paul Whitely (ed.), *Models of Political Economy*. London: Sage Publications, pp. 121–154.

Jonung, Lars, and Eskil Wadensjoe (1979). "The Effect of Unemployment, Infla-tion and Real Income Growth on Government Popularity in Sweden." *Scandi-navian Journal of Economics* 81:343–353.

Kernell, Sam (1978). "Explaining Presidential Popularity." *The American Political Science Review* 72:506–522.

Kirchgaessner, Gebhard (1976). "Rationales Wählerverhalten und Optimales Regierungsverhalten." Ph.D. dissertation, University of Konstanz, West Germany.

Kirchgaessner, Gebhard (1977). "Wirtschaftslage und Wählerverhalten." *Politische Vierteljahresschrift* 18:510–536.

Kirchgaessner, Gebhard (1980). "The Effect of Economic Events on Votes for President — Some Alternative Estimates." Mimeographed. Zurich: ETH-Zurich.

Kramer, Gerald (1971). "Short-term Fluctuations in U.S. Voting Behavior, 1896–1964." *American Political Science Review* 65:131–143.

Krelle, Wilhelm (1974). *Efrahrungen mit einem ökonometrischen Prognosemodell für die BRD*. Meisenheim an der Glahn: Hain-Verlag.

Lafay, Jean-Dominique (1984). "Important Political Change and the Stability of the Popularity Funktion: Before and After the French General Election of 1981." Mimeographed. Poitiers: University of Poitiers.

Lafay, Jean-Dominique, and Chaubert Aubin (1984). "The Positive Approach to Monetary Policy: An Empirical Study of the French Case." Mimeographed. Poitiers: Université de Poitiers.

Laney, Leroy O., and Thomas D. Willett (1983). "Presidential Politics, Budget Deficits, and Monetary Policy in the United States: 1960–1976." *Public Choice* 40: 53–69.

Lewis-Beck, Martin S. (1980). "Economic Conditions and Executive Popularity: The French Experience." *The American Journal of Political Science* 24:306–323.

Madsen, Henrick J. (1980). "Electoral Outcomes and Macro-Economic Policies: The Scandinavian Cases." In Paul Whitely (ed.), *Models of Political Economy.* London: Sage, pp. 15–46.

Mueller, John (1970). "Presidential Popularity from Truman to Johnson." *American Political Science Review* 64:18–34.

Niskanen, William A. (1979). "Economic and Fiscal Effects on the Popular Vote for the President." In D. W. Rae and Thomas J. Eismeier (eds.), *Public Policy and Public Choice.* London: Sage Publications, pp. 93–120.

Paldam, Martin (1981). "A Preliminary Survey of the Theories and Findings on Vote and Popularity Functions." *European Journal of Political Research* 9:181–199.

Paldam, Martin, and Friedrich Schneider (1980). "The Macro-Economic Aspects of Government and Opposition Popularity in Denmark," 1957–1978," *Nationalokonomisk Tidsskrift* 118:149–170.

Pissarides, Christopher A. (1980). "British Government Popularity and Economic Performance." *The Economic Journal* 90:569–581.

Pommerehne, Werner W. (1978). "Institutional Approaches to Public Expenditure: Empirical Evidence from Swiss Municipalities." *Journal of Public Economics* 9: 255–280.

Pommerehne, Werner W., and Friedrich Schneider (1978). "Fiscal Illusions, Political Institutions, and Local Public Spending." *Kyklos* 31:381–408.

Pommerehne, Werner W., and Friedrich Schneider (1983). "Does Government in a Representative Democracy Follow a Majority of Voters' Preferences? – An Empirical Examination." In Horst Hanusch (ed.), *Anatomy of Government Deficiencies.* Heidelberg, West Germany: Springer-Verlag, pp. 61–88.

Romer, Thomas, and Howard Rosenthal (1979). "The Elusive Median Voter." *Journal of Public Economics* 12:143–170.

Rosa, Jean J. (1980). "Economic Conditions and Elections in France." In Paul Whitely (ed.), *Models of Political Economy.* London: Sage, pp. 101–120.

Schneider, Friedrich (1978). *Politisch-Ökonomische Modelle: Theoretische und Empirische Ansätze.* Koenigstein, West Germany: Athenäum-Verlag.

Schneider, Friedrich, and Bruno S. Frey (1983). "An Empirical Study of Politico-Economic Interaction in the United States: A Reply." *Review of Economics and Statistics* 65:178–182.

Schneider, Friedrich, and Joerg Naumann (1982). "Interest Group Behavior in Democracies: An Empirical Analysis for Switzerland." *Public Choice* 38:281–304.

Schneider, Friedrich, and Werner W. Pommerehne (1980). "Politico-Economic Interactions in Australia: Some Empirical Evidence." *Economic Record* 56:113–131.

Schneider, Friedrich, Werner W. Pommerehne, and Bruno S. Frey (1981). "Politico-economic Interdependence in a Direct Democracy: The Case of Switzerland." In Douglas A. Hibbs, Jr., and Heino Fassbender (eds.), *Contemporary Political Economy.* Amsterdam: North-Holland, pp. 231–248.

Ursprung, Heiner W. (1983). "Macroeconomic Performance and Government Popularity in New Zealand." Mimeographed. Victoria University of Wellington, New Zealand.

Whitely, Paul (ed.) (1980). *Models of Political Economy.* London: Sage Publications, pp. 155–160.

van Winden, Frans (1981). *On the Interaction between the State and Private Sector. A Study in Political Economics.* s'Gravenhage: Pasmans.

Wright, Gavin (1974). "The Political Economy of New-Deal Spending: An Econometric Analysis." *The Review of Economics and Statistics* 56:30–39.

CHAPTER 2

Party Strategies, World Demand and Unemployment in Britain and the United States, 1947–1983

James E. Alt
Department of Political Science, Washington University

Students of economic voting assume that voters expect some payoff from the election of one candidate or party rather than another, either in the form of increased personal income or changes in national conditions like the level of aggregate economic activity or the stability of prices. But are voters' expectations fulfilled? Does the election of one party rather than another affect economic conditions consistently? Continuing interest in this question arises from Hibbs's (1977) thesis that the disproportionate burden of unemployment borne by blue-collar workers and their disproportionate support for left-wing parties meant that left-wing parties would organize platforms to elicit this working-class support and reward their supporters by reducing unemployment while in office. But under what circumstances do changes of party control cause sustained changes in the level of unemployment? For example, if President Reagan had not been elected in 1980, is there any reason to believe that unemployment would have risen less in

1981–82 than it did? Or that unemployment would be lower in 1984 than it was?

Alt and Chrystal (1983, chaps. 5 and 6) reviewed the literature in political economics which relates changes in party control to economic outcomes and the reactions of political decision makers to economic structure. Specifically on unemployment, Beck (1982) argued that idiosyncracies of separate administrations explain unemployment variations better than party. Nevertheless, the outline of Hibbs's conclusion appears robust (Hibbs, 1983; Chappell and Keech, 1984). Its relevance to other countries has been both supported (Cameron, 1978) and challenged (Castles, 1982; Rose, 1980; Keman and Braun, 1984; Schmidt, 1983, 1984), though the results in the latter most clearly indicate the absence of many appropriate controls. Limited support also appears in the policy studies of Beck (1983) and Woolley (1984), though these refute theories of electoral-cyclical manipulation (see also Paldam, 1979) more than provide positive accounts of partisan shifts in policy.

Alt (1984) extended the earlier models to include the effect of reelection strategies implied by different party systems and economic constraints and the impact of changes in the level of world trade. The key premise is the rationality of parties' maintaining political support by keeping promises to core supporters in class-based electoral systems. Based on econometric analysis of unemployment rates in 14 countries from 1960 to 1983, the conclusions were that changes of government in which parties of the Left improve their position result in reduced levels of unemployment, provided that (1) the change in the level of unemployment is measured relative to the level of demand for a country's goods in its trading environment, (2) no effects are expected where no such effects were promised by the new government before taking office, (3) in party systems where one-party or dominant-partner coalitions form, the effect should be sustained, and (4) effects are more likely where governments secure parliamentary majorities.

The purpose of this paper is to complement the results in Alt (1984). It will replicate and extend the original Hibbs and Beck results to the case of the United States, while providing extended results for Britain for the whole period 1947–1983.[1] The relationship between American and world economic activity is better specified. However, the economy is consistently an issue in Britain and the United States, the differences between two-party and broad coalition systems do not arise, and minority governments do not form. Hence the political focus changes. The expectations are that changes of party control in Britain and the United States should mean that unemployment falls when Left (Labour, Democrat) parties are elected and rises when Right (Conservative, Republican) parties are elected. However, the following factors should be noted:

1. Partisan differences in Britain can only be isolated and estimated when effects of world economic activity are controlled. American economic activity has major effects on world activity but is itself also affected by feedback from the rest of the world, independent of its own past history.
2. Politicians' strategic incentives and economic regime constraints make the impact of changes of party control transitory rather than sustained. "Transitory" effects can still be large and present for considerable periods, but there is no evidence that partisan changes produce permanent changes in the equilibrium level of unemployment.

THEORY

Equilibrium Unemployment

Market mechanisms imply that unemployment over time should be an autoregressive process (McCallum, 1978). This is because whether an individual is employed depends on many things. Some are economic (aggregate activity, investment), some demographic (location, age, skill), and some institutional (employment policies). These determinants of employment are incentives or forces tending to increase or decrease aggregate employment and unemployment at any time. There is an equilibrium level of unemployment at which these forces balance. If unemployment moves above or below its equilibrium, it will be drawn back toward it. For example, if stable inflation were a strong attracting force, the monetarists' "natural rate" of unemployment would be an equilibrium. In discrete time series analysis, if unemployment is at any time drawn toward its equilibrium level by an amount proportional to its distance from that equilibrium level (an arbitrary but inoffensive assumption), then unemployment can be represented by a first-order autoregressive process.[2]

Clearly, other representations are possible. In a decentralized economy, it might be desirable to represent reequilibration by a series of cascaded filters, or higher-order autoregressive process. Structural change may cause the equilibrium level to trend permanently though gradually upward or downward. But some such equilibrium model forms a natural baseline against which to test for political and other effects on domestic economic activity. This paper is concerned with two sources of such effects: changes in world economic activity and changes of party control of government.

Openness and World Unemployment

In a world of interdependent trading partners, if a country with a large economy enters a recession, the economies of other countries will slow down. The uniquely large size of the United States economy has made it a dominant actor in Western trade relations. However, two trends have been marked over the last 30 years. First, other countries' economies have grown faster than that of the United States. The American economy has thus become smaller relative to the rest of the West. In 1981, American GDP was about 40% of total OECD GDP. In 1960 it was 55%, and larger still a decade earlier. In 1950, American GDP was 2.5 times as large as the combined GDP of the present European Economic Community. Over the last few years, they have been of a comparable order of magnitude, though the exact relationship fluctuates with the strength of the dollar. Japan's economy, insignificant in 1951, is now somewhere between a third and half the American economy in size, again depending on exchange rates. From being the dominant actor, at least in terms of size, in the post-World War II years, the United States has declined to a position of one among a few large actors.

At the same time, the American economy has become more open or dependent on external trade and has actually increased its contribution to world trade. American exports totalled 4% of GDP in 1950, but 10% in 1981. The American economy (like the Japanese) is still relatively closed, but American exports as a fraction of OECD GDP have increased from perhaps 2.5% in 1951 to over 4% recently. Four percent of OECD GDP may seem small, but it cannot be overlooked. It is about the size of the whole Canadian economy. Too small, perhaps, to be hegemonic[3]; large enough to be a significant source of disturbances for the rest of the world.

Transitory and Sustained Effects of Changes of Party Control

Most countries' economies are small and open enough relative to the rest of the world that external shocks would both constrain domestic policy and affect domestic economic activity, and even change the equilibrium level of unemployment (Nickell, 1982). Could government policy changes also produce equilibrium changes? This is a source of contention in modern macroeconomic theory, though most theories permit government policy to have some effects.[4] This paper discusses political as well as economic incentives behind transitory and sustained effects. Two assumptions are central. First, political effects do not arise automatically from class interests. Parties are organizations of politicians. They have their own interests as well as ideological commitments to class-based policies (Frey, 1978). These interests and commitments can diverge. Second, reducing unemployment requires calculated intervention. Intervening costs something politically, in the form of either bargaining to create a supporting coalition or the opportunity cost of foregone alternative policies. Politicians seek ways to increase political benefits while reducing political costs of intervention.

There is no difficulty about why victorious parties at least initially keep promises made to core supporters. Keeping promises to core supporters is a form of support-maximizing (Cox, McCubbins, and Sullivan, 1984). The need for credibility to implement future policies and the desire to have future promises believed require not starting a term of office by breaking too many highly visible promises. The so-called mandate or honeymoon of a government immediately after election makes this a particularly cheap time to pursue policies which might be more strenuously opposed at other times. If a party has promised to reduce unemployment, it should initially take actions to do so, and might continue to take those actions throughout its incumbency. But why might parties, having initially kept their core-supporter promises, cease to do so later on? Many answers are possible. Two are given here.

Party Strategies

If sustaining reduced unemployment requires repeating interventions from period to period and repeatedly bearing the costs of such interventions, transitory changes become more likely. The response of unemployment to a sustained intervention which Hibbs describes displays diminishing marginal returns, since as the new steady-state level is approached, a further period's input generates virtually no further change in unemployment (a formal treatment appears in Alt, 1984). Not only does unemployment cease to change, but voters may become accustomed to the new equilibrium and cease to give the government credit for it. While there would be popularity costs in abandoning the new level of unemployment, it may be possible to mask them or to shift the blame. At least promises will have been kept when they were most visible.

Not only the real political costs but also the opportunity costs of sustaining an intervention in particular may grow very large. If a party has a core class of support whose interests it serves, but this core class is not large enough to provide an electoral majority, when seeking reelection the government must bid for the support of other groups. Parties which seek votes across several distinct social constituencies will try different policies, some of which involve abandoning the commitment to reduce unemployment. Moreover, the agenda will change. Opposition parties will try to fight the next election on advantageous grounds. A party which succeeds in reducing unemployment will be opposed by parties stressing other problems. These things make intervention costs increase during an incumbency. Eventually these costs will exceed even the steady-state benefits of policy and exceed the marginal benefits much sooner. If intervention costs increase during an incumbency, the incentives for transitory impacts grow. Thus electoral strategies give good reasons for expecting party changes to produce transitory rather than sustained changes in unemployment.

Economic Constraints

There are other reasons to expect transitory impacts. Policy may be severely constrained either by the structure of the domestic labor force or by international financial regimes. A fixed exchange rate regime like the Bretton Woods system forced any government running sustained expansionary programs (relative to the United States, which printed the reserve currency) to lose currency reserves and introduce austerity programs in the face of exchange rate crises. Moreover, as one economic problem is solved, others arise. Dow (1968) described how in 1952 the British Conservative government raised interest rates to counter "too much demand," and promptly lowered them a year later (when Australia reduced quotas for British imports) to stimulate economic activity.

But this was not a unique event. The Labour commitment to expansion and growth of October 1964 disappeared in the freeze and severe restraint of July 1966, in the face of currency reserve losses. The Heath commitment to reduce inflation through public sector restraint of June 1970 evaporated in the "go for growth" of 1971–72, after public and media unrest over rising unemployment. The subsidies and voluntary "Social Contract" of the 1974 Labour government turned into the incomes policies and monetarist budgeting of 1976–79. Only the Thatcher government of 1979–1983 did not obviously change course in midterm, possibly only because they were never on course to begin with (Alt, 1985). There are some cases of clear reversals in the United States as well. The Carter years, for example, saw initial stimulation give way to anti-inflationary controls and austerity, particularly in the wake of the 1978–79 oil price increases. As the inflation rate fell, the Reagan commitment to reduce inflation gave way to a sustained expansion fueled by deficit spending which rapidly reduced the extremely high levels of unemployment of 1981–82.

However, operationalizing the way economic constraints produce transitory political effects on unemployment is difficult. First, it is hard to predict when the constraints finally bind. Indeed, as Cairncross and Eichengreen (1983) pointed out, the actual event triggering devaluation of the pound (in 1931 and 1949 as well as 1967) seems small and insignificant in retrospect, particularly in comparison with earlier crises which were survived. Moreover, constraints can be self-imposed or invented to solve internal political problems, like Labour's recourse to borrowing from the International Monetary Fund (IMF) — on terms imposed by the IMF—in 1976. To make inferences about the operation of economic constraints requires a systematic economic model. This paper therefore confines political effects to the impact of early-term policies on unemployment. Any effects from domestic policy other than at the beginnings of terms are treated as residual.

DATA AND ESTIMATION

Data and Measurement

Unemployment Rates

Data for this study are monthly unemployment rates for Britain and the United States, published in the United Nations *Monthly Bulletin of Statistics,* collected from January 1947 to December 1983 to permit replication and extension of Hibbs's work. Monthly figures provide as accurate as possible an estimate of the dynamic structure of the unemployment series.[5] Unemployment rates for the two countries are shown in Figure 1. Both trend upward during the last four decades, though the pattern in the United States oscillates far more. The American series has a long upward trend in the 1950s and long downward trend in the 1960s (both broken by shorter cycles of boom and slump) followed by a pronounced upward trend over the last 15 years. The upward movement in British unemployment is more recent but also more severe. There are some obvious *prima facie* correspondences between changes in unemployment rates and incumbencies (Eisenhower and Kennedy-Johnson in the United States, Thatcher in Britain). This paper estimates how consistently such party-coincident shifts arise, and to what extent they exist independent of trends in the world economy and special factors like overseas military involvement.

Changes of Party Control

Party control of government is assumed to reside in control of the executive. For the United States this is taken to change whenever there is alternation between parties of successive presidents, defining six separate instances of party control: the Truman years up to January 1953 (Democratic), the Eisenhower years 1953–61 (Republican), Kennedy-Johnson 1961–69 (Democratic), Nixon-Ford 1969–77 (Republican), Carter 1977–81 (Democratic), and Reagan since February 1981 (Republican). In Britain the periods are the Attlee government through November 1951 (Labour). Churchill-Eden-Macmillan-Home until October 1964 (Conservative), Wilson's first Labour government until June 1970, Heath's Conservative government until February 1974, the Wilson-Callaghan Labour government until June 1979, and

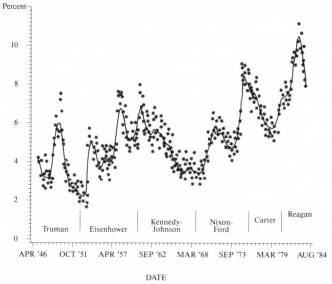

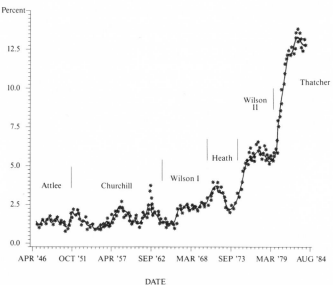

FIG. 1. Unemployment rates in the United States (top) and Britain (below), 1947–83.

Thatcher's Conservative government since then. No change of party control occurs when a party wins reelection or one leader succeeds another of the same party.

Sustained impacts are represented by separate variables for each period of party control coded one throughout the incumbency and zero otherwise. This representation should produce a pattern of gradual increase or decrease to a new equilibrium level of unemployment. The transitory model is represented by a variable with 12 ones at the beginning of each incumbency[6] and zeroes otherwise. This length is arbitrary but not unreasonable. This would result in a pattern of gradual increase or decrease for a year, followed by gradual return to the original equilibrium level. These two representations will be tested in separate models, with the choice of representation based on a combination of goodness-of-fit of the model and recovery of coefficients consistent with expectations. Cases which result in significant effects with signs contradicting these expectations even with better fit will lead to rejection of the model, since these contradict the underlying theory.

World Demand

If a new government forms in a country with a small open economy and the next month the world's largest economies slow down, that country's unemployment will probably rise. The rise will appear to reflect the policy of the new government, since nothing in the past history of that country's unemployment rate predicts a rise at that time — unless the model of unemployment rates explicitly incorporates a term representing the level of economic activity in that country's trading environment. The relative level of economic activity is measured by a trade-weighted average of unemployment rates in nine major economies. World demand of some country m (with time subscripts omitted) is defined as the average of other major countries' unemployment rates U, weighted by the extent of exports X from country m to each of the others:

$$W_m = \sum_i \left(X_i \bigg/ \sum_j X_i \right) U_i, \qquad i,j \neq m \tag{1}$$

The countries are Belgium, Britain, Canada, France, West Germany, Italy, Japan, the Netherlands, and the United States, all of whose unemployment figures were collected back to January 1947. For example, "world demand" with respect to Britain is average unemployment in the other eight countries, with each country's unemployment rate weighted in the average by that country's share of Britain's exports. Alternative measures of world demand could be based on personal consumption or GDP, but these are not available monthly. (For some periods, only quarterly figures are available for West Germany and Italy.) World demand operates on domestic unemployment rates like any other shock. Any month's change in world demand has its largest effects initially, and continues to have effects which decay exponentially over time. However, there will be misspecification bias if all the apparent correlation between world demand and domestic unemployment reflects only shared trends, or if (omitted) mutual feedback relations exist between each domestic economy and the world demand series. Freeman (1983) gave a careful and insightful review of the econometric literature relating to this problem. Before incorporating world demand in the analysis of unemployment, we will investigate whether it appears to be "causally" related to domestic unemployment rates.

Special Considerations

War. A minor element in the controversy between Hibbs (1977, 1983) and Beck (1982) is whether or not to eliminate the effects of war before estimating the effects of party changes on American unemployment. No one would seriously argue that either the Korean or Vietnam wars were undertaken principally — few would argue even incidentally — to promote economic recovery, even though an obvious side effect of having many soldiers in uniform is increased demand for the labor of the rest of the work force. Both wars confound estimates in critical periods, particularly the coincidence of the end of the Korean War and the early months of Eisenhower's term. Since estimates of the unemployment-reducing effects of wars are significant throughout this study, a dummy variable indicating a large number of combat troops engaged overseas is included in all American models. (Since American unemployment is incorporated in world demand, war is implicitly in the British models as well.) The variable is defined as one for the periods June 1950–July 1953 and July 1965–December 1972 and zero otherwise.

Social welfare policy. Hibbs (1977) argued that British unemployment rose sharply because of the extension of supplementary benefits (welfare) to the unemployed beginning in October 1966. As he noted, however, there were also economic policy changes at the time. Their effects on estimates of consequences of party change are cancelled out by attribution of rising unemployment to this social policy innovation. In Hibbs's data, the series for the wholly unemployed, there was a sudden rise in unemployment in late 1966, coincident with the change in benefits. Examination of Figure 1 above shows that the increase in unemployment (including the temporarily stopped, as defined in this paper) began in July 1966, coincident with a national dock strike and unprecedentedly severe fiscal austerity measures to support the pound. These temporarily unemployed left work in July but *by definition* only became wholly unemployed three months later. Since it is unlikely that they left work in anticipation of benefits received later, the rise in unemployment should be attributed directly to economic policy and thus not controlled. The variable is therefore omitted from all models below.[7]

Estimation

ARIMA Processes

This paper isolates and estimates two regular components of the shocks (or two sources of disequilibrium), world demand and changes of party control. These will be sought independent of the (largely autoregressive, as explained above) processes ordinarily changing unemployment, which will be modeled using ARIMA techniques.[8] The purpose of ARIMA modeling is to reduce an observed series (called "realizations" or "manifestations") to a white noise or random series ("innovations") plus a set of processes by which the random input becomes the observed series. The models are conventionally described by the notation (p,d,q) where p is the order of the autoregressive and q the moving-average process (if any) and d the degree of differencing. If some determinants of unemployment have shifted "permanently," causing equilibrium unemployment to increase, the unemployment series is said to be "integrated," and such series must be "differenced" to achieve stationarity before attempts are made to estimate autoregressive parameters. Seasonally dependent monthly series are often adjusted by applying a $(P,D,Q)_{12}$ model multiplicatively with the main model. A model which contains an AR (1) parameter, is differenced once and seasonally adjusted by applying an MA (12) parameter to twelfth differences is denoted $(1,1,0) \times (0,1,1)_{12}$. The noise term in equation (2) below is of the form $(1,1,1) \times (0,0,1)_{12}$.

The first step is to create a "noise" model for unemployment in each country. Such a model contains only a random input plus the processes allowed by ARIMA methodology. Visual diagnosis and statistical confirmation of various autocorrelation functions are used to identify the processes which optimally reproduce the observed unemployment series from a random ("white noise") input. The substantive variables (party control, world demand) are then added. Parameter values are estimated by nonlinear least squares. The algorithm used takes advantage of the fact that the autoregressive process $y_t = bx_t + dy_{t-1}$ may also be represented by the infinite sum $y_t = b \sum_i d^i x_{t-i}$.

A finite approximation of this sum may easily be programmed as a loop, in which first-order dynamic processes involving discrete changes (intervention analyses for party control), continuous inputs (transfer function analysis for world demand), or past errors (autoregression) may be accumulated. Moving-average and seasonal adjustment terms are estimated by adjusting the errors before accumulation. The equation used for estimating the British model is:

$$\text{(2)}$$

$$U_t = \frac{b_w}{(1 - d_w L)(1 - d_0 L)} W_t + \sum_i \frac{b_i}{(1 - d_i L)(1 - d_0 L)} G_{t-1} + \frac{\Theta + \mu L + \epsilon L^{12}}{(1 - \phi L)(1 - d_0 L)} a_t$$

with d_0 set initially to 1.0, μ and ϵ are moving-average parameters, and ϕ the autoregressive parameter. Estimating a "quasi-differencing" parameter d_0 compromises risks of eliminating true partisan effects by misspecified differencing and inclusion of irrelevant terms through not differencing.[9]

The American unemployment series is demonstrably a second-order autoregressive process (both Hibbs and Beck agree), possibly owing to a more decentralized economic structure. However, the same loop structure can be extended to the AR (2) case. MacKuen (1981, pp. 41–42) gave an example of the relationship between AR (2) processes and cascaded filters. In such a two-step feedback model, with $Y = b_1 b_2 / (c_1 + D)(c_2 + D)$, where D is the differencing operator, one can derive an AR (1) parameter d_1 equal to $2 - c_1 - c_2$ and an AR (2) parameter d_2 equal to $(-1)(1 - c_1)(1 - c_2)$ so that the noise term in the American model becomes

$$\frac{\Theta + \mu L + \epsilon L^{12}}{(1 - d_1 L - d_2 L^2)(1 - d_0 L)} a_t \qquad \text{(3)}$$

with all other calculations unaffected.

Since the data begin in the middle of an incumbency in each country, any sustained political impact of the first incumbency is assumed to begin at steady-state level, and the impact of subsequent administrations is estimated relative to this (unidentified) initial steady-state level. Transitory impact parameters for political terms will be presented as 12-month cumulative impacts, the maximum. For world demand and war variables, parameter estimates for the impact parameter b and dynamic parameter d will be presented. These define the familiar initial surge and gradual decay of the first-order dynamic response profile.[10]

Every care has been taken to generate sensible estimates without data mining, including the use of multiple procedures, and so on. Some problems remain. The estimated political effects could be exaggerated, for two reasons. First, estimated standard errors are approximate (Ralston and Jennrich, 1978) and could be exaggerated. Second, the specification of world demand is not ideal. Some form of structural estimation might improve estimation of world demand effects and thereby give a clearer picture of the size of partisan effects. Not much can be done about this at present.

Granger Causality, World Demand, and Domestic Unemployment

Any attempt to model the impact of world demand on British and American unemployment is open to two separate objections. First, there is the problem that all unemployment rates may appear to trend or cycle together, with no evidence that changes in one country's unemployment *cause,* as opposed to coincide with, changes in unemployment somewhere else. World demand in this paper is measured by averages of unemployment rates, and unemployment rates have risen more or less everywhere in the last few years. A rigorous test is required to separate causation from shared trends. Second, the United States economy is large. Even with imports equal to only 10% of GDP, it is so large that trade with the United States is more important for many countries than trade with any other (even much more open) smaller economy. This sheer scale of economic enterprise is a source of what is sometimes called American dominance or hegemony in international trade: but does it insulate the United States from external disturbances?

Granger causality analysis (see Feige and Pearce, 1979; Freeman, 1983) is used in conjunction with ARIMA modeling to examine these problems, to see whether changes in American and/or British unemployment cause changes in world demand or vice versa. Granger causality analysis systematically isolates significant relationships between time series by testing whether the past behavior of one series X significantly adds to the explanation of the present behavior of another series Y, independent of and beyond what can be explained by the past behavior of Y. If X does so, it is said to "Granger cause" Y. While one can argue about this interpretation of causality, finding a Granger-causal relationship assures that apparent correlation is more than common background trends and cycles. For example, if American unemployment Granger causes world demand, then shocks from the United States have effects on world demand over and above what can be explained from the past history of world demand. Then models of unemployment in many countries with interdependent open economies should control for this American factor.

This paper employs an ARIMA-innovation approach to Granger causality.[11] To examine Granger causality between two time series, a noise model for each series is first estimated, as above, through diagnosis and identification of appropriate autoregressive, differencing, and moving-average components. In the case of the United States and world demand, residuals from the noise model for American unemployment and an analogous model for world demand (excluding American but including British unemployment) are the basis of the test. These residuals—"shocks" or "innovations"—are *random*: no shock is systematically predictable from the past history of other shocks.

The Granger causality test is based on the cross-correlations between the two series of innovations, over some long finite period of leads and lags. To determine statistical significance, one evaluates Haugh's test statistic

$$S = N \sum_k r^2_{\hat{x}\hat{y}} (k) \tag{4}$$

with x lagged from one to m periods, where S is distributed as X^2 with m degrees of freedom and $\hat{x}$ and $\hat{y}$ are the residuals from noise models for x and y. S is the sum of squared cross-correlations at these lags. If S exceeds the critical value for χ^2 with m degrees of freedom, x Granger causes y. To see if y Granger causes x, evaluate the analogous S statistic with k varying from $-m$ to -1, that is, with x *leading* rather than lagging. Temporal precedence determines the direction of causality. American unemployment Granger causes world demand if lagged innovations in United States unemployment correlate significantly with world demand innovations. If world demand shocks correlate with American unemployment shocks at some *lead,* the flow of causality is the other way. If the correlations are significant at both leads and lags, there is feedback.[12] There is no causality if neither is significant. Significant *negative* cross-correlation at short lags should not contribute to the finding of Granger causality, as this is inconsistent with the underlying trade-constraint explanation of the effects of world demand.

RESULTS

World Demand Causal Analysis

Expectations differ for the British and American cases. The British economy is small and open, so it is reasonable to expect a large effect from world demand on British unemployment, but less reason to expect independent feedback from changes in British unemployment onto the world rate (world demand for any country *excludes* that country's unemployment rate). The opposite holds for the United States. Here there should be a strong effect from American unemployment onto the rate for the rest of the world, reflecting America's size. But since the rest of the world's economy is now larger than that of the United States, there is also reason to expect feedback onto the American unemployment rate. However, since other countries respond to changes in American economic activity at different rates and to different degrees (Alt, 1984), this feedback may be small and erratic.

Tables 1 and 2 show the results. Table 1 is the estimates of the "noise" models. The British unemployment series is reduced to random residuals by the filter shown in Table 1(a). In the notation described above, this is a $(3,1,0) \times (0,1,1)_{12}$ ARIMA model. First and twelfth differences achieve stationarity and remove annual seasonal dependence. Seasonal adjustment is achieved by adding a 12th-order moving-average term. First- and third-order autoregressive parameters of .29 and .20, respectively, complete the model

TABLE 1. Noise Models for Domestic and World Unemployment, 1947–83

Term	Domestic Unemployment		World Demand	
(a) *Britain*				
d_0	1.0		1.0	
d_1	0.29	(6.3)	0.53	(1.8)
d_2	0.01	(0.3)	0.07	(0.9)
d_3	0.20	(4.3)		
d_{12}	1.0		1.0	
ma_1			0.41	(1.4)
ma_{12}	0.65	(15.1)	0.68	(18.1)
Constant	0.003	(0.6)	0.00	(0.1)
lag 24 χ^2 (prob)	28.4	(0.1)	18.1	(0.5)
resid. sum. sq.	10.98		23.70	
R^2	0.997		0.986	
(b) *United States*				
d_0	1.0		1.0	
d_1	0.14	(2.9)		
d_2	0.17	(3.6)		
d_{12}	1.0		1.0	
ma_1			−0.15	(4.0)
ma_2			−0.09	(2.7)
ma_{10}			−0.05	(1.4)
ma_{11}			−0.17	(4.5)
ma_{12}	0.75	(22.5)	0.63	(16.6)
Constant	0.005	(0.9)	0.00	(0.1)
lag 24 χ^2 (prob)	21.2	(0.4)	27.3	(0.07)
resid. sum. sq.	40.04		7.98	
R^2	0.972		0.993	

Note. Data are 444 monthly observations, January 1947–December 1983. Estimation used the SAS ARIMA package. T-statistics are in parentheses.

(the second-order term is never significant). The model explains 99.7% of the original variance of the unemployment rate. The residuals are satisfactorily random by a chi-squared test. The residual sum of squares serves as a goodness-of-fit benchmark with which to compare the success of later models. Table 1(b) shows that United States unemployment can similarly be modelled by a $(2,1,0) \times (0,1,1)_{12}$ filter: first and twelfth differences and seasonal correction as before but an AR (2) structure, consistent with the published analyses of Hibbs and Beck. The fit is good, though not quite as good as in the British case.

Noise models are also provided for the world demand series. Recall that different series represent world demand for different countries. British unemployment is in America's world demand but not Britain's. United States unemployment is in Britain's world demand but not its own. World demand with respect to Britain (Table 1(a)) is modeled by a process close to that of American unemployment, though with an extra first-order moving-average term. World demand with respect to the United States is an untidy collage of moving-average terms, possibly reflecting different responses to shocks from American unemployment in different countries (Alt, 1984). Both these noise models produce residuals satisfactorily devoid of any systematic process components.

The Granger causality analysis using the residuals from these noise models is summarized in Table 2. Looking at the British case, the largest amount of cross-correlation is at short positive lags, indicating that a shock from world demand affects British unemployment after a short delay, in fact, 1 to 3 months. There is no evidence of external effects with longer delays, and indeed eventually the cross-correlations become predominantly negative. At negative lags (implying causality in the opposite direction) the S-statistic indicates the possibility of effects from Britain onto the rest of the world after a delay of some 6 to 10 months. Some of these effects are negative, inexplicable within our model. There is probably no significant effect from British aggregate demand onto world demand. There is a significant effect from the rest of the world onto British unemployment after a short delay.

The American case is different. There is a strongly significant effect at short negative lags. Changes in American unemployment *lead* changes (of the same direction) in world demand by a few — particularly 1 to 2 — months. Effects disappear at longer delays. However, there is also some evidence of a change in world demand causing a change in American unemployment. The larger correlations from lags 1 to 10 are predominantly positive, though none are particularly large. Given the low power of this test and the fact that world demand is an average of different countries' unemployment rates which may themselves respond to common shocks at different rates, it appears safer *not to exclude* the possibility of feedback from the rest of the world when modeling United States unemployment.

Thus, changes in American unemployment affect world demand with a short delay, which in turn has further effects on the unemployment rates of individual countries with open economies like Britain. This is confirmed for other countries in Alt (1984). However, these changes in world demand may also feed back onto the United States after a further delay. This complicates modeling the impact of world demand on American unemployment, since care must be taken to avoid confusing feedback from the rest of the world with the domestic consequences of changes in American unemployment.

TABLE 2. Granger Causality Analysis

Lags	S^a	df	prob $<^b$
(a) *Britain*			
− 11 to − 15	2.28	5	0.80
− 6 to − 10	9.09	5	0.20
− 1 to − 5	6.75	5	0.30
+ 1 to + 5	12.43	5	0.03
+ 6 to + 10	1.40	5	0.95
+ 11 to + 15	3.27	5	0.70
(b) *United States*			
− 11 to − 15	8.77	5	0.20
− 6 to − 10	5.95	5	0.40
− 1 to − 5	16.96	5	0.005
+ 1 to + 5	9.35	5	0.10
+ 6 to + 10	11.98	5	0.05
+ 11 to + 15	4.28	5	0.60

Note. Data are the 444 monthly observations from January 1947–December 1983. Estimation used the SAS ARIMA package.
[a] The S statistic is the sum of squared correlations at the lags given between the residuals from the noise models for domestic and world unemployment given in Table 1.
[b] Probability is that for a chi-squared variate are large as the value of S in column 1 with 5 degrees of freedom.

Say a shock or change in American unemployment causes a change in world demand the next month, and this subsequent change feeds back onto American unemployment the month after. Thus a shock in month t would have a discernible feedback effect in month $t + 2$. But the same effect would be predicted from the noise model for American unemployment described above, which is a modified AR (2) − second-order autoregressive − process. Here as well a shock in month t has an effect in month $t + 2$. In order to isolate the feedback effects of world demand on United States unemployment, the world demand series will first have to be purged of the effects of lagged American unemployment. This is described in the discussion of the United States unemployment model, below.

British Unemployment, World Demand, and Party Changes

Earlier work has raised many relevant points. Beck (1982) showed that the impact parameters for party changes are somewhat variable in the United States, though parties are still clearly separated. Alt (1984) showed that if administrations are modeled separately in Britain, in the early period

(1947–72) only the Churchill government had a significant impact, large enough to carry the other episodes. Moreover, when more recent data were considered, any attempt to model all party changes with a single parameter gave wrongly signed or at best insignificant parameter estimates. Worse, omission of world demand regularly produced estimates of party change effects which had wrong signs. Moreover, in all cases models with transitory impacts performed as well as or better than did models with sustained impacts.

The same problems of suppression and misspecification arise in the full period estimates, but there is no need to expand on them. Instead, only the full model results for Britain 1947–83 are presented in Table 3. Regardless of the choice of final model, both the transitory-impact and sustained-impact model have much in common. In each of them both the differencing parameter d_0 and first-order autoregressive parameter d_1 are slightly reduced relative to the noise model, doubtless by the inclusion of so much extra information (world demand, party control) which represents part of the autoregression. Both models contain similar MA (1) and seasonal adjustment parameters. World demand in each is estimated to have an impact parameter value of .05 and a reequilibration parameter on the order of 0.8. This means that the cumulative effect of a one percentage point increase in world demand is to increase British unemployment by $.05/(1 - .8) =$ about .25 of a percentage point, the effect being largely complete within 12 to 18 months. This is slightly less than the estimate for the years since 1960 reported in Alt (1984). Finally, the sustained-impact model fits the data somewhat better than the transitory model and is preferred in this respect. The reduction in the sum of squared residuals is on the order of 4%.

There are big differences between party control terms of the sustained and transitory models, however. The sustained-impact model estimates fewer significant effects, and many of them are of the wrong sign. According to Table 3, relative to the steady state at the end of the Attlee government in November 1951 (which cannot strictly be separated from the constant term), the long-run effect of the Conservative Churchill government was to reduce unemployment by about six-tenths of a percentage point rather than to increase it. A glance at the low levels of unemployment between 1951 and 1964 in Figure 1 confirms that this estimate is reasonable. The fall in unemployment is the effect *relative to world demand,* whose effects are controlled in this model and which would have (owing to the rise in American unemployment and the recessions of the late 1950s and early 1960s) led one to expect larger increases in British unemployment than actually occurred.

Similarly, the first Wilson government had no long-run effect (positive, or wrong-sign coefficient but insignificant) on unemployment, and the Heath government effect was also of the wrong sign, showing a decline between

TABLE 3. Full Models for Britain, 1947–83

Term	Model	
	Sustained	Transitory
Party parameters		
Impact Δg or b_{12}		
Churchill (+)	− 0.639x+	0.493 +
Wilson I (−)	0.083x	− 0.608+
Heath (+)	− 1.802x	1.319*
Wilson II (−)	2.173x*	− 0.290*
Thatcher (+)	12.412*	1.954*
Dynamic		
Churchill	0.467+	0.880*
Wilson I	0.622	0.910*
Heath	1.012*	1.006*
Wilson II	0.604*	0.718*
Thatcher	0.971*	1.016*
World demand		
Impact (+)	0.051*	0.050*
Dynamic	0.807*	0.781*
Noise term		
d_1	0.262*	0.258*
d_0	0.975*	0.990*
Constant	3.47	1.75
ma_1	− 0.181*	− 0.188*
ma_{12}	0.456*	0.460*
Resid. sum of squares	9.78	10.23
R^2	0.998	0.998
lag 24 χ^2 (prob)	36.2 ($p < .06$)	33.9 ($p < .09$)

Note. Data are 444 monthly observations, January 1947–December 1983. Estimation is by non-linear least squares. Partisan impact coefficients are changes in equilibrium unemployment levels between administrations (Δg) or twelve-month impacts (b_{12}). Their expected signs are in parentheses. "x" denotes wrong sign, + denotes coefficient significant at .1 level or less, * indicates significance at .05 level or less. Statistical significance is based on approximate asymptotic standard errors (Ralston and Jennrich, 1978).

1970 and 1973 of 1.8 percentage points, also statistically insignificant. Again, while the Heath government actually did achieve a slight reduction in unemployment during its tenure, the magnitude of this estimated reduction has to be set against the increase in unemployment that would have been expected to follow the recession attendant on the end of the Vietnam War and the Nixon incomes policy. In other words, the first Wilson government had higher unemployment, and the Heath government lower (but neither significantly) than developments in the rest of the world might have made one expect. The long-run level of unemployment also increased under the second Labour government (contrary to expectations, and significantly). Here again the estimated steady-state change (2.2 percentage points) is *smaller* than the actual change in unemployment during their incumbency (closer to 3.5 percentage points), implying that some of the observed increase reflects world trends and that British unemployment fared slightly better than the world rate might have made one expect. Finally, the Thatcher government's effect is significant and of the expected sign. It is far larger than other party effects, because British unemployment does worse than the world rate, though that itself demands an explanation. In sum, four of the five incumbencies result in long-run effects contrary to the party change hypothesis expectations. In most cases, this is evidently because of previously ignored effects of world demand.

Quite the opposite happens with the transitory model. Table 3 gives the impact coefficients after one year, the cumulative effects of the first year in office, which will then dissipate over the rest of the incumbency at a rate given by the dynamic parameter. All the effects are consistent with theoretical expectations. All but two are strongly significantly estimated, and even the other two are weakly significant. The Churchill government's policies raised unemployment by half a percentage point in a year, *ceteris paribus*. The effect dissipated fairly rapidly and was by and large gone after two years, in time not to be distorted by the extremely low unemployment rates of the mid-1950s. The Labour government took over in 1964 and reduced unemployment by six-tenths of a point in a year. This effect too was largely gone by the devaluation of 1967. The Heath government's first year policies raised unemployment by 1.3 percentage points (starting from a higher base), but there is no evidence of subsequent reequilibration, though the government ended after only two- and a half years.[13] The second Labour government, as expected, reduced unemployment initially, at least relative to the OPEC-induced increases in unemployment taking place everywhere else in 1974, though as one sees from the sustained model, they could not sustain the reduction in the long run. Finally, the early-term effects of the Thatcher government are of the right sign. They are larger than those of previous incumbents (though unemployment is considerably higher already), though not so glaringly much larger as in the case of the sustained-impact model. Like the Heath government parameters, they show no sign of reequilibration, at least through their first term.

The fit of this model is not quite as good as that of the sustained-impact model. However, its interpretability and consistency with expectations (as a model rather than a test) is much better. The sustained-impact model was therefore reestimated with the erring coefficients restricted to an admissible range.[14] The result was an error sum of squares equal to that of the transitory impact model and only the Thatcher effects significant. The indicated choice of final model is to prefer (i) a transitory-impact model, which confirms expectations in each case, but confines party change effects on unemployment to those of early-term promise keeping — to (ii) a sustained-impact model, which has one significant effect, the Thatcher government, and an identical fit to (i) — to (iii) a sustained-impact model with better fit, but with unexplained long-run effects on unemployment which contradict expectations four times in five.

United States Unemployment

Table 4 lists the estimates for the United States unemployment model. The error term parameters are estimated in the underlying dynamic model form, but they can readily be translated into the notation of equation (3) above.[15] As in the British case, the incorporation of extra information results in an improvement in fit over the noise model 5% to 10% and a reduction in the magnitude of the autoregressive parameters. Moving average and seasonal parameters are significantly estimated, the residuals are satisfactorily random, and the overall fit is good. In spite of Beck's (1982) comments to the contrary, the effects of wars are clearly and significantly estimated. Presence of a major overseas military commitment reduces unemployment initially by .17 of a percentage point, but ultimately (after 2 to 3 years) by $.17/(1 - .9)$ or over one-and-a-half percentage points. Given that both wars overlap party changes, their effects should obviously be controlled.

The feedback effects of world demand are also clear. To generate the feedback, world demand is first modeled as a transfer function with lagged United States unemployment as the input, since this is what the analysis of cross-correlations suggested, and various autoregressive and moving-average processes removed.[16] The residuals from this transfer function are what is left after all the impact of American unemployment is removed from world demand (which average in this case, recall, does not contain the American rate). Moreover, these residuals are demonstrably uncorrelated with any lag of American unemployment less than 24 months, so no longer-term effects have been overlooked. The residuals are then entered into the final model for American unemployment, as world demand was into the British model, with the results shown in Table 4.

Both impact and dynamic parameters are significantly estimated. The impact parameter looks large, since it appears that a one percentage point increase in (residual) world demand increases American unemployment by a quarter of a percentage point. However, the residuals themselves are small. One percentage point is the maximum rather than a common size change in the world demand residuals once the effects of American unemployment are

TABLE 4. Full Models for United States, 1947–83

Term	Model	
	Sustained	Transitory
Party parameters		
Impact Δg or b_{12}		
Eisenhower (+)	5.618*	1.300 +
Kennedy-Johnson (−)	− 4.282 +	0.348ˣ*
Nixon-Ford (+)	4.091 +	0.635
Carter (−)	− 1.473	− 1.567*
Reagan (+)	1.347	0.473*
Dynamic		
Eisenhower	0.971*	0.977*
Kennedy-Johnson	0.103	0.049
Nixon-Ford	0.974*	0.993*
Carter	0.990*	0.975*
Reagan	0.985*	0.952*
World demand (residual)		
Impact (+)	0.254*	0.358*
Dynamic	0.992*	0.993*
War		
Impact (−)	− 0.170*	− 0.170*
Dynamic	0.895*	0.907*
Noise term		
c_1	− 0.096*	− 0.133*
c_2	1.207*	1.231*
d_0	0.183*	0.157*
Constant	− 0.053	− 1.860
ma_1	− 0.084*	− 0.074*
ma_{12}	0.547*	0.565*
Resid. sum of squares	38.03	36.97
R^2	0.973	0.974
lag 24 χ^2 (prob)	33.1 ($p < .10$)	31.9 ($p < .13$)

Note. Data, estimation, and notation follow Table 3.

removed. The standard deviation of these residuals is about one-twelfth that of the original world demand variable itself. Dividing the estimated impact coefficient in Table 4 (.254 or .358) by 12 gives an impact of .02 or .03, about 40% to 60% of the impact of raw world demand on British unemployment. At a rough guess, then, the impact of world demand — once the effects of past American unemployment are eliminated — on American unemployment is about half the initial impact of world demand on the British unemployment rate. The very large dynamic parameter in the American case makes the cumulative impact much larger, but it is reached very slowly indeed. This is a clear demonstration that American policy has consequences for the rest of the world but is itself affected in turn by external shocks.

Turning to the party change parameters, the sustained model produces large estimates of implicit steady-state changes, perhaps unreasonably large. However, they are in exact accord with the expectations of the original party change hypothesis and offset each other from one administration to the next. Relative to Truman, unemployment rose under Eisenhower, and the steady-state level would have been 5 percentage points higher, though it would not have been reached for many years. Most of this was offset under Kennedy-Johnson (though equilibrium here is reached in an unrealistically short time) and restored under Nixon-Ford. Presidents Carter and Reagan appear to have had little or no sustained effect on unemployment. The steady-state level falls a little under Carter and rises a little under Reagan, but after 8 years the party-political aspects of unemployment (net of any residual war effects and changes in world demand) are back at the level of the end of Ford's tenure.

The transitory-impact model fits the data better (the residual sum of squares is about 3% smaller) and gives estimates which are no less interpretable. Unemployment moves up initially under the Republican Presidents Eisenhower, Nixon, and Reagan, independent of all other effects. It moves down under Carter, though this effect was not sustained. Only under Kennedy are the early-term expectations contradicted, though the reequilibration rate is so quick that the small positive impact disappears almost immediately. The impacts are similar in size, and of reasonable magnitudes. As in the British case, the transitory impact model offers at least as good, if not a better, representation of political effects on unemployment. At least it is able to discern effects in changes since 1968, so there is no reason to think that party change effects disappeared with the advent of monetarism in the mid-1970s.

CONCLUSIONS

Several themes emerge from the results discussed in the previous part. First, models of transitory impacts from changes of party control perform as well or better than models with sustained impacts. There is a lot of evidence for consistent party-political effects on unemployment, and the effects are both large and long-lasting. However, changes of party control do not affect long-run unemployment equilibria. Such transitory effects are consistent with views of domestic policymakers as constrained by economic structure or international regimes, but also with competitive incentives in two-party systems. Second, models of the impact of party change on unemployment should always include the effects of external shocks to avoid misspecification. In Britain, it is impossible to obtain sensible estimates without considering world economic activity. In the United States, feedback from the rest of the world helps explain why, at least recently, party change impacts on unemployment have been transitory rather than sustained. The absence of controls for international factors underlies inconsistent results found in other studies.

Third, does it matter whether attention is focused on changes to the left or right? Is it more difficult for parties of the Left to make (even transitory) reductions in unemployment than for parties of the Right to allow unemployment to rise? There are reasons to expect this asymmetry. Whereas left-wing parties may promise to lower unemployment immediately, right-wing parties do not in general promise to raise it. Rather, they promise to do something which involves unemployment rising later in consequence. Controlling inflation is a common example of this. Moreover, structural resistance from approaching full employment may be encountered more quickly than dangers from the political upper limit to unemployment. A fixed exchange rate regime like the Bretton Woods system forced a government with expansionary programs (relative to the United States) to lose currency reserves and introduce austerity programs in the face of exchange rate crises. Inflows of reserves and upward pressure on exchange rates need not frustrate Right parties as much as the opposite effects frustrate Left parties. Finally, if people become accustomed to sustained conditions, then steady unemployment at any level stops hurting right-wing governments (who persist in policy) and stops helping left-wing governments (who desist), providing further incentives for the asymmetric behavior described above. Evidence from retrospective support models (Hibbs, 1982) that right-wing parties' constituencies are less concerned with unemployment is another asymmetry, producing a situation in which the incentives facing Right and Left governments are different.

Some evidence can be given about this asymmetry between parties of the Left and Right. In the transitory model for Britain, it is clear that in general reequilibration is slower in the cases of parties of the Right. Two administrations (Heath and Thatcher) showed no evidence of reequilibration at all, and the third (Churchill) reequilibrated slowly. By contrast, after initial reductions, one Labour administration returned to equilibrium at the speed estimated for the Churchill government, and the other much faster. (The sustained impact model contains too many wrong signs to analyze the dynamic parameters.) The same differences cannot readily be observed in the American data, where most dynamic parameters are extremely slow. However, in the sustained model, the two cases which confirm the original expectations best (large changes reached gradually) are both Republican, Eisenhower and Nixon-Ford. Effects in the transitory model are correctly signed in all the Republican cases. So there may be something in the conjecture that Right parties can raise unemployment more readily than Left parties can lower it, but further analysis is clearly called for.

The clear connection between changes of party control of government and changes in economic policy has several general implications. First, there is the implication for democratic theory that some degree of public control of policy is evident. Politicians keep election promises, even if the direction in which this leads policy is not sustained throughout incumbencies. Moreover, the government should be seen as responsible for changing economic conditions, at least to some extent, and the methodology of this paper offers a means toward assessing the extent to which changes in unemployment arise explicitly from political and nonpolitical sources.

There are also two clear implications for political economics. One is that concern with political influences on the economy should be oriented to post-election as well as pre-election changes. Effects reported here and in Alt (1984) for postelection trends in unemployment are more widespread than any evident pre-election trends in unemployment sought by students of the political business cycle. Second, there is a contribution here toward better specification of the economics of voting. Kramer (1983) pointed out that a critical role in the observed scale of economic voting is played by the size and variability of the "government-induced economic changes." Economic change would not have electoral consequences if the change were seen as originating in circumstances beyond the control of any government (Alt, 1979, chap. 8). If the extent of economic voting depends on the share of economic change attributable to government policy, one must estimate systematically how far different parties or administrations are associated with differences in economic outcomes. This paper does exactly that, for the unemployment rate.

The finding of party differences in the ultimate economic outcomes like unemployment only emphasizes the need to find similar partisan differences in the instruments by which governments make economic policy. Few published studies have found such effects consistently. Frey's (1978) estimates of party differences in income shares spent were not significant. Nor were Cowart's (1978) fiscal or monetary policy estimates. Beck's (1983) study of monetary policy finds no significant administration-related changes in British interest rates, a finding echoed in other studies of the United States like Chappell and Keech (1984). Alt and Chrystal (1983) found a significant difference in transfer payments under the 1964 Labour government, but in no other case, nor were there significant party or administration differences in public consumption or investment once economic constraints were allowed for. (Of course, the further one moves toward instruments whose final effects are measurable like the full employment surplus, the less these instruments resemble the tools actually controlled by policymakers.)

However, the situation of finding party differences in the ultimate outcomes but not the instruments is highly unsatisfactory. Differences in neither (economic structural dominance) or both (political discretion) would be easy to accept. Differences in the instruments but not the outcomes would lead one to believe that the authorities tried but were unable to affect outcomes systematically, owing to the strength and rigidity of other economic constraints or a misunderstanding of the nature of the economy. Party differences in the outcomes but not the instruments must involve misspecification. Since the outcome effects have been demonstrated in ARIMA models, they are likely to be robust. Hence richer systematic models of the instruments must be developed in order to find the means by which the party differences in outcomes arise.

NOTES

1. The final estimates for Britain 1960–83 (Alt, 1984, table 4, model 2) suggested that each percentage point increase in unemployment in Britain's trading partners raised British unemployment, *ceteris paribus,* by about 0.3 percentage points in the long run and that there were regular partisan effects of the expected sort, save that the effect of the Thatcher regime was about twice as large as the rest.

2. Other derivations of this process are possible. See Alt (1984). MacKuen (1981) gave an accessible treatment of the relationship between an equilibrium or negative feedback dynamic system and the autoregressive process.

3. Hegemony depends on America's position in NATO and military aid, its key position in Bretton Woods, etc., as well as size.

4. On the one hand, Keynesians who subscribe to the possibility of multiple employment equilibria believe that government manipulation of aggregate demand can shift employment permanently to a new equilibrium level. Monetarists argue that accelerating inflation would eventually cancel out government initiatives to reduce unemployment below the "natural rate," making only transitory political changes in unemployment possible. Extreme versions of the rational expectations hypothesis, in which policy changes are anticipated and offset, would preclude any partisan effects, though more moderate versions would allow transitory effects arising from unanticipated or changing behavior.

5. Cross-national differences in methods of counting the unemployed are not an insuperable difficulty, since the analysis focuses on comparing time-series analyzed within individual countries. Recent comparisons to the OECD's "standardized" rate show that the distortions caused by different methods of counting are no longer as large as some years ago. The data were checked for changes in counting to avoid confounding these with changes of party control. Such a change occurs near the end of the British series, and the last year's published figures have been adjusted.

6. Twelve-month transitory inputs were used because the complexity and federalism of the U.S. political system imply a slower start even if all goes well. The same length was used for Britain for comparability. Six months was used in Alt (1984), but gave similar results to those reported here.

7. Repeated estimation with restrictions on the cumulative impact of the social welfare variable showed that party change parameter estimates were robust unless social welfare was restricted to have virtually no effect at all, at which point the party change parameter for the 1964 Labour government became insignificant.

8. The techniques originate with Box and Jenkins (1976) and are reviewed in McCleary and Hay (1980). The normal strategy estimates parameters relating to the errors and the substantive inputs of world demand and party control simultaneously. But the inputs are driven by processes isomorphic to those of the errors (essentially autoregressive or first-order dynamic processes). Simultaneous estimation will probably result in making estimates of the effects of world demand and party control coefficients which would be significant in the realizations (observed series) insignificant in the presence of the modeled noise process. In such a case the extra information in the inputs does not improve forecasts which could have been made from information in the unemployment series alone. However, these forecasts contain not just the noise, but also a powerful endogenous process on whose elements we are trying to cast some light. This problem is especially acute when the noise model involves complex processes whose origins are not understood. The magnitude of the problem was illustrated in preliminary British estimates, where the parameters relating to world demand and party control could explain 75% of the variance in unemployment 1960–83 if separately estimated first, with the residuals from these models subsequently whitened. The standard error of the separately estimated model was not markedly inferior to the standard error of the simultaneously estimated model.

9. For instance,

   ell = e;te = phi*le; to = d0*lo;ema = mu*ell;
   tg = bl*G + dl*lg;
   tw = bw*W + dw*lw;
   lg = tg;lw = tw;
   uh = theta + te + tg + tw − ema;
   e = u − uh;a = e − ema;le = te + a;
   uh = theta + te + tg + tw + to;
   o = u − uh;lo = to + o;retain le e lo lg lw;

   is a loop sufficient to estimate a first-order transfer function on world demand W, intervention for party control G, and ARMA $(1,d_0,1)$ process on the random errors "a". This loop (plus initial conditions and seasonal adjustments) can be entered into the SAS-NLIN procedure to give nonlinear estimates and asymptotic confidence intervals on the model described above.

10. The procedure by which estimates were actually obtained is as follows: *Step 1:* Initial parameter estimates for the noise term were taken from preliminary SAS-ARIMA estimates, with d_0 set to 1.0, while all other impact parameters were started at .01 and all dynamic parameters started at .5. Each model was estimated using a nonlinear minimization procedure. *Step 2:* The resulting residuals from step 1 were examined for evidence of non-randomness. With any necessary adjustment made to the noise term (and small alterations made to other coefficients to avoid local minimum problems), the model was rerun. *Step 3:* If the residuals from step 2 were not white, step 2 was repeated once more. Then each model was rerun, if necessary, with any insignificant noise term parameters omitted. *Step 4:* As confirmation, the final solution was rerun with a different minimization routine. If major discrepancies were observed, analysis returned to step 2.

11. The alternative "direct Granger" method consists of testing for x causing y by adding many lags of x to the right-hand side of an equation already containing many lags of y and testing (by an F-test) the joint contribution of these many lags of x. This method is less likely to

reject a true causal relationship, but more likely to fail to control for shared trends or moving-average errors. Because the ARIMA approach treats *all* process (ARIMA terms) correlation as spurious, it is of lower power than alternative approaches: there is a good chance that it may reject a significant relationship where one truly exists. However, the use of averages makes it imperative to control rigidly for process correlation, and the use of ARIMA models fits comfortably into the estimation strategy for the rest of the paper.

12. The unidirectional test is also conservative in eliminating all contemporaneous correlation from the tests of significance. Only theory would indicate the direction of causality in that case. We will concentrate on a relatively short set of leads and lags (up to plus or minus 5 months) in interpreting the results.

13. The absence of reequilibration means effectively that the one-year impact is sustained at a constant (if $d = 1.0$) or slightly increasing (if $d > 1.0$) level for the rest of the incumbency.

14. Estimation is actually done of the underlying impact and dynamic coefficients, which are then converted to relative steady-state values. The significance of the changes in steady state refer back to the significance of the underlying b coefficients. When restricted estimation is performed, two of these coefficients become (restrictedly) equal to zero and two are greater than zero in magnitude, but insignificant.

15. The denominator polynomial of the noise model in Table 1 for American unemployment is $(1 - d_1L - d_2L^2)$ $(1 - L)$, where L is that lag operator. Multiplying this through gives $(1 - (1 + d_1)L + (d_1 - d_2)L^2 + d_2L^3)$. Introducing the "quasi-differencing parameter" d_0 (i.e., substituting $1 - d_0L$ for $1 - L$), makes this $(1 - (d_0 + d_1) L + (d_0d_1 - d_2)L^2 + d_0d_2L^3)$, where $d_1 = 2 - c_1 - c_2$ and $d_2 = (-1)(1 - c_1)(1 - c_2)$ where c_1 and c_2 are the negative feedback parameters from the underlying cascaded dynamic model. The estimates in Table 1 make the denominator polynomial for the noise model equal to $(1 - 1.14L - .03L^2 + .17L^3)$, while from Table 4's estimates for the sustained-impact model it is $(1 - 1.072L - .064L^2 + .042L^3)$ and for the transitory-impact model it is $(1 - 1.059L - .12L^2 + .041L^3)$. There is a marked similarity among all three models.

16. The transfer function takes first and twelfth differences of world demand and United States unemployment. The input is American unemployment lagged one period, with an impact parameter of 0.08 (highly significant) and dynamic parameter of 0.20 (insignificant). AR (1) and AR (2) and MA (12) parameters are also estimated (that is, their effects removed) to eliminate the process driving the American unemployment rate. This model has residuals (to be used as input into the American unemployment model) uncorrelated with any lag of American unemployment up to 3 years. The transfer function explains over 99% of the original variance of world demand, outperforming the noise model of Table 1(b) by about 2%.

REFERENCES

Alt, J. (1979). *The Politics of Economic Decline.* Cambridge: Cambridge University Press.

Alt, J. (1984). Political parties, world demand, and unemployment: domestic and international sources of economic activity. *American Political Science Review,* forthcoming.

Alt, J. (1985). The political economy of Thatcher's Britain: a comparative perspective. Mimeo., Washington University, St. Louis.

Alt, J., and Chrystal, K. A. (1983). *Political Economics.* Berkeley: University of California Press.

Beck, N. (1982). Parties, administrations, and American macroeconomic outcomes. *American Political Science Review* 76:83–93.

Beck, N. (1983). Domestic politics and monetary policy: a comparative perspective. Paper presented at the annual meeting of the American Political Science Association, Chicago.

Box, G., and Jenkins, G. (1976). *Time Series Analysis.* San Francisco: Holden-Day.

Cairncross, A., and Eichengreen, B. (1983). *Sterling in Decline.* Oxford: Blackwell.

Cameron, D. (1978). The expansion of the public economy: a comparative analysis. *American Political Science Review* 72:1243–1261.

Castles, F. (1982). *The Impact of Parties.* Beverly Hills: Sage.

Chappell, H., and Keech, W. (1984). Party differences in macroeconomic policies and outcomes. Paper presented to the annual meeting of the Public Choice Society, Phoenix.

Cowart, A. (1978). The economic policies of European governments. *British Journal of Political Science* 8:285–312 and 425–439.

Cox, G., McCubbins, M., and Sullivan, T. (1984). Policy choice as an electoral investment. *Social Choice and Welfare* 1:231–242.

Dow, J. (1968). *The Management of the British Economy 1945–60.* Cambridge: Cambridge University Press.

Feige, E., and Pearce, D. (1979). The causal relationship between money and income: some caveats for time series analysis. *Review of Economics and Statistics* 61: 521–533.

Freeman, J. (1983). Granger causality and time series analysis of political relationships. *American Journal of Political Science* 27:327–358.

Frey, B. (1978). *Modern Political Economy.* London: Martin Robertson.

Hibbs, D. (1977). Political parties and macroeconomic policy. *American Political Science Review* 71:1467–1487.

Hibbs, D. (1982). Economic outcomes and political support for British governments among occupational classes: a dynamic analysis. *American Political Science Review* 76:259–279.

Hibbs, D. (1983). Communication. *American Political Science Review* 77:447–451.

Kramer, G. (1983). The ecological fallacy revisited: aggregate- versus individual-level findings on economics and elections and sociotropic voting. *American Political Science Review* 77:92–111.

Keman, H., and Braun, D. (1984). The limits of political control: a cross-national comparison of economic policy responses in eighteen capitalist democracies. *European Journal of Political Research* 12:101–108.

McCallum, B. (1978). The political business cycle: an empirical test. *Southern Economic Journal* 44:504–515.

McCleary, R., and Hay, R. (1980). *Applied Time Series Analysis for the Social Sciences.* Beverly Hills: Sage.

MacKuen, M. (1981). *More Than News.* Beverly Hills: Sage.

Nickell, S. (1982). The determinants of equilibrium unemployment in Britain. *Economic Journal* 92:555–575.

Paldam, M. (1979). Is there an electional cycle? *Scandinavian Journal of Economics* 81:323–342.

Ralston, M., and Jennrich, R. (1978). DUD: a derivative-free algorithm for non-linear least squares. *Technometrics* 20:7–14.

Rose, R. (1980). *Do Parties Make a Difference?* Chatham, N.J.: Chatham House.

Schmidt, M. (1983). Politics of unemployment rates and labour market policy in OECD nations. Presented to the Conference on Public Policy to Combat Unemployment, Nürnberg.

Schmidt, M. (1984). The welfare state and the economy in periods of economic crisis: a comparative study of twenty-three OECD nations. *European Journal of Political Research* 12:1–26.

Woolley, J. (1984). Political factors in monetary policy. In D. Hodgman (ed.), *The Political Economy of Monetary Policy: National and International Aspects.* Federal Reserve Bank of Boston Conference Series, Number 26.

CHAPTER **3**

Perceptions of Economic Performance and Voting Behavior in the 1983 General Election in Britain

Paul Whiteley
Department of Politics, University of Bristol, England

Some of the earliest research into the question of the influence of the economy on electoral support related to Britain. This was true both in the case of individual-level analysis (Butler and Stokes, 1974) and the aggregate analysis of popularity functions over time (Goodhart and Bhansali, 1970). However, unlike the United States, where aggregate and individual-level analyses have developed side by side and where there are methodological disputes about which is most appropriate, research in Britain has been largely at the aggregate level (Frey and Schneider, 1978, 1981; Chrystal and Alt, 1981; Whiteley, 1980, 1984). This is rather curious in a way, since when Butler and Stokes developed their "valence" model of the effects of economic conditions on electoral support, this appeared to open up a rich variety of research possibilities. However, subsequent work on the effects of the economy on electoral behavior using individual-level survey data is relatively thin and confined to a few writers (Alt, 1979; Crewe and Särlvik, 1983; Whiteley 1983).

The purpose of this paper is to develop and test a model of the effects of voters' perceptions of economic performance on electoral behavior in the 1983 general election. This election was a particularly suitable opportunity to test the impact of voters' evaluations because it was one in which the relationship between social class and party, the traditional determinant of elections in Britain, was fractured by a realignment of the party system. The relationship between class and party had been declining for a number of years (Franklin and Mughan, 1978; Crewe and Särlvik, 1983), but it declined precipitously at the 1983 general election following the split in the Labour party in 1981 and the emergence of the Social Democratic and Liberal party alliance. Moreover, a "center-periphery" geographical cleavage in electoral behavior emerged more clearly from this election than ever before, and to a significant extent this followed regional variations in economic prosperity (McAllister and Rose, 1984). Thus the decline in class voting and the emergence of a geographical cleavage made economic performance a very significant influence on electoral choice in 1983.

INDIVIDUAL RESPONSES TO ECONOMIC CONDITIONS

The starting point of research into economic effects on voting in Britain was the Butler and Stokes "valence" model. The basic model is very simple: social class largely determines partisanship, which largely determines voting behavior.[1] To support this model, they showed that in 1963 about 79% of the respondents with a middle-class self-image were Conservative identifiers, and 72% with a working-class self-image were Labour identifiers (Butler and Stokes, 1974, p. 77). Thus, the relationship between social class and partisanship, though not perfect, appeared to be quite strong. Moreover, this picture does not change if one measures social class by some objective measure such as occupational status. Furthermore, with very few independents in the electorate, party identification is a very strong predictor of voting behavior.

In the Butler-Stokes model, issues play very much a subsidiary short-term role in comparison with party identification. They are most important for voters with weak partisan attachments. Among the influential issues, the economic performance of the incumbent party is seen as the most important and is also regarded as purely a valence issue; that is, the overwhelming majority of voters prefer a good economic performance to a bad one; therefore, there is no division of opinion within the electorate on the goals of economic policy. In assessing economic performance, Butler and Stokes argued that voters operate with a relatively simple reward-punishment model, very similar to that postulated by Key (1966) in the United States. Voters tend to support the party that makes them feel better off and punish the party that makes them feel worse off. The impact of the economy on elections is reduced by the fact that strong partisans tend to ignore such considerations, and in any case, most respondents to their surveys thought that their own economic prospects would remain unchanged under either of the major parties. However, as Butler and Stokes pointed out: "Among those who felt that their well-being would change, there was a marked tendency to see one party or the other as more likely to improve their economic condition" (1974, p. 380).

Butler and Stokes supported the valence model with both individual-level and aggregate-level data. On the whole, their individual-level survey analysis is more convincing than their aggregate analysis, despite the lack of proper controls. This is because they did not attempt to model the relationships between the time series in the aggregate analysis, except for the relationship between party lead and the balance of payments (1974, p. 399), which is impossible to evaluate anyway, since they report no coefficients or test statistics.

Alt criticized this model, largely in relation to the aggregate analysis (1979, pp. 16–21). He also developed his own model, which is based on the notion of an individual's "economic outlook." Alt defined this as follows: "The economic outlook of an individual is taken to be, at its broadest, a subjective assessment of economic well-being: an evaluation filter through which external events pass. Economic outlook is an evaluation of economic conditions" (1979, p. 89).

In Alt's model, the voters' evaluations of government popularity are determined by their approval of its record, which is, in turn, determined by economic outlooks. Thus, the concept is at the center of the model. Economic outlook is, in turn, determined by voters' perceptions and expectations of economic performance, which is determined by actual economic outcomes. Thus, the model is essentially a recursive causal chain running from actual economic outcomes to government popularity (1979, p. 127). Alt did not apply his model to estimate a vote function. In other words, we do not know from his analysis how economic outlooks influence voting behavior, as distinct from government popularity in the polls.

Since Alt's work, there have been two other investigations of the relationship between perceptions of economic performance and electoral behavior that do specify and test a vote function. Crewe and Särlvik (1983) have developed a multivariate model of voting behavior that they applied to the general election of 1979. They predicted the probability of voting Conservative, Liberal, and Labour from three classes of variables: First, there is the voters' views on the two major parties' handling of economic problems when they were in office; second, the voters' perceptions of political issues such as racial and sexual equality, permissiveness, and social welfare spending; and third, the voters' attitudes about policy positions taken up by the different parties in 1979 on issues like incomes policy, the European Economic Community, trade union legislation, and public ownership of industry.

All the various attitude measures in their model together explain 59% of the variance in voting behavior in 1979, and the economic issues alone explain 48% (Crewe and Särlvik, 1983, p. 266). The economic performance indicators that relate to inflation, unemployment, and strikes are the most significant predictors of voting behavior in 1979 out of the three groups of issues.

There are, however, two serious defects with the Crewe and Särlvik model. First, they assume that the three parties are distributed evenly along a monotonically increasing unidimensional scale. Conservatives are arbitrarily assigned a score one, Liberals two, and Labour supporters three (1983, p. 381). This is a very strong assumption, which is not really justified in the absence of any attempt to scale these parties. But, perhaps more seriously, they fail to control for partisanship in the model, and so the estimates of the effects are unreliable if one wants to determine the influence of issues on voting behavior independently of partisan attachments.

Such a model was specified and tested by Whiteley (1983), using data from the 1979 British Election Study. This is a linear probability model testing for a vote function of support for the Labour party. The probability of voting Labour is predicted from four classes of variables. First, there are voters' social attributes that concern their relationships to the means of production and consumption in society; this includes such variables as occupational status, sectoral status,[2] trade union membership, and home ownership. Second, there is an affective evaluation scale, which is a thermometer measure of respondents' liking of the Labour party along a 10-point scale and which is, of course, highly correlated with party identification. Third, there are prospective evaluations of various salient policy proposals made by the major political parties. And fourth, there are retrospective evaluations of Labour's performance in handling the economy. Thus, in this model, economic assessments appear as retrospective evaluations.

Altogether there are 18 different variables in the model, which together explain 47% of the variance in the probability of voting Labour in 1979. Social attributes are relatively poor predictors, and the affective evaluation scale is the best predictor. However, retrospective evaluations, or assessments of economic performance, are easily the strongest predictors after the affective evaluation scale. Thus, voters judged the Labour party on its record and not on the promises it made. Overall, the evidence pointed to a rather instrumental electorate whose support did not strongly reflect social class divisions and who were strongly influenced by economic performance.

Since the 1979 election the British party system has undergone a major upheaval. In 1981 the Labour party split, and the Social Democratic party (SPD) was founded by four former Labour cabinet ministers. This had a drastic effect on public opinion in the short run. In December 1981, the SDP had the support of 36% of the electorate in the Gallup voting intention series (Gallup, 1981) compared with 23% for the Conservatives and 23.5% for Labour. This was an unprecedented shift in opinion, and although the new party quickly began to lose ground relative to the two major parties, it quickly formed an electoral alliance with the Liberals, which had a longer-term effect on voting behavior. In the 1983 general election, the Liberal/SDP alliance received 26% of the popular vote, some 2% behind Labour. This compares with the Liberals' solo performance of just under 14% in the 1979 election. Traditional voting patterns had clearly shifted.

In the subsequent sections of this paper, we specify and test a multivariate model of the influence of voters' perceptions of economic conditions on electoral behavior in the 1983 general election. We then use survey data obtained at the time of the election to examine this model. The aim is to estimate the importance of economic perceptions in relation to other factors in determining the vote for the Conservatives in 1983.

THE THEORETICAL MODEL

All the economic variables in the model to be tested refer to voters' perceptions of economic performance rather than to any objective measure of performance such as changes in real incomes. Kramer (1983) has convincingly shown that individual-level survey models of economic influences on voting behavior are likely to be thoroughly misleading when they use objective measures of performance. He recommended aggregate time series analysis with this type of data. In the present case Kramer's incisive critique does not apply, since we are using subjective evaluations of performance.

In the model, voting behavior is seen as a product of long-term predispositions that are summarized by the party identification variable, and short-term issue perceptions that are summarized by the three classes of attitude indicators. This model is an extension and development of the one outlined in the previous section (Whiteley, 1983). The main difference between this and the earlier model is that this one omits indicators of socioeconomic status. This is because such measures, particularly occupational status, contribute very little to explaining voting behavior in 1983. Accordingly, these variables are omitted from the model. This in itself is an interesting finding, since social class has been at the center of research into electoral behavior in Britain for many years. Occupational status, the standard measure of social class, is not remotely statistically significant in the full model.

We estimate the model using data from a Gallup survey of more than

4,000 respondents, which was carried out for the BBC on the eve-of-poll and on election day.[2] It was very accurate in forecasting the final vote,[4] and so provides a reliable report of public opinion at the time of the general election.

The dependent variable in the model is a dummy variable measuring the probability of voting Conservative. As is well known, there can be statistical problems with such a specification,[5] but a reanalysis of the results with a probit model revealed no significant differences. Accordingly, we use the linear probability specification for reasons of ease of interpretation. The analysis is carried out with those respondents who had already voted or said they would definitely vote.

The party identification variable and the indicators of noneconomic issues in the election are included in the model primarily as controls. Party identification is measured with the standard 7-point scale, in two different versions. The first version is a Conservative-Labour identification scale, and the second is a Conservative-Alliance identification scale.

The salient noneconomic issues in the campaign are identified from an open-ended question in the survey about voters' concerns over issues. There are four noneconomic issues altogether, two of them relating to defense. The first is a general question that asked respondents to indicate which party was best at "ensuring that Britain is safely defended"; the second is concerned with the introduction of cruise missiles into Britain, asking respondents if they thought this was a good idea or not. The third is concerned with financial support for the National Health Service, which became a point of contention between the parties during the campaign; and the fourth is an attitude scale that measures the respondents' views on laws to regulate trade unions.

Both sets of economic indicators have retrospective and prospective dimensions, although the emphasis is on the former rather than the latter. In the case of personal economic circumstances, respondents were asked "how does the financial situation in your own household compare with what it was twelve months go?;" and also "how do you think the financial situation in your household will develop over the next twelve months?." In the case of national economic circumstances, respondents were asked the same two questions except the phrase "in this country" was substituted for "in your own household." This close similarity in the wordings together with the fact that these questions were all asked at the same point in the interview schedule have implications for the reliability of the answers, as we shall see below.

In addition to the two questions about evaluations of national economic conditions, respondents were also asked three additional questions about the comparative performance of the political parties in three areas. First, there was a general question about which party was best at "making Britain more prosperous"; second, a question on the party best at "keeping prices down"; and third, a question on the party best at "reducing unemployment." Altogether then, there are five indicators of attitudes to national economic circumstances. Each of the party questions has been recorded into a dummy variable to make them suitable for quantitative analysis.

THE MULTIVARIATE ANALYSIS OF THE MODEL

As a first step toward defining the multivariate model, we consider the bivariate relationships between voting behavior and the other predictor variables. This is done in Table 1, which also includes bivariate correlation coefficients. The percentages in this table refer to those respondents with or without that particular attitude who did or did not vote Conservative in 1983. Thus 95.2% of the very strong Conservative identifiers voted Conservative, and 4.8% did not; 46.1% of nonidentifiers voted Conservative and 53.9% did not, and so on.

All the bivariate relationships in Table 1 are highly significant, though some correlations are stronger than others. Not surprisingly, the relationships between the party identification scales and voting behavior are very strong, although the Conservative-Labour scale is more highly correlated with voting than the Conservative-Alliance scale. Overall, the indicators of national economic circumstances are more highly correlated with voting than are the other issue indicators; this is true of the prosperity indicator as well as unemployment and inflation. The lowest correlations are between the personal economic circumstances indicators and voting behavior. The noneconomic issues are also significantly related to voting, particularly the issue of financial support for the National Health Service.

Since we are using a variety of observable indicators of three underlying or latent variables, we require a technique that allows us to estimate the relationships between observable and unobservable variables as well as the causal links specified. Accordingly, we use the full information maximum likelihood estimation procedure available in the LISREL program (Jöreskog, 1973, 1977; Jöreskog and Sörbom, 1981). However, before examining the model, which includes latent variables, we estimate the relationships between the observables first, making each of the variables discussed above a predictor of voting behavior. These estimates appear in Table 2 which contains two models, one for each of the party identification scales.

The overall goodness of fit of the models in Table 2 is very high in both cases. In both models party identification is the strongest predictor of voting, followed by the "prosperity" indicator, which is a general measure of voters' evaluations of economic performance. Unemployment and inflation are also highly significant predictors of voting. Altogether 48% of respon-

TABLE 1. The Relationship Between Party Identification, Attitudes to the National Economy, Personal Economic Circumstances, Noneconomic Issues and Voting Behavior in 1983

		Vote[a]	
		Conservative	Non-Conservative
Variable	Coding	(1)	(0)
1. Party identifica- tion (Con-Lab)	1 Very strong Conservative	95.2%	4.8%
	2 Fairly strong Conservative	92.2	7.8
	3 Not very strong Conservative	71.0	29.0
	4 None	46.1	53.9
	5 Not very strong Labour	13.4	86.6
	6 Fairly strong Labour	4.7	95.3
	7 Very strong Labour $r = -.82$	1.5	98.5
2. Party identifica- tion (Con- Alliance)	1 Very strong Conservative	95.2%	4.8%
	2 Fairly strong Conservative	92.2	7.8
	3 Not very strong Conservative	71.0	29.0
	4 None	46.1	53.9
	5 Not very strong Alliance	12.5	87.5
	6 Fairly strong Alliance	11.2	88.8
	7 Very strong Alliance $r = -.75$	4.1	95.9
3. Party best at making Britain more prosperous	1 Conservative 0 Non-Conservative $r = .78$	80.9% 2.6	19.1% 97.4
4. Party best at reducing unem- ployment	1 Conservative 0 Non-Conservative $r = .72$	93.5% 17.6	6.5% 82.4

TABLE 1. (*Continued*)

		Vote[a]	
Variable	Coding	Conservative (1)	Non-Conservative (0)
5. Party best at keeping prices down	1 Conservative 0 Non-Conservative $r = .72$	80.7% 8.9	19.3% 91.1
6. How did the national economy change over last 12 months?	1 Got a lot better 2 Got a little better 3 Stayed the same 4 Got a little worse 5 Got a lot worse $r = -.59$	87.0% 72.5 48.8 18.8 4.9	13.0% 27.5 51.2 81.2 95.1
7. How will the national economy change over next 12 months?	1 Get a lot better 2 Get a little better 3 Stay same 4 Get a little worse 5 Get a lot worse $r = -.49$	81.9% 67.0 37.2 13.0 3.4	18.1% 33.0 62.8 87.0 96.6
8. How did the respondents' personal financial situation change in last 12 months?	1 Got a lot better 2 Got a little better 3 Stayed same 4 Got a little worse 5 Got a lot worse $r = -.41$	78.9% 64.8 49.9 25.0 11.1	21.1% 35.2 50.1 75.0 88.9
9. How will the respondents' personal financial situation change in next 12 months?	1 Get a lot better 2 Get a little better 3 Stay same 4 Get a little worse 5. Get a lot worse $r = -.34$	72.6% 59.6 43.9 17.0 7.2	27.4% 40.4 56.1 83.0 92.8
10. Party best at ensuring Britain's defence	1 Conservative 0 Non-Conservative $r = .62$	67.7% 3.1	32.3% 96.9
11. Party best at providing for the Health Service	1 Conservative 0 Non-Conservative $r = .71$	94.8% 18.8	5.2% 81.2

TABLE 1. (*Continued*)

		Vote[a]	
Variable	Coding	Conservative (1)	Non-Conservative (0)
12. Cruise missiles should be allowed in to Britain	1 Very good idea	71.5%	28.5%
	2 Fairly good idea	59.9	40.1
	3 Fairly bad idea	30.3	69.7
	4 Very bad idea	12.1	87.9
	$r = -.50$		
13. There should be stricter laws to regulate trade unions	1 Very strongly agree	67.3%	32.7%
	2 Fairly strongly agree	49.0	51.0
	3 Mildly agree	32.5	67.5
	4 Mildly disagree	24.1	75.9
	5 Fairly strongly disagree	13.1	86.9
	6 Very strongly disagree	7.6	92.4
	$r = -.44$		

[a]Average $N = 2,780$.

dents thought that the Conservatives were best at making Britain more prosperous, and 42% thought they were best at keeping prices down. Some 28% thought they were best at reducing unemployment. With the exception of the unemployment issue, opposition support was divided fairly evenly between Labour and the Alliance on these issues, so that, for example, 20% of respondents thought that Labour is the best party on making Britain more prosperous, and 15% thought the Alliance. Thus, on balance, the Conservatives had a big advantage on these retrospective issue indicators of economic performance.

However, there appears to be something of a paradox in Table 2 in the voters' evaluations of national and personal economic conditions. In the Conservative-Labour model in this table, the personal financial situation indicators are statistically significant, but the national economic indicators are not. This is also true of future evaluations of the national economy in the Conservative-Alliance model of Table 2. This appears to be inconsistent with the earlier evidence on evaluations of national economic performance, and it is also at odds with Alt's analysis referred to earlier (Alt, 1979). He showed that personal financial conditions are unrelated to assessments of party performance. However, as we shall see below this apparent paradox

TABLE 2. Party Identification and Attitudes as Predictors of the Probability of Voting Conservative in 1983 (standardized coefficients)

Party Identification and Attitudes	Conservative-Labour Model	Conservative-Alliance Model
Conservative-Labour identification	− 0.283 (19.9)[a]	
Conservative-Alliance identification		− 0.263 (24.8)[a]
Party best at prosperity	0.229 (18.4)	0.221 (18.3)
Party best at reducing unemployment	0.158 (14.3)	0.150 (13.9)
Party best at keeping prices down	0.095 (8.2)	0.106 (9.5)
Change in national economy in last 12 months	− 0.010 (0.9)	− 0.053 (5.2)
Change in national economy in next 12 months	− 0.002 (0.2)	0.004 (0.3)
Change in personal finances in last 12 months	− 0.022 (2.4)	− 0.034 (3.9)
Change in personal finances in next 12 months	− 0.026 (2.7)	− 0.022 (2.4)
Party best at defense	0.056 (5.5)	0.030 (3.0)
Party best at providing for the NHS	0.169 (15.7)	0.158 (15.0)
Cruise missiles should be allowed in Britain	− 0.061 (6.9)	− 0.089 (10.6)
Stricter laws to regulate trade unions	− 0.061 (1.8)	− 0.089 (10.9)
R^2	0.81	0.82

[a]T statistics in parentheses.

comes about because of the failure to take account of the reliabilities of these different indicators in relation to the underlying latent variables. In Table 2 we are assuming that all indicators are equally reliable, which in the event, produces a misleading picture.

Because it proves impossible to obtain sensible estimates of the model with four latent variables (the estimates are badly distorted by multicollinearity), we adopt the alternative strategy of carrying out an exploratory factor analysis of the predictor variables, before respecifying the model in the light of this analysis. The results of the exploratory factor analysis in the case of the Conservative-Labour identification scale appear in Table 3. This is done with a standard principal components analysis followed by a varimax rotation. The results of the factor analysis are most revealing, since they demonstrate the existence of two latent variables underlying the data, not four as previously postulated. The first latent variable, which is easily the most significant, is highly related to party identification, to most of the indicators of national economic conditions, and also to the indicators of noneconomic issues. We can describe this as a general "partisanship and perceptions of

TABLE 3. Exploratory Factor Analysis of Observable Predictor Variables

Variable	Factor 1[a]	Factor 2[a]
Conservative–Labour identification	0.81	0.32
Party best at prosperity	−0.81	−0.29
Party best at unemployment	−0.76	−0.23
Party best at keeping down prices	−0.80	−0.27
Change in national economy in last 12 months	0.60	0.53
Change in national economy in next 12 months	0.36	0.76
Change in personal finances in last 12 months	0.31	0.63
Change in personal finances in next 12 months	0.10	0.87
Party best at defense	−0.74	−0.19
Party best at providing for NHS	−0.76	−0.15
Cruise missiles should be allowed in Britain	0.56	0.30
Stricter laws to regulate trade unions	0.55	0.32
Eigenvalues	6.34	1.10
percentage of variance explained	52.8	9.2
percentage of common variance explained	85.2	14.8

[a]Varimax rotated factor matrix.

national economic conditions" variable. The second factor, which is much less significant, is an indicator of personal economic circumstances, and it is also related to changes in the national economy in the future. The indicator of changes in the national economy over the previous 12 months is moderately related to both factors.

The most plausible explanation of these results is that there are two separate latent variables underlying the predictor set, but that the reliability of the two national economy indicators is rather low as a measure of the national economy latent construct. It may be recalled that these two indicators have virtually the same question wording as the personal finance indicators and that they all appeared together in a group in the interview schedule. Most probably, respondents mixed up personal and national economic circumstances in their minds when answering these questions and, in the case of the "national economy in the future" indicator, answered it very much like a question about personal finances.

In the light of the exploratory factor analysis, we respecified the relationships between the observable and latent constructs, and then reestimated the full model. The results of this appear in Table 4. "Partisanship and perceptions of the national economy" (Factor 1) is a very significant predictor of the probability of voting Conservative, whereas "personal economic circumstances" (Factor 2) is not a statistically significant predictor at all. However,

TABLE 4. **The Two-Latent-Variable Model as a Predictor of Voting Conservative in 1983 (full information likelihood estimates)**

Variable	Partisanship & Perceptions of National Economy (First Factor)	Personal Economic Circumstances (Second Factor)	Probability of Voting Conservative
Party identification	1.00		
Prosperity	− .93		
Unemployment	− .84		
Prices	− .88		
Defense	− .76		
National Health Service	− .82		
Cruise missiles	.60		
Trade union laws	.55		
National economy − past	.40	.54	
National economy − future		.90	
Personal finance − past		1.00	
Personal finance − future		.77	
Partisanship and perceptions of national economy (1st latent construct)		.76	− 1.081
Personal economic circumstances (2nd latent construct)			.06*
$R^2 = .94$			

Note. All coefficients are statistically significant $(p > .05)$ except *.

the two latent constructs are highly interrelated, which suggests that the latter exercises a small influence on voting via the former. The loadings or correlations between the observable variables and the latent constructs are also included in the table. The relationship between party identification and Factor 1 was set to equal 1, in order to define a scale for the latent variable. This follows standard practice in LISREL modeling (Jöreskog and Sörbom, 1981, p. 17). The same is done with the perceptions of personal finances in the past and the second latent construct (Factor 2). The square of each correlation measures the variance explained in the observable variable by the latent construct; in most cases the construct explains a highly significant percentage of the variance in the observable variable. We are justified in interpreting Factor 1 as "partisanship and perceptions of the national economy," even though some noneconomic issues are related to it. This is because the correlations between the economic indicators and Factor 1 are significantly larger than the correlations with the noneconomic issues. The exception to this is perhaps the National Health Service indicator, but even this can be defined partly as an economic issue, since it refers to financial support for the health service.

If the model is reestimated with the Conservative-Alliance party identification scale instead of the Conservative-Labour scale, the results are very similar to those in Table 4. If anything, in the Alliance model the economic issues are more strongly correlated with Factor 1 than in the Labour model, except that the relationships are only marginally stronger than those in Table 4.

CONCLUSIONS

These results show that issues, particularly economic performance issues, played a very significant role in influencing the outcome of the general election of 1983. The events in the years immediately before the election probably served to further fracture the relationship between social class and party, which had been declining for more than a decade and which in the past had served to reduce the significance of issues in electoral behavior. The two major events that stand out particularly were the unprecedented dissension within the Labour party, which lead to the split with the Social Democrats, and the victory in the Falklands War of 1982. The first effectively divided the opposition to the Conservative government, and the second gave an immediate boost to the Conservatives, which was sustained until the general election a year later.

The economic issues discussed in this paper were predominantly retrospective issues relating to the performance of the political parties in handling inflation and unemployment and in creating prosperity. The accuracy of voters' perceptions in terms of the actual performance of the economy is, of course, another question. Between 1979, when the Conservative party came into office, and 1983, unemployment more than doubled. However, the Conservatives had a moderately good record on inflation, and they succeeded in improving the living standards of those who were working, so public perceptions may have been a reasonable approximation to the reality. At all events, whether perceptions were accurate or not, they clearly played a decisive role in explaining the Conservative victory of 1983.

NOTES

1. Butler and Stokes' theoretical framework was inherited from Campbell (1960).
2. The notion of a sector was developed by Habermas (1976) and others and refers to vertical divisions in society that represent cleavages that crosscut social class. Generally these have been defined in terms of production sectors, i.e., whether the individual works in the corpor-

ate, private market, or public sectors; or in terms of consumption sectors, i.e., whether the individual owns a house or a private means of transport.

3. The data are available from the Economic and Social Research Council archive at the University of Essex, England.
4. The error in forecasting the lead of the Conservatives over Labour was 0.7%, and the average error per party in forecasting the vote share was 0.4%.
5. The main problem is heteroscedasticity (see Finney, 1964). However, the alternative of using a probit or logit model poses the problem that the estimates are very difficult to interpret.

REFERENCES

Alt, J. (1979). *The Politics of Economic Decline*. Cambridge: Cambridge University Press.

Butler, D., and Stokes, D. (1974). *Political Change in Britain*. London Macmillan.

Campbell, A., Converse, P. E., Miller, W. E., and Stokes, D. (1960). *The American Voter*. New York: Wiley.

Chrystal, K. A., and Alt, J. (1981). Some problems in formulating and testing a politico-economic model of the United Kingdom. *Economic Journal* 91: 730–736.

Crewe, I., and Särlvik, B. (1983). *Decade of Dealignment*. Cambridge: Cambridge University Press.

Finney, D. J. (1964). *Probit Analysis*. Cambridge: Cambridge University Press.

Franklin, M., and Mughan, A. (1978). The decline of class voting in Britain: problems of analysis and interpretation. *American Political Science Review* 72: 523–524.

Frey, B., and Schneider, F. (1978). A politico-economic model of the United Kingdom. *Economic Journal* 88: 243–253.

Frey, B., and Schneider, F. (1981). A politico-economic model of the UK: new estimates and predictions. *Economic Journal* 91: 737–740.

Gallup Polls. (1981, December). *The Gallup Political Index*. No. 256. London: Gallup Polls.

Goodhart, C. A. E., and Bhansali, R. J. (1970). Political economy. *Political Studies* 18: 43–106.

Habermas, J. (1976). *Legitimation Crisis*. London: Heinemann.

Jöreskog, K. G. (1973). A general method for estimating a linear structural equation system. In A. S. Goldberger and O. D. Duncan (eds.), *Structural Equation Models in the Social Sciences*. New York: Seminar Press, pp. 85–112.

Jöreskog, K. G. (1977). Structural equation models in the social sciences: specification, estimation and testing. In P. R. Krishnaish (ed.), *Applications of Statistics*. Amsterdam: North-Holland, pp. 265–287.

Jöreskog, K. G., and Sörbom, D. (1981). *LISREL V User's Guide*. Department of Statistics, University of Uppsala.

Key, V. O., Jr. (1966). *The Responsible Electorate*. New York: Vintage.

Kramer, G. (1983). The ecological fallacy revisited: aggregate versus individual-level findings on economics and elections and sociotropic voting. *American Political Science Review* 77: 92–111.

McAllister, I., and Rose, R. (1984). *The Nationwide Competition for Votes*. London: Frances Pinter.

Whiteley, P. (ed.) (1980). *Models of Political Economy.* London and Beverley Hills: Sage.

Whiteley, P. (1983). *The Labour Party in Crisis.* London: Methuen.

Whiteley, P. (1984). Inflation, unemployment and government popularity — dynamic models for the United States, Britain and West Germany. *Electoral Studies* 3: 3–24.

CHAPTER 4

Political Change and Stability of the Popularity Function: The French General Election of 1981

Jean-Dominique Lafay
Faculté des Sciences Economiques et de Gestion,
University of Poitiers, France

There is much to learn from great changes, and far from being seen as abnormal situations to be disregarded, they deserve a detailed analysis precisely because of their high information content. In May, 1981, the Fifth French Republic experienced, for the first time, a drastic political change: the socialist F. Mitterrand succeeded the "liberal" V. Giscard d'Estaing as president of the Republic.[1] After the anticipated dissolution of the National Assembly, a new one was elected in June, with a large majority of socialist and communist representatives in support of the government. The new political authorities benefited initially from exceptional popular support. In June, 1981, popularity indexes for the president rated F. Mitterrand higher than V. Giscard d'Estaing had been one month before, throughout *all* age ranges and *all* socioeconomic classes. Even among respondents supporting the Gaullist party (R.P.R.), the socialist prime minister P. Mauroy was more popular than his "liberal" predecessor, R. Barre. Above all, the complete reshuffle of the social structure of governmental support should be noted.

What have the consequences of these huge structural changes been for the links between political support and the economic situation? Now that we have nearly three years of data at our disposal, what can we say about the temporal stability of the popularity functions, a crucial problem in general, as Paldam (1981) noted in his excellent survey? These two questions have served as a departure point for this paper. First, existing econometric estimates based on French time series data are summarized. Next, a theoretical framework which takes the effect of governmental change on popularity function coefficients into account is developed. Such a framework provides a basis for the empirical analysis then presented. Finally, conclusions are drawn.

POPULARITY FUNCTION ESTIMATES IN FRANCE

General problems about popularity functions will not be discussed here.[2] Instead, this section presents, as summarized in Table 1, time series empirical results concerning the effect of macroeconomic variables on political support in France and discusses their specific problems. Though centered on the influence of the "big three" (inflation, unemployment, and real income growth), Table 1 has a column reserved for other noticeable characteristics of the studies reviewed.

The first studies on French data go back to the mid 70s (Lafay, 1973; Rosa and Amson, 1976). This preliminary work has been followed by numerous estimates of vote or popularity functions (Lafay, 1977, 1981; Giraud, 1980; Hibbs, 1981; Kernell, 1980; Lecaillon, 1980a, 1981, 1982; Lewis-Beck, 1980; Lafay et al., 1981). Interest in the problem has lessened in the past two years, essentially because the data available to measure the effect of the socialist advent to power were not sufficient. But now this last constraint is disappearing, as the empirical analysis presented here will show, and renewed interest can be expected in the near future. The growing interest of French political scientists in this kind of time series empirical work is also worth noting.[3]

Contrary to economic data, which are available for a long period and from a unified source (i.e., National Institute, I.N.S.E.E.), political data are more difficult to gather. The longer series are those of I.F.O.P.[4] They go back to the beginning of the Fifth Republic in 1958. Some data are missing and, therefore, only quarterly series for the global indexes of the President and the Prime Minister can be established on a regular basis.

The beginning of the tenure of V. Giscard d'Estaing (June, 1974) coincided with a noticeable improvement in political statistical material. Not only did I.F.O.P. monthly data come to be gathered on a regular basis, but disaggregated figures, according to age, socioeconomic status, urban size, and party affiliation, became available. Also, there was the beginning of regular publication of the useful S.O.F.R.E.S. "barometer",[5] which includes detailed questions concerning the judgments of the electorate on perceived political priorities, the efficiency of the government, and the popularity of the parties and politicians. This last statistical material, still improved after the legislative election of 1978, can serve as a basis for a complete model of popularity (Lafay, 1980).

Table 1 shows that French empirical results for popularity functions are very similar to those obtained for other countries and present a comparable degree of precision. However, there are important divergences or even contradictions between some of the studies. Below the key findings are reviewed.

Unemployment is almost always statistically significant, whether the number of unemployed or the unemployment rate is used. Some questions have, however, been raised about the validity of this result, because of the strong trend which creates problems with this variable. The effect is much less evident when trends are removed, as in the multispectral analysis of Giraud (1980). Moreover, and at least for periods before 1981, when a simple dummy variable is introduced to separate Pompidou's tenure from Giscard's, the unemployment variable no longer has a significant impact (Hibbs, 1981; Lewis-Beck, 1980). This raises the general problem of the use of dummies or time trends as separate variables and shows that the real problem with unemployment is to have at one's disposal sufficient data to avoid strong collinearity with time.

Inflation does not appear statistically significant in all functions. In particular, we can contrast Lewis-Beck (1980), for whom inflation is more decisive than unemployment, and Hibbs (1981), for whom the price variable appears insignificant and with the wrong sign. As Table 1 indicates, income growth and inflation are often mutually exclusive. Because they generally don't use an income variable, studies on monthly data always show a significant impact for inflation. For longer basic periods, all possible situations arise: inflation and income can both be significant (Lafay, 1977, 1981; Lecaillon, 1981), or only income (Hibbs, 1981; Lecaillon, 1980a,b), or only inflation (Lecaillon, 1981, 1982).

With the important exception of Hibbs (1981) for whom the *memory of the electorate* goes back three or four years, the *estimated* lags for economic variables have tended to shorten since the initial studies. For a large part, this phenomenon, which occurred in other economic domains, results from an increase in the number of observations available: more sophisticated lag structures can be tested and differentiation between trends is easier. Present results for France are then closer to those obtained for other countries and confirm the idea of a rather short-sighted electorate. A possible explanation of this myopia in *popularity* function, as opposed to *vote* functions, is given by Paldam (1981, p. 188): "When a poll is taken the respondents have less than five minutes to react to the unexpected question, that is, here we get a straight reaction. A vote takes place after a considerable period where people know that they have to choose."

Nevertheless the question remains of the long lags estimated by Hibbs (1981). As this author obtains similar results for other countries (Paldam, 1981; Hibbs, 1982a,b), one may suspect that the model specification plays a great role. Hibbs' model is based on the assumption of an electorate behaving in a sophisticated way, with a unified discount rate and taking precise account of governmental changes. From a purely statistical point of view, this results in smoothing — with geometrically decreasing weights — all the explaining variables and in introducing temporary upswings in periods following the elections lost by incumbents.

As with any distributed lag model, it is difficult to discriminate between a simple inertia explanation and hypothesized sophisticated adaptive behavior. Logically, one might think that the length and sophistication of the memory of an elector, in Hibbs' model, should correlate with the degree of his education. In fact, the disaggregated estimates of Hibbs (1982a) for the United States show precisely the reverse pattern, finding blue collars workers to have the longest memory. This result is much more in line with the inertia explanation. If so, the estimates of Hibbs do not necessarily exclude shorter-term independent influences for variables (as is the case when the sophisticated behavior explanation is retained).

An important deficiency in present French popularity functions is their lack of external variables, such as the balance of payments or the exchange rate. Indeed, and except for Great Britain (Paldam, 1981; Hibbs, 1982b), the evidence for other countries is rather weak. This kind of variable may, however, have an influence in France for at least two reasons. The first is an economic one: foreign trade is relatively important (18% of GNP), particularly for farm produce, and Common Market rules create considerable interdependence with other European countries. The second reason is purely political: estimates linking the global popularity of the president to opinions which concern different policy categories[6] show that judgments about *foreign policy* play a significant independent role (Lafay et al., 1981). Then, it could be that a variable such as the rate of exchange is perceived as indicative of the international strength of the country.[7]

Table 1 reproduces only those studies directly linking global popularity and macroeconomic data. Other lines of French research should be mentioned, however. Lecaillon (1982) introduces income distribution as an independent

TABLE 1. Summary of Previous Empirical Results for Popularity Functions in France

References	Period	Dependent variable	Influence of economic variables			Other characteristics
			Inflation	Unemployment	Income	
Lafay (1973)	61–71	Prime minister's popularity IFOP, quarterly	–	+ +	+	No political variables. Long lag for unemployment.
Lafay (1977, 1981)	61–77	Prime minister's popularity IFOP, quarterly	+ +	+ +	+ +	Specific dummies for each prime minister. Long lag for unemployment. (Real wage index as income variable.)
Lecaillon (1980a)	65–77	President's popularity IFOP, annual	–	+ +	+	Long lag for unemployment. Inflation insignificant.
Lecaillon (1980b)	73–79	Prime minister's popularity IFOP, quarterly	–	+ +	+ +	Long lag for unemployment. Inflation insignificant.
Kernell (1980)	59–79	President's popularity IFOP, monthly	+	+ +	–	No income variable. Low influence of economic variables.
Lewis-Beck (1980)	60–78	President's popularity IFOP, monthly	+ +	+	–	No income variable. Lags of a few months. High influence of inflation.
Lewis-Beck (1980)	66–78	Prime minister's popularity IFOP, monthly	+ +	+	–	Unemployment just significant. Greater influence of economic variables on prime minister's popularity than on president's popularity.
Hibbs (1981)	69–78	President's popularity IFOP, quarterly	–	+	+ +	Values of variables before the beginning of the tenure are introduced. With a negative sign. Elaborated lag structure, logit estimates by weighted least squares, very long memory of the electorate.

Study	Period	Variable				Comments
Giraud (1980)	74–79	President's popularity IFOP, monthly	+ +	+	–	Multispectral analysis on filtered data. No income variable.
Lafay-Berdot-Giraud (1981)	77–81	Prime minister's popularity SOFRES, monthly	+ +	+	–	Lagged endogenous variable significant, short instantaneous lags.
Lecaillon (1981)	60–79	President's popularity IFOP, annual	+ +	–	+ +	Unemployment insignificant. Lagged endogenous variable.
Lecaillon (1981)	60–79	Prime minister's popularity IFOP, annual	–	–	–	Only the lagged endogenous variable significant.
Lecaillon (1981)	69–80	Mean popularity of the president and the prime minister IFOP, quarterly	+	+ +	–	Lagged endogenous variable.
Lecaillon (1981)	73–80	Mean popularity of the president and the prime minister IFOP, quarterly	–	+ +	+ +	Income variable is real wage index growth. Lagged endogenous variable. Comparison with the preceding estimate illustrates the collinearity between the income variable and inflation (changing the period gives very different results for these variables).
Lecaillon (1982)	74–80	President's popularity IFOP, quarterly	+ +	+ +	–	Significant influence of the wage hierarchy

Notes. +: Significant (5% level or more). + +: Highly significant (about the 1% level or more). –: Not significant (about the 1% level or more). –: Not significant or not introduced. All estimates with an endogenous variable different from the level of popularity of the prime minister or of the president are excluded. This is the case for the vote functions of Rosa and Amson, 1976, Lecaillon, 1980a, Lewis-Beck and Belluci, 1982, and for functions using variables such as the ratio between satisfied and dissatisfied (Lecaillon, 1981, 1982).

variable. According to the empirical results of Lecaillon, when wage hierarchy narrows, the popularity of the president goes down. This indicates that people strongly defend their sectional interests and is parallel to the findings of Lewis-Beck (1983). Using the rich statistical material gathered in "Euro-Barometers," Lewis-Beck stressed the influence of the personal situation on the vote of the French electorate, as opposed to their judgments on global economic questions.[8]

The S.O.F.R.E.S. surveys allow one to test a more detailed model of popular support formation. A first attempt at this is Lafay (1980), where the popularity problem is formulated in terms of supply and demand for the different public policies and takes into account the specific French institutional dichotomy between the president of the Republic and the prime minister. The economic variables are used to explain only judgments about relative policy *priorities* and perceived *efficiency* of the government in the different policy domains. Popularity indexes are explained at a later stage.

The effect of tax increases and forced subscriptions to public borrowing[9] on popularity are an important (and often neglected) problem. The long term fiscal history of France often coincides with that of popular revolts (Ardant, 1976). To a lesser degree, the 1976 "Plan Barre" and the socialist "politique de rigueur," applied since 1982, has had a discernible impact on popularity indexes (at least at the moment of their implementation and for the few months after). Gilbert (1979), though in the limited frame of a simulation model, is an interesting first examination of this problem.

EFFECTS OF POLITICAL CHANGE ON THE STABILITY OF THE POPULARITY FUNCTION

People generally admit that governmental change has two effects on the popularity function: a displacement effect, i.e., a change in the intercept for each administration, and a "honeymoon" effect, i.e., an initial strong upward movement followed by a steady return of popularity indexes to "normal" levels. Appropriate trends and dummies have been extensively used to model these phenomena, but their ad hoc nature can be criticized.

A more satisfying solution is to suppose that a government is judged only on the difference between the present situation and the situation at the beginning of its tenure. Let

$$Y_{it} = a + b(Z_{it} - Z_{i-1,t_0-1})$$

where Y_{it} is a support index for the government i in t, Z is a vector of performance variables, and Z_{i-1,t_0-1} is the value of Z at the end of the tenure of the government, $i-1$ (i.e., at the period just before the election date, t_0).

This formulation is such that a newly elected government will benefit from a *sizeable* popularity supplement:

$$Y_{it_0} - Y_{i-1,t_0-1} = b(Z_{it_0} + Z_{i-1,t'_0-1} - 2Z_{t-1,t_0} - 1)$$

where t'_0 refers to the second to the last election. As it is logical to suppose that the government $i-1$ was defeated because of its bad performance, the right side of the equation is positive.

The popularity supplement concerns only new governments, not reelected ones, and is acquired definitively. No endogenous return movement to a "normal" level is allowed after the "honeymoon." Furthermore all the newly elected governments will experience the same level of support at the origin of the axis ($=a$). This last problem can be solved by introducing a different intercept (a_i) for each government, but note that the differential nature of Z will then become purely formal because full identification of parameters is no longer possible in the equation.

Hibbs' distributed lag model of popularity has a priori more interesting consequences for periods of government change (Hibbs, 1982a,b). The model can be developed as follows:

$$Y_{it} = a_i + b (Z_t + gZ_{(t-1)} + \cdots + g^{(t-t_0)}Z_{t_0} - g^{(t-t_0+1)}Z_{(t_0-1)} - g^{(t-t_0+2)}Z_{(t_0-2)} - \cdots)$$

where g is the rate of decline of the lag weights, and the performance of the preceding government is supposed to be counted negatively in the memory of the voters, i.e., they judge the new government differentially. For this last reason, "the worse (better) the prior government, the higher (lower) will be the initial support of the new government" (Hibbs, 1982a). A second interesting characteristic is that, with the passing of time, the government's popularity will depend more and more on its own performance, permitting a progressive return to a long term equilibrium. However, as Keech (1982) noted, the time profile generated by the Hibbs model is not always adequate. To show it simply, we suppose that $Z_t = \overline{Z} \; \forall t \; (\overline{Z} > 0)$ and that the intercept remains the same from one government to the other ($a_i = a \forall i$).

Summing up geometrical progressions:

$$Y_{it} = a + b \left(\frac{1 - g^{(t-t_0+1)}}{1-g} - \frac{g^{(t-t_0+1)}}{1-g} \right) \overline{Z}$$

$$= a + b \left(\frac{1 - 2g^{(t-t_0+1)}}{1-g} \right) \overline{Z}$$

If the previous government was at its long term equilibrium, then

$$Y_{i-1,t_0-1} = a + \left(\frac{b}{1-g}\right)\overline{Z}$$

Compared to the previous government period, the difference in popularity after an election will be

$$t_0 \quad \to \left(b \times \frac{1-2g}{1-g} - \frac{b}{1-g}\right)\overline{Z} = \frac{-2bg}{1-g}\overline{Z}$$

$$t_0+1 \quad \to \left(b \times \frac{1-2g^2}{1-g} - \frac{b}{1-g}\right)\overline{Z} = \frac{-2bg^2}{1-g}\overline{Z}$$

$$\cdots\cdots \to \cdots\cdots\cdots \qquad\qquad = \cdots\cdots$$

$$t_0+\infty \to \left(b \times \frac{1}{1-g} - \frac{b}{1-g}\right)\overline{Z} = 0$$

If $b<0$ (i.e., coefficients for variables such as unemployment or inflation), the time profile is adequate. Popularity is higher first and decreases to return to its steady state level. On the contrary, if $b>0$ (i.e., coefficients for variables such as income growth), the cycle generated by the model is *inverted*. Popularity will be lower first and increases further to its steady state level. In the multivariate model, where b and Z are vectors, the *net* profile generated for the honeymoon period will depend on the relative weight of the variables with negative and positive coefficients. Hibbs claims that this profile is *empirically* correct, but strong spurious effects remain. In particular his model implies that the lower the income growth under the previous government, the milder the *net* honeymoon effect for the new one. This result does not fit well with the supposed *differential* aspect of popular judgments when the government changes.

In fact, the interesting idea in Hibbs' model is the possibility of endogenously predicting the "honeymoon period" using a distributed lag model. However, the oversimplifying assumption that individuals just reverse the signs corresponding to the former government after an election creates severe theoretical problems. Additional research is clearly necessary on this subject. Consequently, we decided to limit our empirical analysis of the honeymoon effect to tests grounded on simple dummy variables (the first with value 1 at the moment at the election, the second with value 1 at the period immediately after, etc.).

TABLE 2. Mean Values of Popularity Indexes for Subperiods (Percentage of Persons Satisfied with the President)

Group[a]	Giscard period (74/10 to 81/05)	Mitterand period (81/10 to 83/12)	Difference
CSUP	48.6	40.4	− 8.2
COMM	50.0	24.7	− 25.3
EMPL	43.0	46.4	+ 3.4
OUVR	39.1	48.8	+ 9.7
INAC	61.0	44.7	− 16.3
AGRI	55.9	29.5	− 26.4
TOTAL	48.8	43.3	− 5.5

[a]CSUP, management class, executives, professional people; COMM, businessmen, tradesmen; EMPL, clerks, lower level management; OUVR, blue collar workers; INAC, population out of the work force; AGRI, farmers.

All the preceding analysis concerns the global explanations of the effects of governmental change. In spite of their interest, such explanations completely disregard what are perhaps the most important effects of great political changes, at least in countries where ideological attachment to parties is strong, their *distribution effects*. A simple look at Table 2 will show the extent of the long term modification in the *structure* of the support to the President in France before and after May 1981.

The simple theory of aggregation teaches us that a *global* function will remain stable through time if either all the individuals demonstrate *similar behavior* or the internal distribution of the population remains the same *(no structural change)*. Estimates for disaggregated popularity functions on the Giscard period show that the first proposition is false (see Table 5 below). The previous look at Table 2 has already shown that the second proposition was also not fulfilled. What could be, then, the distribution effect of the May, 1981, change on the popularity function?

A first possibility is to suppose that the electorate is divided into three separate groups: two ideologically motivated voting groups and a third group voting according to the economic situation.[10] The first two groups have their preferences represented in the constants of the aggregate popularity functions (and in the error terms), and the significant economic variables correspond exclusively to the third group behavior. So, the only distribution effect of a change in government is to modify deeply and definitively all the intercepts.[11] This type of aggregation effect is a good candidate to rationalize the ad hoc practice of differentiating intercepts according to administrations.

A completely different hypothesis is to suppose that all individuals react to economic variables, but not in the same way. For example, left-wing voters may have a tendency to react more strongly to unemployment and right-wing voters to inflation. However, if their preferred party is in power, voters will react less severely. Then, political change will correspond to a modification in the *slopes* of the variables. Under a right-wing government, the coefficient of the inflation variable would tend to be lower, and that of unemployment higher, than under a left-wing government. Note that, supposing that governments are popularity maximizers, this could help to rationalize the old saying that left-wing governments generally have to perform a right-wing policy and vice versa.

To summarize, purely aggregate explanations are insufficient when, for ideological reasons, the structure of the support for the new government is deeply modified. Then, distribution effects are present and may correspond to change either in the value of the intercept or in the value of all the other coefficients.

EMPIRICAL ANALYSIS

This section presents empirical estimates of monthly popularity functions using I.F.O.P. indexes, for two different periods: October, 1974, to May, 1981, a period corresponding to Giscard d'Estaing's presidency, and October, 1974, to December, 1983, a period including the available data for the socialist administration. (See Appendix for data sources.) No estimates are given for the strict socialist period (May, 1981 to December, 1983) because of the insufficient number of degrees of freedom and multicollinearity problems. The explained variable is the logit

$$\log\left(\frac{pop}{1-pop}\right)$$

of the proportion of people who are satisfied with the President (*pop*). The estimation method is weighted least squares, to take into account the heteroscedasticity problems raised by the transformation of the dependent variable into logit. (See Pindyck and Rubinfeld, 1981, and Hibbs, 1982a,b, for detailed justification of all these technical choices.)

All the variables introduced in the function (inflation, unemployment rate, real disposable income growth rate, and exchange rate for the dollar) are highly significant during the first period (Giscard's tenure). Note that a dummy is introduced to take into account a sharp decrease in the President's popularity at the moment of the severely restrictive "Plan Barre" (value of the dummy = 1 from October, 1976 to January, 1977, and zero elsewhere).

The estimates presented here contain no "honeymoon" variables: the specific dummies did not appear significant. We cannot say whether this negative result is linked to the lack of data (the period contains only one change from a right-wing to a left-wing government) or corresponds to the absence of a deep and lasting honeymoon effect in France. What has been called in France "état de grâce," as separated from the longer term effects shown below, seems to have been only a very short term and limited surplus in popularity.

The analysis concentrated then on the effects of the May, 1981, change on the structure of support. All variables were lagged systematically by one month because popularity surveys (dependent variable) are generally performed at the very beginning of each month. The choice of the specific forms for variables was based on polynomial estimates of lag structures, with no restrictions at end points (Pindyck and Rubinfeld, 1981, p. 238). Only the one month lag coefficient was significant for unemployment and the exchange rate. For the two other variables (inflation and income growth), the number of lags was increased by one month each time. The process was ended just before the last term became not significant.

Results presented in Table 3 (col. 1) are rather clear-cut. There is no significant move in the lagged coefficients, as opposed to the regular decay implied by geometrically distributed lags. The electorate appears to judge the President with a stable but differentiated retrospective horizon: it looks back to the performance of the last six months for inflation and to that of the last 15 months for real income growth. Consequently, semestrial growth in prices was taken as the inflation variable and growth in real income for the last 15 months as the income variable.

One may question the rationale for the differences in the memory horizon according to the variable considered. If distributed lags are interpreted as a simple memory of the past, the horizon for all the variables must be the same. This is the logic of the unique rate of decay, g, chosen by Hibbs. However, if distributed lags are considered as a process of expectation building, the horizon for each independent variable will generally differ (according to its perceived volatility or to the perceived economic structure).

The same function estimated for the Giscard period was then estimated for the whole period. The resulting coefficients are quite different and the quality of the relation is distinctively lower (Table 4, cols. 1 and 2). All the parameters are then allowed to be different from one period to the other. The new function could be written as follows:

$$Y = \sum_{i=1}^{n} a_i X_i + \sum_{i=1}^{n} a'_i \cdot D_{soc} \cdot X_i$$

D_{soc} is a dummy variable with value 1 for the whole socialist period (June, 1981 to December, 1983) and zero elsewhere. A value of a'_i significantly different from zero means that the coefficient for X_i has changed from Giscard to Mitterrand. The resulting estimate (Table 4, col. 3) indicates a severe prob-

TABLE 3. Lag Structure for Inflation and Real Income Growth[a]

		Period 1974/10–1981/05 (Giscard)		Period 1974/10–1983/12 (Giscard + Mitterrand)	
Constant		1.83	(4.9)	1.82	(6.0)
Dummy "plan Barre" (76/10–77/01)		− 0.35	(4.6)	− 0.32	(4.5)
Dummy 1981/06 to 1983/12				+ 0.69	(6.6)
Exchange rate	$t-1$				
(francs per dollar)		− 0.237	(4.2)	− 0.255	(6.8)
Unemployment rate	$t-1$	− 0.105	(5.8)	− 0.100	(5.9)
Inflation	$t-1$	− 0.007	(1.7)	− 0.007	(2.0)
(Second order	$t-2$	− 0.004	(1.5)	− 0.004	(2.2)
polynomial	$t-3$	− 0.002	(0.8)	− 0.003	(1.3)
lag)	$t-4$	− 0.003	(1.0)	− 0.003	(1.4)
	$t-5$	− 0.005	(2.3)	− 0.004	(2.4)
	$t-6$	− 0.010	(2.4)	− 0.007	(2.1)
[Σ for inflation]		[− 0.031	(2.8)]	[− 0.028	(3.3)]
Real disposable	$t-1$	+ 0.0019 (1.3)		+ 0.0018 (1.5)	
income growth	$t-2$	+ 0.0017 (1.4)		+ 0.0018 (1.9)	
(second order	$t-3$	+ 0.0016 (1.5)		+ 0.0019 (2.3)	
polynomial	$t-4$	+ 0.0015 (1.5)		+ 0.0019 (2.5)	
lag)	$t-5$	+ 0.0014 (1.4)		+ 0.0020 (2.5)	
	$t-6$	+ 0.0014 (1.4)		+ 0.0020 (2.5)	
	$t-7$	+ 0.0014 (1.4)		+ 0.0020 (2.4)	
	$t-8$	+ 0.0014 (1.4)		+ 0.0020 (2.4)	
	$t-9$	+ 0.0014 (1.5)		+ 0.0021 (2.4)	
	$t-10$	+ 0.0015 (1.6)		+ 0.0021 (2.5)	
	$t-11$	+ 0.0017 (1.8)		+ 0.0021 (2.6)	
	$t-12$	+ 0.0018 (2.0)		+ 0.0021 (2.6)	
	$t-13$	+ 0.0020 (2.2)		+ 0.0020 (2.5)	
	$t-14$	+ 0.0021 (2.1)		+ 0.0020 (2.1)	
	$t-15$	+ 0.0024 (2.0)		+ 0.0020 (1.7)	
[Σ for real income]		[+ 0.0253 (2.1)]		[+ 0.0298 (3.0)]	
Correlation between fitted and actual proportions (R^2)		0.714		0.772	
Degrees of freedom		70		100	

[a]Weighted least-squares estimates. The dependent variable is the logit of the proportion of persons satisfied with the President of the French Republic (monthly data). t values in parentheses.

lem of multicollinearity between all the newly introduced variables (i.e., for the Mitterrand period). Consequently, we decide to limit the test to the simplest hypothesis, difference in intercept, and to allow for only one more coefficient change (Table 4, cols. 4, 5, 6, and 7).

Results given in Table 4 show clearly that (1) differences in intercepts are important from one period to the other, and no difference in other coefficients appears significant, and (2) the coefficients estimated for the earlier

(Giscard) period remain particularly stable during the later (Mitterrand) period. On the basis of Table 4 we cannot reject the perfect stability hypothesis of the popularity function, except indeed for the intercept. (The stability of the global popularity function is also confirmed for the more general formulation presented in Table 3; compare cols. 1 and 2.)

Table 5 presents results for socioeconomic categories. Although the coefficients are not all strictly significant, the results look rather satisfying. The more severe problems are for income growth. But it is important to note that this variable represents *global* income and not the particular income of the category in question. The mere fact that this variable gives relatively worse results on disaggregated data could be seen as an indirect index of the "personal situation orientation" of the French electorate (Lewis-Beck, 1983).

The differences in the value of the intercept illustrate the differences in the pure ideological support for the two governments: blue collar workers (OUV), clerks (EMP), and surprisingly though less intensively, management class and executives (CSUP) give more support to the socialist government than to the preceding one, on this ground. It is also important to notice the high sensitivity of this last class to unemployment. Farmers (AGRI) and, to a lesser degree, businessmen and tradesmen (COMM) are particularly sensitive to price movements and to exchange rate fluctuations. They have indeed a privileged position to observe the effects of these variables on their costs. Moreover, the EEC support price system for agriculture works in such a way that national farm products become less competitive when the national exchange rate goes down (costs of imported raw products are higher, and the price advantage of currency depreciation is "compensated" by the system). In general, and even for disaggregated results, the coefficients remain fairly stable from one period to the other.

CONCLUSIONS

The analysis of French monthly data shows that a very stable popularity function for the president can be obtained. The unemployment rate and the exchange rate have a very significant short run impact. The influence of inflation is of longer term. Real disposable income growth is clearly the variable for which the retrospective horizon of the electorate is the largest. The results for disaggregated data according to socioeconomic groups satisfyingly confirm the global results.

When the time span is broadened to include the socialist period (from June, 1981 to December, 1983) the coefficients of all the functions remain very stable, except for a modification in the constant. Correspondingly, it seems that people judging politics more on the basis of the economic situation have continued to behave in the same way since May, 1981. A nonnegli-

TABLE 4. Estimates for France of the Global Popularity Function for the President and Stability of the Coefficients over the Whole Period (1974/10–1983/12)

Period	(1) G	(2) G+M	(3) G+M	(4) G+M	(5) G+M	(6) G+M	(7) G+M	(8) G+M
Constant	1.845 (5.2)	−0.002 (0.01)	1.845 (5.2)	1.869 (6.3)	1.829 (6.1)	1.840 (6.1)	1.793 (5.5)	1.839 (6.3)
$\dot{P}_{t-1/6}$	−0.031 (2.4)	+0.007 (0.9)	−0.031 (2.4)	−0.031 (3.1)	−0.028 (3.3)	−0.028 (3.3)	−0.029 (3.4)	−0.028 (3.4)
u_{t-1}	−0.103 (6.3)	−0.033 (2.3)	−0.103 (6.3)	−0.103 (6.6)	−0.102 (6.4)	−0.103 (5.6)	−0.103 (6.5)	−0.103 (6.6)
$\dot{y}_{t-1/15}$	+0.027 (2.4)	+0.072 (6.2)	+0.027 (2.4)	+0.027 (2.6)	+0.029 (3.1)	+0.029 (2.8)	+0.028 (2.8)	+0.029 (3.1)
$\$_{t-1}$	−0.245 (4.5)	−0.032 (1.4)	−0.245 (4.5)	−0.249 (6.6)	−0.250 (6.0)	−0.253 (5.6)	−0.240 (4.5)	−0.253 (6.8)
D_{BARR}	−0.317 (4.6)	−0.335 (4.2)	−0.317 (4.5)	−0.316 (4.8)	−0.312 (4.7)	−0.310 (4.6)	−0.317 (4.6)	−0.310 (4.7)
D_{LEFT}			+0.522 (0.4)	+0.601 (2.9)	+0.819 (1.1)	+0.708 (5.3)	+0.817 (2.4)	+0.707 (7.0)

$D_{LEFT} \cdot \dot{p}_{t-1/6}$			+0.008 (0.4)	+0.008 (0.6)			
$D_{LEFT} \cdot u_{t-1}$			+0.039 (0.3)		−0.014 (0.2)		
$D_{LEFT} \cdot \dot{y}_{t-1/15}$			−0.008 (0.2)			−0.0003 (0.01)	
$D_{LEFT} \cdot \$_{t-1}$			−0.035 (0.3)				−0.021 (0.3)
Fit of actual and estimated proposition R^2	0.705	0.663	0.771	0.771	0.770	0.770	0.770
Degrees of freedom	74	105	100	103	103	103	104

Notes. See Table 3 for definition of the dependent variable and estimation method. G corresponds to 1974/10–1981/05. G + M corresponds to 1974/10–1983/12.

$\dot{p}_{t-1/6}$ Inflation on six months (lagged by one month), percentage annual equivalent.
u_{t-1} Unemployment rate (lagged by one month), percentage.
$\dot{y}_{t-1/15}$ Real disposable income growth on fifteen months, percentage, annual equivalent (lagged by one month).
$\$_{t-1}$ Number of francs per dollar (lagged by one month).
D_{BARR} Dummy variable, value 1 from 1976/10 to 1977/01 and 0 elsewhere.
D_{LEFT} Dummy variable for the left wing administration, value 1 from 1981/06 to 1983/12 and 0 elsewhere.

TABLE 5. Disaggregated Popularity Function Estimates for the President of France

Independent variable Period	$\dot{P}_{t-1/16}$ G	$\dot{P}_{t-1/16}$ G+M	u_{t-1} G	u_{t-1} G+M	$\dot{y}_{t-1/15}$ G	$\dot{y}_{t-1/15}$ G+M	$\$_{t-1}$ G	$\$_{t-1}$ G+M	D_{BARR} G	D_{BARR} G+M	D_{LEFT} G	D_{LEFT} G+M	Constant G	Constant G+M	R^2 G	R^2 G+M
CSUP	-0.014 (0.7)	-0.021 (1.5)	-0.182 (6.4)	-0.190 (7.1)	+0.025 (1.3)	+0.011 (0.7)	-0.352 (3.7)	-0.289 (4.5)	-0.552 (4.5)	-0.595 (5.2)		+0.926 (5.4)	2.542 (4.1)	2.420 (4.9)	0.582	0.659
COMM	-0.036 (1.7)	-0.043 (2.4)	-0.143 (4.3)	-0.144 (4.3)	+0.038 (1.7)	+0.022 (1.1)	-0.458 (4.1)	-0.302 (3.7)	-0.396 (2.8)	-0.476 (3.5)		0.044 (0.2)	3.09 (4.2)	2.513 (4.0)	0.521	0.795
EMPL	-0.019 (1.5)	-0.014 (1.4)	-0.126 (6.5)	-0.128 (6.4)	+0.043 (3.2)	+0.046 (3.8)	-0.281 (4.9)	-0.290 (6.0)	-0.408 (4.8)	-0.400 (4.6)		+1.253 (9.6)	1.719 (4.0)	1.702 (4.5)	0.702	0.732
OUVR	-0.033 (2.6)	-0.024 (2.8)	-0.107 (5.4)	-0.108 (3.7)	+0.010 (0.7)	+0.024 (2.0)	-0.181 (2.7)	-0.335 (7.0)	-0.289 (3.4)	-0.209 (2.4)		+1.514 (11.6)	1.257 (2.9)	1.212 (4.8)	0.511	0.753
INAC	-0.032 (2.2)	-0.030 (2.8)	-0.043 (1.9)	-0.034 (1.6)	+0.015 (0.9)	+0.014 (1.1)	-0.319 (4.2)	-0.185 (3.7)	-0.141 (1.5)	-0.192 (2.2)		-0.118 (0.9)	2.423 (4.9)	1.753 (4.5)	0.331	0.780
AGRI	-0.091 (4.5)	-0.087 (5.7)	-0.116 (3.8)	-0.111 (3.9)	+0.017 (0.8)	+0.020 (1.1)	-0.426 (4.1)	-0.350 (5.0)	-0.392 (0.7)	-0.119 (1.0)		+0.075 (0.4)	3.688 (5.5)	3.267 (6.1)	0.545	0.848
Total	-0.031 (2.9)	-0.028 (5.7)	-0.103 (3.8)	-0.103 (6.6)	+0.027 (2.4)	+0.029 (3.1)	-0.245 (4.5)	-0.253 (6.8)	-0.317 (4.6)	-0.311 (4.7)		+0.707 (7.0)	1.793 (5.5)	1.840 (6.1)	0.685	0.757

Notes. See Tables 2, 3, and 4 for definition of variables and estimation method. G corresponds to 1974/10 to 1981/05 (74 degrees of freedom for functions estimated on this period). G+M corresponds to 1974/10 to 1983/12 (104 degrees of freedom for functions estimated on this period).

gible part of the move in the constant can be interpreted as the net result of changes in attitude of the more ideologically oriented electors, from before to after the election.

Acknowledgments. I wish to thank the participants of the Shambaugh conference (University of Iowa, March, 1984) and of the European Public Choice Society meeting (Munich, May, 1984) for comments and suggestions, particularly R. Jankowski, M. Lewis-Beck, M. Gaertner, and B. Blankart. This study has also benefited from extensive discussions with Ch. Aubin, J. P. Berdot, D. Goyeau, D. Hibbs, H. Rosenthal, and A. Cukierman.

NOTES

1. "Libéral" according to the French meaning of the word, i.e., politically near U.S. Republicans or English Conservatives.
2. The reader is referred to Paldam (1981) for this.
3. The conference "Chômage et politique," held in March 1982 at Fondation nationale des sciences politiques and organized by J. L. Parodi, is most representative of this (cf. Schnapper, 1982).
4. Published in the daily newspaper *France-Soir* up to January, 1983, and, since then, in the weekly newspaper *Journal du Dimanche*.
5. In the daily newspaper *Le Figaro*.
6. Questions asked in S.O.F.R.E.S. surveys are: "Have you got confidence in the President concerning economic policy (or social policy, foreign policy, etc.)?"
7. For a review of the international aspects of politico-economic problems, cf. Frey (1983). A first attempt to introduce the rate of exchange in the French popularity function is May, 1983.
8. "Eurobarometers" are published twice a year by the E.E.C. under the direction of J. R. Rabier. Lewis-Beck gives a "cultural explanation" of his results which raises interesting questions, but these are beyond the scope of this paper.
9. A device used in 1976 and 1983 in France.
10. Indeed, less extreme hypotheses are possible, but the core of the argument will not be changed.
11. Except if the numbers of ideological supporters of the preceding government and of the new one match exactly.

REFERENCES

Ardant, G. (1982). *Histoire financière de l'Antiquité à nos jours.* Paris: Gallimard.

Frey, B. (1983). The public choice view of international political economy. University of Zürich.

Gilbert, G. (1979). Economie politique des structures fiscales. Thesis, Université de Paris.

Giraud, R. (1980). L'analyse spectrale: théorie et application à l'étude des interactions politico-économiques. Thesis, Université de Paris II.

Hibbs, D. (1981). Economics and politics in France. *European Journal of Political Research* 9 (June).

Hibbs, D. (1982a). The dynamics of political support for American presidents among occupational and partisan groups. *American Journal of Political Science* 26: 312–332.

Hibbs, D. (1982b). Economic outcomes and political support for British governments among occupational classes: a dynamic analysis. *American Political Science Review* 76: 259–279.

Keech, W. (1982). On honeymoons and economic performance: comment on Hibbs. *American Political Science Review* 76: 280–281.

Kernell, S. (1980). Unemployment, inflation and party democracy Mimeo, University of California, San Diego.

Lafay, J. D. (1973). Comportements politiques et conjoncture économique. Miméo, Université de Poitiers.

Lafay, J. D. (1977). Les conséquences électorales de la conjoncture économique. *Vie et Sciences Economiques* 75: 1–7.

Lafay, J. D. (1980). Demandes de politiques économiques et mouvements de popularité. Mimeo, Université de Poitiers.

Lafay, J. D. (1981). The impact of economic variables on political behavior in France. In D. Hibbs and H. Fassbender (eds.), *Contemporary Political Economy*. New York: Elseoier North-Holland.

Lafay, J. D., Berdot, J. P., and Giraud, R. (1981). Popularity functions and models for France: tables of preliminary results, Mimeo, Université de Poitiers.

Lecaillon, J. (1980a). *La Crise et l'Alternance*. Paris: Cujas.

Lecaillon, J. (1980b). Salaires, chômage et situation politique. *Revue d'Économie Politique* 5: 615–627.

Lecaillon, J. (1981). Popularité des gouvernements et popularité économique. Consommation 3: 17–50.

Lecaillon, J. (1982). Disparité de revenus et stratégie politique, Mimeo, Université de Paris I.

Lewis-Beck, M. (1980). Economic conditions and executive popularity: the French experience. *American Journal of Political Science* 24: 306–323.

Lewis-Beck, M. (1983). Economics and the French voter: a micro-analysis. *Public Opinion Quarterly* 47: 347–360.

Lewis-Beck, M., and Belluci, P. (1982). Economic influences on legislative elections in multiparty systems: France and Italy. *Political Behavior* 4: 93–107.

Paldam, M. (1982). A preliminary survey of the theories and findings of vote and popularity functions. *European Journal of Political Research* 9: 181–189.

Pindyck, R. and Rubinfeld, D. (1981). *Econometric Models and Economic Forecasts*. New York: McGraw-Hill.

Rosa, J. J., and Amson, D. (1976). Conditions économiques et élections. *Revue Française de Science Politique* 26: 1101–1124.

Schnapper, D. (1982). Chômage et politique: une relation mal connue. *Revue Française de Science Politique,* (August, October):

APPENDIX

Economic variables are taken from I.N.S.E.E. statistics. Unemployment rate is the ratio of "Demandes d'emploi non satisfaites," seasonally adjusted, and monthly interpolations of annual figures concerning active population. The monthly estimates for nominal disposable income are based on the I.N.S.E.E. quarterly figures for this variable. A monthly wage index, adjusted for seasonal fluctuations, is used for monthly allocation of the quarterly total. Real disposable income is obtained by using the price index as deflator. Some missing data in I.F.O.P. surveys, particularly in August, are replaced by simple interpolation based on the two nearest existing figures.

CHAPTER 5

Economic Concerns in Italian Electoral Behavior: Toward a Rational Electorate?

Paolo Bellucci
European University Institute, Florence, Italy
Centro Studi Investimenti Sociali, Rome, Italy

The issue of the relevance of economic considerations for electoral behavior in Italy has not received much attention from scholars and Italian specialists. Studies on the Italian case have only recently appeared (Santagata, 1981, 1982; Lewis-Beck and Bellucci, 1982; Bellucci and Lewis-Beck, 1983; Bellucci, 1984). Their exploratory nature implies that the presence and the impact of economic concerns among Italian electors is still far from being a settled issue.

Many elements have contributed to the scarcity of research on the relationship between economic conditions and electoral behavior in the Italian system. The single most important one, however, is the diffuse belief that the main feature of the Italian party system and of its electoral behavior, i.e., the ideological dimension, makes irrelevant any consideration of economic conditions. The centrality of ideology finds a confirmation in the two most influential interpretations of Italian politics, i.e., Galli's (1968) imperfect bipartitism and Sartori's (1976) polarized pluralism, where the ideological dimension is found to be the key variable capable of accounting for the (un-satisfactory) operation of the Italian political system. Galli attributes the lack of real government alternation to the presence of a strongly ideological Communist party which, through its monopolistic opposition role, has prevented the emergence of a bloc capable of alternating in government with the Christian Democrats. Expanding the analysis, Pasquino (1980) finds in this lack of government alternation the source of most of the Italian party system's problems, with its low turnover of political personnel and difficulties in structuring alternative policies and policy outputs. Though from a different perspective, Sartori's argument attributes the low viability of the Italian system to the high level of ideological polarization (Sartori, 1976).

If we move from the analysis of the party system to electoral behavior, ideology again plays a central role: the current paradigm finds in the ideological attachment and identification of the electorate with the parties the basic determinants of Italian voting behavior. After these, political culture and tradition, party predispositions traditionally rooted in different social groups and in geographical areas, and parties' organizational networks become the main variables employed in explaining Italian electoral behavior (Galli, 1968; Galli and Prandi, 1970; Sani, 1973). Of course, studies which have focused on socioeconomic variables are not lacking, but their main concern is to identify the social and economic features of the parties' electoral base, assessing the propensity for given social strata to be supporters of different parties (see, among others, Galli, 1968; Bartolini, 1977; Mannheimer et al., 1978; Mannheimer, 1980).

If economic concerns have rarely been included in analyses as potential explanatory variables, this seems to have been due to electoral behavior being "shaped" by ideological identification and partisan attachment, where an almost psychological relationship between voters and political families (left- and right-wing parties) had supplemented and reinforced, through political socialization and the strengthening of political subcultures, the freezing of early social cleavages on which the parties have developed in Italy as well as in other European countries (Lipset and Rokkan, 1967). Given these molding forces, it is not surprising that Barnes and Sani found only minor differences among partisans' evaluations of their economic situations in 1972 as compared to five years earlier (Barnes and Sani, 1975). Personal economic conditions, though they might have been important for the people, were not politically relevant for the vote choice, at least in 1972.

The author's aim in this paper is to show that the assumed irrelevance of economic conditions in past electoral behavior is not absolute, since it has been possible to detect a clear, moderate correlation between electoral out-

comes and the state of the national economy. Moreover, and most important, the influence of economic conditions on voting is very likely to increase
since the basic attitude of the Italian electorate, i.e., ideological polarization
and partisan identification, seems to have undergone an important transformation, and since it appears now more feeble than ever before (Putnam
et al., 1981).

THE IMPACT OF ECONOMIC CONDITIONS ON ELECTORAL BEHAVIOR

Assessing the relationship between economic conditions (either personal
or collective) and party preference in a multiparty system like Italy it is not
an easy task. Besides the problems related to the highly ideologized style of
politics, systemic factors also contribute to make things more complex. While
in two-party systems the parties' alternative in power enables us to test the
influence of economic conditions on electoral behavior with respect to both
policy issues and incumbency, in Italy such a distinction is much more
blurred. First, Italy has not experienced yet actual government alternation.
Second, in such a system elections do not automatically "produce" majorities
and governments. They only distribute "weights" to parties which, through
complex bargaining, form ruling majorities. This implies that a voter un-
happy with the policy of one of the frequent coalitions in power might not
be able to recognize which of the coalition parties are to be held responsible.
Moreover, an electorate dissatisfied with a party's policy can cast a vote for
a different party of the government coalition, thus affecting the distribution
of votes among the ruling parties, but retaining the coalition as a whole in
power. Most important, such format makes it difficult to distinguish the
relevance of economic concerns on voting *due* to reation (or protest) to incumbent parties, from simple opposition voting based on policy assessments
and a party's traditional attachment. In other words, it is not a straightforward matter in Italy to test the general hypothesis which has guided research in this field, namely, that incumbent parties are hurt by a worsening
economy while the opposition is favored by it (Bellucci, 1984). These problems should be borne in mind during the following discussion.

Research on *aggregate data* shows that there exists a clear relationship
between macroeconomic indicators and the electoral support for the two
major Italian parties, i.e., the Communists (PCI) and the Christian Democrats (DC). In the period between 1953 and 1980, which covers seven national
elections, inflation has emerged as an important element in influencing the
voter's choice. Its impact is in the expected direction: increasing inflation
depresses the national electoral support of the ruling DC, while it is positively associated to the opposition PCI vote. In particular, in the period analyzed, a 1% increment of the inflation rate produces, on average, a drop

of .18% of the DC vote, and increases the PCI vote by .55%. Contrary to expectations, and to standard interpretations of rational voting, the other economic variable included in the regression equation, i.e., the unemployment rate does not behave as expected (Bellucci and Lewis-Beck, 1983).

Increasing unemployment is associated with a stronger support for the DC, while it hurts the Communist vote. Such a finding is clearly "embarassing," at least in terms of standard rational and economic voting theory, which ". . . would assume growing unemployment such an important indicator of government poor economic performance as to push discontented voters to turn to the opposition" (Bellucci and Lewis-Beck, 1983, Part 1, p. 11). The findings have then been tested on the regional level, fitting the same specification of the equation in each of the 19 Italian regions. (Val d'Aosta was excluded from the analysis since regional party politics is too different from the national level.) But, the overall picture did not change: consistently in all regions, between 1953 and 1979, the inflation coefficients are positive for the PCI vote and negative for the DC, while the sign of the unemployment variable is negative for the PCI and positive (with the exception of the Abruzzo region) for the DC.

Clearly, the national trend is not a statistical artifact resulting from aggregation bias. This "unemployment puzzle" needs an explanation which is provided by considering two important factors. The first refers to the uneven geographical distribution of unemployment and of the electoral support of the parties: the DC is electorally stronger in peripheral and rural areas, especially in southern Italy, where unemployment is higher, while the PCI electorate tends to be concentrated in urban areas (Sani, 1978) with low jobless rate, thus yielding the negative correlation. However, this ecological explanation is only preliminary. The second factor takes into account the presence of the "exchange vote," which is seen operating behind the DC-unemployment relationship. Accordingly, such a positive relationship reflects the economic weakness of the region and the people's demand for individualized policies and compensation (transfer payments such as old age pensions, disabled people's compensation, etc.). The DC, through its patron-client network, firmly established since the 1950s, is able to satisfy such demands and, consequently, can reinforce the link between incumbency and its electoral support. Such an explanation also offers a rational framework to account for an apparent irrational behavior, i.e., rewarding electorally the party responsible for mismanagement of the economy. Indeed, it appears quite rational to exchange electoral support for personal economic benefits with the party which can actually distribute them, namely the incumbent one (Bellucci, 1984).

In summary, analysis at the aggregate level shows that for the seven national elections held between 1953 and 1979, the impact of macroeconomic conditions on the electoral support of both the main ruling party and the main opposition one is not irrelevant. However, though the R^2s are fairly high (.94 for the PCI and .43 for the DC), the models developed present serious problems. The regression coefficients are unstable, multicollinearity is fairly strong, and the dependent variable does not incorporate all party choices but considers the DC and the PCI separately. Finally, aggregate analysis does not show how *individuals* behave in response to economic change.

Turning to a *cross-sectional analysis,* still at the aggregate level, units of analysis are the Italian regions, and all indicators employed, i.e., the DC and PCI regional shares of the national vote plus the economic variables (unemployment, per capita income, and inflation), are measured at this level. The findings are again ambivalent: in 1976 no clear economic influence on the vote was detected. None of the economic coefficients in the DC equation reached statistical significance, and their signs were in the wrong direction; clearly the responsibility hypothesis was not confirmed.

The 1979 model performed much better. Increasing inflation and income are positively associated with the Communist vote, which is depressed by higher unemployment rates. A minor image is offered by the DC estimates; unemployment is positively associated with the DC vote while negative signs present the other two economic variables. Moreover, in 1979 the influence of aggregate economic conditions on the vote for the two major Italian parties appears to be rather strong, according to the coefficients of multiple determination ($R^2 = .70$ for PCI and .67 for DC).

The contrasting findings in the two elections (1976 and 1979) seem to confirm, indirectly, the (negative) relationship between ideological polarization and the importance of economic conditions, for electoral behavior. Little evidence of economic effects was in fact found in the 1976 elections, when the process of ideological depolarization of the mass electorate had just begun. Furthermore, in that election the issue of whether the PCI would reach a position of relative majority, which was seen very likely to happen, produced a highly ideological campaign which did attenuate the impact of economic considerations on the vote. These conditions changed significantly in 1979; the PCI was already far from holding a position of power, and ideological polarization was weaker than three years earlier. In this election, economic effects were clearly detected. Santagata (1982), employing different models, also failed to find economic effects in the 1972 and 1976 elections, while in 1979 the impact of macroeconomic conditions on the vote is stronger.

Now let us consider data from the individual level. Analysis of the 1976 and 1979 election year surveys (Eurobarometers) confirms the aggregate level findings, showing that economic concerns do shape the vote choice in Italy (Bellucci and Lewis-Beck, 1983). Economic dissatisfaction moves electors to the left, both for policy-oriented motivations and for incumbency-oriented concerns. Further, economic voting is stimulated by collective economic judgments as well as personal economic circumstances.

In 1976 the vote choice was clearly influenced by personal economic conditions, i.e., voters with a lower income were more likely to vote for a leftist party. Further, they were influenced by collective economic perceptions and attitudes. Those who feel that strikes should not be curbed, that inflation is an important economic problem, and that government should do more to help the poor tend to cast a vote for the left.

In the 1979 survey, collective dissatisfaction again moved electors to the left. Those respondents who felt that greater efforts should be made to reduce income inequality, and those who thought that economic growth should not be the nation's top priority were more likely to favor the left. Turning to personal economic conditions, support for the left came also from those voters who were unemployed. At first sight, this last finding seems inconsistent with the opposite result from the aggregate analysis, which showed a negative aggregate correlation between unemployment and the PCI vote. The two findings, however, can be reconciled if we consider that the aggregate association relates incumbent support and the unemployment *rate*. This means that support for the DC is stronger in those areas where unemployment is at high levels, i.e., it is a structural disease. Then the "exchange vote" is a means to solve the job problem. But Santagata shows that if the yearly change of the unemployment rate is positive, i.e., there is a sharp rise of unemployment above average values, the positive association disappears and the DC vote is depressed (Santagata, 1982, p. 12). From the incumbent's perspective it would seem that the marginal utility, in terms of votes, of an extra person unemployed, is negative. This seems to imply that the incumbent's interest is to keep unemployment high enough to stimulate demands for individual unemployment benefits from the electorate. However, if unemployment rises beyond the average level (for one given geographical area), its impact on incumbent electoral support becomes negative.

The influence of economic conditions on electoral behavior that emerged from the individual level analysis acquires more salience considering that their impact was estimated net of the ideology of the voters, by inserting the left-right ideology scale in the model and holding it constant in a multiple regression equation. Thus an estimate can be provided of the impact of economic dissatisfaction on the vote, by utilizing the ordinary least squares estimates as a probability model. Focusing on the DC–PCI choice, it was found that, for a voter who locates himself at the center of the ideological spectrum, the probability of a DC vote is .91 if he is "economically content," while in case of economic discontent the probability lowers to .42 "The difference between the two estimates $(.91 - .42 = .49)$ is large, indicating that economic discontent can substantially shift the probability of supporting the DC." (Bellucci and Lewis-Beck, 1983, part II, p. 9).

TABLE 1. Italian Voters' Perception of Economic Situation: 1980–1983

	Country's economic condition			Household's economic condition		
	1980	1982	1983	1980	1982	1983
Much worsened	14.1	35.2	28.0	5.8	8.0	6.0
A little worsened	43.4	43.0	40.0	25.8	24.0	23.0
The same	22.0	10.0	18.0	48.0	50.0	53.0
A little better	16.8	8.0	10.0	18.1	15.0	16.0
Much better	1.5	3.0	1.0	1.1	2.0	1.0
Don't know	2.2	1.0	3.0	1.2	1.0	1.0
(N)	(1116)	(1025)	(1031)	(1116)	(1025)	(1031)

Source: Eurobarometer 13 (Fall 1980), 18 (Fall 1982), 19 (Spring 1983).

A major problem with the analyses of the 1976 and 1979 Eurobarometer surveys derives from the economic variables used. The questions available ascertain the respondents' *static* economic conditions and their opinions on broadly defined national economic issues. The early versions of the surveys in fact did not tap the respondents' perceptions of the *change* in personal as well as in national economic conditions. Therefore, it was not possible to relate party choice to such dynamic perceptions. This appears possible now, since such questions have been inserted in later versions of the Eurobarometer. We can thus observe how Italians have perceived economic change, both personal and collective (see Table 1). A striking feature is the difference of perception between the country's economic condition and the respondents' own family economic situation.

In general, Italians are much more pessimistic about the nation than they are with themselves. If we focus first on those who perceived no change since the previous year, we see that, referring to Italy as a whole, only 22% of the Italians shared such a view in 1980, and 18% did the same in 1983. But, evaluating the economic condition of their family, the share of those perceiving no change rises to 48% in 1980, and to 53% in 1983. The percentage of Italians who thought that the national economy had worsened (a little or much more) since the previous year was 57.5% in 1980, but only 31.6% reported the same evaluation for the family. Three years later such gap has increased: 68% see the country's economy as worse than in 1982; however, only 29.1% think the same about the family financial situation. In the same year, 17% of the respondents reported an improvement of the family's economy since 1982, but only 11% were willing to extend such evaluation to the national economy.

Such striking differences in the perception of economic change pose intriguing questions. They may reflect either a cognitive difference or actual rational evaluations on two separate economic actors. We will not examine

TABLE 2. Correlation coefficients matrix for 1980 Eurobarometer survey no. 13 (Italy)[a]

	1	2	3	4	5	6
1. Party choice		.82	.09	.08	− .01	.03
2. Ideology scale			.11	.04	− .03	.02
3. Italy's standard of living				.05	.21	.33
4. Personal economic hardship					.15	.07
5. Family financial situation since last year						.29
6. Italy's economic situation since last year						

[a]*Definition of variables.* Party choice: 1 = DP; 2 = PCI; 3 = PR; 4 = PSI; 5 = PSDI; 6 = DC; 7 = PLI; 8 = DN; 9 = MSI. Ideology scale: 1 to 10, left to right. Italy's standard of living: 1 = it is worsening; 2 = it is the same; 3 = it is better. Personal economic hardships, 4 point scale: 1 = I cannot make it; 4 = I can save money. Family financial situation since last year, 5 point scale: 1 = it has much worsened; 5 = it has much improved. Italy's economic situation since last year, 5 point scale: 1 = it has much worsened; 5 = it has much improved.

the issue here, but such differences obviously must be taken into account when assessing the relevance of economic conditions on the vote. While Kinder and Kiewiet (1979) report for the U.S. only weak correlations between collective and personal economic judgments, in Italy the link between collective and personal judgments seems stronger: in 1980 (the only year for which data were available until recently) the Pearson's correlation between personal and national economic conditions is .29 (see Table 2). However, the correlation between these two variables and party choice appears almost nonexistent, i.e., $r = − .01$ with the family financial situation, and $r = .03$ with the country's economic situation. Also, when they are used to predict party choice in a regression equation, they fall short of statistical significance.

In the same 1980 survey, two other questions tapped the perceptions of the respondents with respect to Italy's standard of living and to personal economic problems. Both questions did not imply comparisons with any point in time: they just ascertained the person's satisfaction at the time of the survey. Their intercorrelation is very weak ($r = .05$), but they correlate slightly better with party choice than the previous ones. We can then try to insert them in a multiple regression model, together with the left-right ideology scale (to exert a statistical control for the ideology of the respondent), and a government priority variable. The estimates from OLS appear in Table 3, in standardized form. The results are consistent with those of the earlier 1976 and 1979 models: those who are troubled by family expenditures and cannot save some money every month (P) are likely to select a leftist party, as well as those who are not happy about Italy's standard of living (C).

Economic dissatisfaction then, either collective or personal, pushes voters toward the left. Fighting inflation, as the government's top priority, is a goal

TABLE 3. An Economy-Ideology Model of Party Choice in 1980[a]

$V = .81^*I$	+	$.05^*P$	+	$.03C^*$	−	$.04^*G$
(38.4)		(2.3)		(1.6)		(−2.0)
$N = 728$	$R^2 = .68$	t ratios in parentheses				

*Entries are standardized regression coefficients.

[a]*Definition of variables.* V = party choice; I = ideology scale; P = personal economic hardship; C = Italy's standard of living; G = Government should give priority to fighting inflation (0); to something noneconomic (1). For variables coding see Table 2. *Source:* Eurobarometer no. 13 and DOXA.

selected more likely by voters for the center and center-right parties. The model fits the data quite well ($R^2 = .68$), and the coefficients are statistically significant (at the .05 level, one tail, $t > 1.61$). The standardized coefficients, however, show that much of the explanatory power of the model is due to the ideology variable, while the contribution of the three economic variables is much smaller.

Our hypothesis is that, if the depolarization of the Italian electorate is, as we think, an indicator of the declining strength of ideological, traditional, and subcultural voting, the emergence of a more rational and secular electorate should increase the importance of economic voting. Therefore, future research should discover an increase of the effect of economic variables on party choice.

CONCLUSIONS

The sharp decline of ideological polarization observed in recent years among the Italian mass electorate is an important consequence of the attenuated role played by "institutionalized traditions" in shaping electoral behavior. Ideological identification and tradition do not seem any longer the exclusive determinants of partisan choice, since the secularization of the electorate has allowed other factors to intervene. The *opinion vote* and the *exchange vote* are both increasing in importance, thus indicating the presence of more rational evaluations by the voters when casting their ballots.

More freedom from subcultural barriers implies more attention to parties' performance but also increasing political alienation. In the 1983 national elections, abstention and spoiled or blank ballots reached a high level: 16% of the electorate as compared to an average 10% in the previous eight elections in republican Italy. At the same time electoral volatility has also increased: from an average of 6.8% in the period 1970–1977 to 8.3% in 1983. And the subcultural vote is progressively losing strength: in the stronghold of Catholic subculture, the Veneto region, the DC's loss in 1983 was 8.6%, which was 3.2 percentage points above the national mean loss of 5.4%.

To be sure, ideology is still a key feature of Italian electoral behavior, though its impact is now mediated through other not strictly ideological elements. And the issue of the economy is surely among these. But the economy seems to have always played a role, though a minor one, in electoral behavior. Temporal analyses have shown a relationship between macroeconomic indicators and aggregate electoral returns. Cross-regional analyses also show this relationship. Moreover, the findings point to a stronger economic impact in recent elections than in early ones. Last, individual level research shows that economic dissatisfaction reduces electoral support for the incumbent party, i.e., the DC.

Nevertheless there are at least two aspects of the relationship between economic conditions and party choice in Italy which need to be clarified, if we want to achieve a better understanding of the nature of the relationship. First, research so far has shown that economic dissatisfaction tends to be associated with the choice of a leftist party. But this is not a clear test of antiincumbent voting, since the left was never in power. While waiting for actual government alternation to take place, we must then devise alternative strategies. One of these alternatives is to analyze how erosion or increase of electoral support for incumbent parties takes place among these parties' sympathizers, assessing through surveys and panel studies whether economic conditions matter. A second possible strategy is to step down to a level, from the national one, where alternation in government did take place, i.e., by focusing on regional elections or even province or city elections.

Second, it appears that both collective and personal economic conditions influence the Italians' partisan choice. There is a moderate correlation between the two factors. What is not clear yet is whether there is a correlation between actual economic conditions and their subjective perception. In other words we do not know whether actual experience or rather its perception *is politically* relevant. The Italian case seems to suggest that, at least in 1980, the *perception of economic change,* both personal and collective, is unrelated to the vote, while actual conditions are so for both. Of course, if it is possible to distinguish between experience and perception with respect to individuals' economic conditions, an analogous distinction is not possible for the nation's economy; here only perception is possible.

But while perceptions of the state of the national economy are mainly derived from information diffused by the media, the process through which perceptions of personal economic conditions are formed is less known. Do they reflect simply satisfaction or discontent with the individual's own economic situation, or are they referred, or compared, also to a wider context, i.e., one's friends, the city, etc.? Also, what about the widening gap observed between the share of Italians who evaluate positively change in the family's economic situation and those who think the same about the national economy? Is this due to actual differences in economic well-being, or merely to an inability to relate to an abstract concept such as the national economy? Research on these questions would appear important, since they can illuminate the way through which economic concerns translate into issues and, eventually, into voting.

REFERENCES

Barnes, S. H., and Sani, G. (1975). Nuovi movimenti politici e partiti tradizionali. In Mario Caciagli and Alberto Spreafico (eds.), *Un Sistema Politico alla Prova.* Bologna: Il Mulino.

Bartolini, Barbara (1977). Insediamento subculturale e distribuzione dei suffragi. In A. Parisi and G. Pasquino (eds.), pp. 103–144.

Bellucci, Paolo (1984). The effect of aggregate economic conditions on the political preferences of Italian electorate: 1953–1979. *European Journal of Political Research* (forthcoming).

Bellucci, Paolo, and Lewis-Beck, Michael (1983). Economics and the vote in Italy. Paper delivered at the Conference Group on Italian Politics Workshop on "Institutional Performance in Italy," Bellagio, Italy, June 1983.

Galli, Giorgio, ed. (1968). *Il comportamento elettorale in Italia.* Bologna: Il Mulino.

Galli, Giorgio, and Alfronso Prandi (1970). *Patterns of Political Participation in Italy.* New Haven: Yale University Press.

Kinder, Donald R., and D. Roderick Kiewiet (1979). Economic discontent and political behavior: the role of personal grievances and collective economic judgments in congressional voting. *American Journal of Political Research* 23: 495–526.

Lewis-Beck, Michael S., and Bellucci, Paolo (1982). Economic influence on legislative elections in multiparty systems: France and Italy. *Political Behavior* 4: 93–107.

Lipset, S. M., and S. Rokkan (1967). Cleavage structures, party systems and voter alignments: an introduction. In S. M. Lipset and S. Rokkan (eds.), *Party Systems and Voter Alignments.* New York: Free Press.

Mannheimer, Renato, Micheli, Giuseppe, and Zajczyk, Francesca (1978). *Mutamento sociale e comportamento elettorale.* Milano: F. Angeli.

Mannheimer, Renato (1980). Un'analisi territoriale del calo comunista. In A. Parisi and G. Pasquino (eds.), pp. 79–102.

Parisi, Arturo, and Pasquino, Gianfranco, eds. (1977). *Continuità e mutamento elettorale in Italia.* Bologna: Il Mulino.

Parisi, Arturo, and Pasquino, Gianfranco (1977). 20 giugno: struttura politica e comportamento elettorale. In A. Parisi and G. Pasquino (eds.), pp.

Pasquino, Gianfranco (1980). *Crisi dei partiti e governabilità.* Bologna: Il Mulino.

Putnam, Robert, Leonardi, Robert, and Nanetti, Raffaella Y. (1981). Polarization and depolarization in Italian politics. Presented at APSA Meeting, New York.

Sani, Giacomo (1973). Fattori determinanti delle preferenze partitiche in Italia. *Rivista Italiana di Scienza Politica* 3: 129–143.

Sani, Giacomo (1978). La composizione degli elettorati comunista e democristiano. In Alberto Martinelli and Gianfranco Pasquino (eds.), *La politica dell'Italia che cambia*. Milano: Feltrinelli.

Santagata, Walter (1981). Ciclo politico-economico: il caso italiano. *Stato e mercato* 2: 257–259.

Santagata, Walter (1982). On the demand for macroeconomic outcomes and politicians' beliefs: the Italian case. Working Paper n. 4 Laboratorio di Economia politica, Università degli Studi di Torino.

Sartori, Giovanni (1976). *Parties and Party Systems. A Framework for Analysis*. Cambridge: Cambridge University Press.

CHAPTER **6**

Economics, Democracy, and Spanish Elections

Thomas D. Lancaster
Department of Political Science, Emory University

Empirical comparative studies have greatly advanced our theoretical and substantive knowledge of the effects economic conditions have on electoral politics in firmly established liberal democracies. But what are the effects of economic conditions on electoral outcomes when democratic legitimacy has not yet been clearly established? Does the economy influence electoral politics differently in a Western European country that does not have a fully developed democratic tradition? This essay addresses these general questions of economic influences on elections by considering the Spanish case. Spain's recent democratic reforms provide an example that may be generalizable to other European systems, e.g., Portugal and Greece, and possibly to some African and Latin American countries' experiments with liberal democracy. Analysis of Spain and other similar cases should increase our understanding of the relative importance of economc conditions when elections themselves are relatively new to the political system.

The post-Franco transition to democracy since 1975 began just as the world economic crisis reached Spain, hauntingly parallel to the Second Republic's beginning in 1931, which coincided with the Great Depression's impact. The ultimate success of Spain's current democractic system may well depend upon the country's economic conditions, the government's ability to address the country's economic crisis, and the degree to which the electorate holds the government accountable for economic conditions. Previous studies on Spain's elections have analyzed the parties and other political forces, generally from a sociohistorical perspective (Maravall, 1979; Gunther et al., 1980; Pollack, 1983; Marcus, 1983). A few good quantitative studies have been undertaken on the Spanish parties' ideological space (Linz, 1980), their ideological base (Maravall, 1981), and public attitudes toward democracy (McDonough et al., 1981; Linz et al., 1982). Scarce attention has been paid, however, to the nexus between Spanish economic conditions and the country's three general elections.

This essay advances the argument that economic conditions have played an important role in Spanish elections but, until recently, one secondary to the establishment of democracy itself. This argument is advanced first by considering the Spanish economy's development at the time of these elections and the Spanish public's response to it. Spain's three national elections and significant economic policy activities and conditions are then analyzed. The third section considers unemployment's emergence as the central economic influence on recent Spanish elections. Finally, Spain's politics of consensus is presented as an explanation for the economic conditions' initial lack of influence on Spanish elections.

ECONOMIC PERFORMANCE AND ATTITUDES

Spain's "economic miracle" of the 1960s and early 1970s brought the country's economy to a level comparable with the other Western European countries (Harrison, 1978; Lieberman, 1982; Wright, 1977). Between 1960 and 1973, the Spanish economy grew faster than any other European system, with a real gross domestic product (GDP) annual growth rate of 7.16% (OECD, 1983). This economic boom came to a halt equally rapidly and intensely. The 1973 energy crisis economically exposed Spain's nearly complete dependence on imported petroleum and the country's susceptibility to the world's business recession (Lancaster, 1983). "Soft" economic transfusions had "existed in the form of tourism, immigrant remittances in foreign currency, and foreign investment" (Maravall, 1982, pp. 206–207). Franco's early 1970s economic policies had also aggregated Spain's economic conditions. Many economic sectors stimulated during the economic miracle could only survive with strong state protection. Furthermore, when the economy stagnated, greater inequalities existed in the distribution of material resources in Spain than in the other advanced European countries (Maravall, 1982, pp. 130–131). Spain's unemployment rate began to rise to unprecedented levels.

TABLE 1. Spanish People's Worries about the Future

Issues[a]	1975[b]	1976[b]
Unemployment	74%	71%
Inflation	63	61
Social inequalities	34	36
Strikes and demonstrations	29	27
Lack of freedom	24	24
Loss of moral values	30	20
International situation	18	11
Too rapid change	12	11
Don't know/no response	2	9

[a]Multiple response, closed-ended question.
[b]$N = 2,500$.
Source. Centro de Investigaciones Sociológicas (reported in Lopez Pintor, 1983, p. 14).

Such economic growth and decline had an enormous impact on Spanish social and political behavioral patterns. The growth of a much larger middle class, of an industrial and state cadre of technocrats, and of educational opportunities transformed the country's socioeconomic structures and the Spanish people's awareness of economic affairs. López Pintor (1981, 1983) reported the Spanish people's awareness of economic performance. More specifically, Table 1 shows that a few years into the country's economic decline, the Spanish people were overwhelmingly preoccupied with such economic problems as unemployment and inflation. These findings of high awareness of and concern over economic issues in relation to other political and social concerns are especially interesting since Spain initiated movement toward political reforms at this time.

The Spanish people's concern about economic issues remained high throughout the transition to democracy. Table 2 presents Spanish survey data across a 2-year period. Economic issues, particularly unemployment, continued to stand out when individuals were asked to identify their central preoccupation in a closed-ended questionnaire. Economic conditions were at the forefront of Spanish public opinion throughout this period, followed distantly by concern over terrorist activities, particularly by the Basque group ETA. Spain's worsening economic conditions only served to solidify economic issues' centrality among the citizenry. Even the unsuccessful February 1981 coup attempt and its sharp reminder of democracy's tenuousness appears to have drawn disproportionately from other issues, not the economy.

Spain's worsening post mid-1970s economic slump did not go unnoticed by the country's citizens. Table 3 reflects a strong trend over time in the Spanish people's responses to the country's economic conditions. An increas-

TABLE 2. Spanish People's Central Worries

Issues[a]	7/1979	5/1980	3/1981	10/1981
Unemployment	45%	60%	58%	62%
Inflation		8	6	5
Energy crisis	9	5	3	3
Terrorism	22	12	20	11
Public order/citizen safety	4	3	3	2
Regional automony	2	1	1	1
Social inequalities	1	2		
Morality in customs	1			
International relations				
Strengthening democracy			5	5
Others		1		
Don't know/no response	16	8	4	2
Totals[b]	100%	100%	100%	100%

[a]Percentage, first mention, closed-ended question.
[b]$N = 1,200$.
Source. Centro de Investigaciones Sociológicas (reported in López Pintor, 1983, p. 14).

ing percentage responded that the economy had worsened. These perceptions of a declining economy and the high degree of concern for economic issues reported in Table 2 together indicate a potential economically induced frustration among the Spanish electorate.

The Spanish people have also created a potentially strong accountability link between economic performance and the government. State management of many parts of the economy, for example, is widely accepted in Spain. Maravall (1982, p. 107) reported that 87% of his respondents agreed that the state should plan the economy. The long period of governmental economic intervention during the Franco regime produced a situation where state control or nationalization of major industry has generally had many partisans (de Miguel, 1976, pp. 229–230). As a consequence, political fallout in Spain occurred when the government did not directly confront the country's declining economic situation. The Spanish electorate's concern for economic problems, however, has coincided with the extremely difficult task of political reform.

NATIONAL ELECTIONS: 1977, 1979, 1982

Table 4 presents the results of Spain's three national elections. Several general trends emerge from these elections: the early strength of Adolfo Suarez's centrist UCD party and its rapid demise; a concomitant strengthening of

TABLE 3. Spanish People's Perception of the Country's Economic Situation Compared with that of the Previous Year

Perception of Country's Economic Situation	1965	1976	1979	1980	1981
Has improved	42%	20%	14%	14%	7%
Is the same	34	35	34	31	37
Has worsened	11	31	39	27	41
No response	13	14	13	28	15
Total	100%	100%	100%	100%	100%

Source. Centro de Investigaciones Sociológicas (reported in López Pintor, 1983, p. 22).

the Socialist party (PSOE); the right-wing Popular Alliance's (AP's) initial struggles replaced by its current role as the leading opposition party; and the Communist party's (PCE's) continued electoral weakness. Spain's economic conditions and the different parties' treatment of economic issues go far in explaining these trends. The following analysis of the economic influences on Spain's three general elections focuses on the major political parties, in part because Spain's use of the d'Hondt system of representation accentuates the outcomes, favoring the larger parties (Pallarés, 1981).

The June 15, 1977, election was the first national election held in Spain since the Second Republic's last election in 1936. Politically, conditions of uncertainty dominated the 1977 election: terrorist bombing in the Basque

TABLE 4. Spanish Election Results

Political Party	1977		1979		1982	
Popular Alliance (AP)	8.4%	(16)[a]	6.1%	(9)	26.6%	(106)
Democratic Center Union (UCD)	34.9	(167)	35.1	(168)	6.9	(12)
Democratic and Social Center (CDS)					2.9	(2)
Socialist party (PSOE)	29.4	(118)	30.5	(121)	48.7	(202)
Communist party (PCE)	9.3	(20)	10.1	(23)	4.1	(4)
Basque Nationalists (PNV)	1.7	(8)	1.7	(7)	1.9	(8)
Democratic Convergence of Catalonia (CiU)	3.7	(11)	2.7	(8)	3.7	(12)
Other regional parties			6.3	(13)	2.2	(4)
Others	12.6	(10)	7.6	(1)	3.1	(0)
Total	100.0%	(350)	100.1%	(350)	100.0%	(350)

[a]Number of seats in parentheses.

country erupted and the party system did not crystallize until late — particularly given that the Communist party was not legalized until late April of that year and President Suarez did not announce his candidacy, along with the UCD's registration, until early May. Spain's economic conditions were also worsening: the annual inflation rate had increased to its highest levels; unemployment had risen to above 7%, with some parts of Andalusia as high as 25%; a structural deficit existed in state finance; the stock exchange fell precipitously; and investment had virtually ceased. Spain's economic deterioration had continued throughout 1976 and the 1977 election year.

Despite these economic problems, politics took an almost obsessional priority over economic issues during this period. The pre-election Suarez government ideologically leaned toward an economic policy combating inflation. Nevertheless, this appointed government could not bring itself to impose the urgently needed economic austerity measures, given its transitional nature. In spite of the serious and worsening economic conditions, neither the government nor the general Spanish population placed the economic crisis at the forefront of Spain's political agenda: economic conditions took a backseat to the political campaign. The newness of an electoral campaign, and the personalities and past memories it aroused, provided the "issues." Democracy itself became the focus of Spain's 1977 election.

The dearth of clear political alternatives in economic policy provided by the newly created political parties rather than the Spanish electorate's disinterest in economic conditions best explains the economic crisis's lack of influence on the 1977 election. As seen in Table 1, economic conditions provided potentially favorable terrain for the different parties to exploit politically. Even Spain's major leftist political parties, nevertheless, intentionally obfuscated many essential economic policy questions. The need to establish political credibility among the plethora of parties that contested this election generally meant forthright economic policy statements would lose votes. Parties tended to opt for electoral strategies that postponed clearer definitions of economic policy positions.

The 1977 election results, however, did not resolve Spain's political direction. The near equal political balance in parliament — the UCD as the largest parliamentary party fell nine votes short of a majority — mandated negotiated governmental, political, and economic solutions. Even after the 1977 election, negotiation remained the norm for decision making (Lojendio, 1979, p. 153). Holding the fabric of democracy together continued to be Spain's central task for the next several years. And since facing the country's grave economic situation required a strong political position, politics continued to take precedence over economic affairs even after the 1977 election. The Spanish people's immediate political concern, which took priority over economic conditions, centered around the drafting of a new constitution. This process took almost a year and a half to complete. In the meantime, the economy received governmental attention only when it threatened to disrupt Suarez's plans for the transition.

As a political agreement, the Moncloa Pact bought Suarez the time he needed to guide Spain's transition to democracy without infringement from the country's economic conditions. The October, 1977, Moncloa Pact helped assuage and, in many aspects, postpone Spain's economic problems as a political issue. With this agreement, Adolfo Suarez's UCD government managed to temper the Left's push for placing economic concerns at the front of Spain's political agenda (Coverdale, 1979, pp. 91–94). The Moncloa Pact formalized, among other things, the political Left's moderation on the economic front and its willingness to work with the government in formulating an economic policy. The opposition agreed to a 20% wage increase ceiling, public expenditure reductions, tax increases, and strong credit restrictions in exchange for a number of political and economic concessions.

The UCD government and the leftist parties and the labor unions continued, nevertheless, to engage in some economically oriented debate following the Moncloa Pact signing. Some non-negotiated aspects of the UCD government's economic policy began to be criticized shortly after this formal agreement. Objections to the government's monetary and fiscal polices began to grow. Inflation, while slightly abating, continued as a serious economic problem during 1978. Furthermore, the UCD government did not respond to the Left's call for employment policies and welfare reforms. Unemployment continued throughout 1978 to be at the heart of the political antagonism between the UCD and the PSOE and PCE.

Spain's major political parties acknowledged the seriousness of these economic problems but reached no consensus for solutions. During 1978, the Socialists increasingly began to distance themselves from the UCD's economic policies, in retrospect a move that ultimately facilitated their coming to power. Whereas the PCE favored extending the Moncloa Pact, the PSOE only accepted an agreement applicable until the next general elections (Kohler, 1982, p. 22). The PSOE desired greater political maneuvering room in many areas, including economic policy, in order to confront the UCD electorally.

President Suarez called new elections almost immediately following Spain's December 1978 ratification of the new constitution. Economic and other issues, nevertheless, received much greater attention in the 1979 campaign than in the 1977 election. Economic issues such as unemployment, housing, education, and public investment and social concerns such as abortion, divorce, public health, and law and order greatly replaced the 1977 campaign's democracy versus dictatorship question. The PSOE's program in particular centered on these economic and social issues (Maravall, 1979, pp. 305–306). Nevertheless, such agreements between the UCD government and the political Left as the 1979–1981 Framework for Collective Agreements, written in the same spirit as the Moncloa Pact, continued to lessen the intensity of the political confrontation over economic issues.

While the 1979 election virtually replicated Spain's political balance, the increasing conflict over economic policy between the UCD government and the PSOE and PCE in opposition continued to dominate Spanish politics. The government's unemployment and conservative socioeconomic policies increasingly antagonized the Left. Many Socialists and Communists argued that the UCD did not possess its own distinctive economic program, that it simply followed the late Franco period's policy direction, and weakly at that. The Suarez government also aggravated political antagonisms when it cut unemployment benefits during an extremely difficult economic period. Such UCD economic policies, along with its foot-dragging on the regional question and political devolution, prompted a PSOE-sponsored motion of censure against the UCD government on May 20, 1980. Although this motion failed to obtain a parliamentary majority, it crystallized public opinion: this parliamentary motion instigated the UCD's and President Suarez's political crisis and significantly increased PSOE's support, both of which ultimately ushered the Socialists into power in October 1982 (Maravall, 1982, p. 59).

The Suarez government's difficulties in dealing with Spain's more overt economic problems such as the high inflation rate and an unemployment rate of over 12% contributed to Suarez's resignation in January 1981. Despite the abortive military coup of February 23, 1981, and the reminder of the still-tenuous nature of Spanish democracy, the new Calvo Sotelo–led UCD government pursued stricter economic policies. Tight credit and a more stringent monetary program reduced Spain's inflation to a little over 15% in 1981. In mid-1981, the Calvo Sotelo government also reach an agreement with organized labor setting wage increases below the inflation rate. Such economic policy effects, however, did not manage to turn around the previous UCD government's weak economic program. Government popularity steadily eroded between 1979 and 1982 because of "its apparent failure to control the twin evils of economic recession and terrorist violence" (Marcus, 1983, p. 281). The 1982 election proved to be the UCD's last.

The PSOE acknowledged its potential for winning Spain's October 1982 general election. The UCD's internal cohesion problem, the PCE's ideological wrangling and its slippage in the trade union elections, the PSOE's earlier success in regional elections, and most public opinion polls signaled a Socialist election victory. As a consequence, under Felipe Gonzalez's leadership, the PSOE contrasted the UCD's continuing lack of creativity in economic policy with a mild economic program. The PSOE offered no radical reforms such as major nationalizations or state takeovers, proposing only slight economic policy changes. Yet economic issues still struck a responsive cord in the electorate. More important, the PSOE appealed to Spain's 2 million unemployed, over 16% of the adult population, with promises of 800,000 new job creations during its 4-year term. Public investment to stimulate demand and the encouragement of private investment were to provide these employment opportunities. The PSOE also promised aid to small and medium businesses through various measures, including more flexible credit and reductions in employers' social security contributions (Marcus, 1983).

THE MAJOR ISSUE: UNEMPLOYMENT

The Socialists' 1982 national victory provided Spain's clearest electoral mandate since the reestablishment of democracy. Many factors contributed to this success: Felipe Gonzalez's youthful and skilled leadership, UCD internal ideological conflict, the PCE's inability to challenge the PSOE's control of Spain's political Left, and other recent governmental activities in such areas as NATO membership, failure to overcome barriers to EEC membership, and continuing terrorist violence. The Spanish people also increasingly blamed the incumbent government for the country's persistent economic problems. Schwartz's (1976, p. 98) belief that Spanish voters would hold their governments electorally accountable for economic performance still appeared correct, even if it is somewhat overestimated.[1] More specifically, Spain appears to have followed the general political economic trend in which unemployment concerns distinguish support cleavages (Alt and Chrystal, 1983, p. 161). Consolidation of Spanish democracy needed to come first, but unemployment eventually proved a major challenge to the UCD government. Many Spanish people respected the UCD's significant role in the democratic transition, yet fears about the growing unemployment ranks led to the belief that the country was ready for a change in power — and thus the successful completion of the transition to democracy.

As seen in Tables 1 and 2, unemployment provided Spain with its fundamental economic issue throughout the transition. Spain's employment situation posed an immediate problem at the time of the initial political reforms. Into the early 1980s, many more Spanish people were concerned about unemployment than about other economic issues such as inflation, as seen in Table 2. More important to our analytical focus, this economic concern was translated into political frustration during the period before the 1982 election. Three-quarters of some survey respondents indicated that unemployment was why expectations at the beginning of the transition had not been met (Maravall, 1982, p. 122). When asked what were the country's principal problems, "98 per cent indicated 'to ensure work for all' and 94 per cent declared the provision of health and housing for all; simultaneously, 91 per cent mentioned public order" (Maravall, 1982, p. 122). The Spanish electorate gave strong political consideration to unemployment and the economic crisis, along with public order and security. Both the basic concern over individual economic security and the years of job security resulting from employers' inability to fire employees under the Franco regime reinforced a low tolerance level in this economic area. This economically induced worry ultimately received its paramount political expression in the 1982 election. The PSOE, as the major opposition party, reaped the electoral benefits of the incumbent government's poor economic policy record. The Spanish Communist party, as the other major oppositional political force, did not successfully compete with the PSOE in this regard. This was in part due to its older leadership under Santiago Carrillo, its internal ideological conflict over Eurocommunism, and its overall failure to generate new party membership and to mobilize groups politically outside its own ranks.

Following its 1982 sweeping electoral victory, the PSOE immediately responded on the economic front. The new government devalued the peseta 8%, announced increased taxes on gasoline and other fuels, and introduced a maximum 40-hour week. The current PSOE government must now forcefully face Spain's difficult unemployment problem. The difficult task of encouraging employment through greater private investment and increased public investment without aggravating Spain's already mounting budget deficit must now be faced. If the PSOE is unsuccessful, the Spanish electorate will most likely become as impatient with it as it did with the UCD. If the PSOE government does not ameliorate Spain's deteriorating economic conditions, the right-wing party Popular Alliance, in its new role as the major oppositional force, may well be able to combine the electorate's economic frustrations and Francoist nostalgia into propelling it to power in 1986.

POLITICS OF CONSENSUS

Why, despite Spain's intensifying economic crisis, did economic conditions only recently come to have a strong influence on the country's electoral outcomes? The tribulations and uncertainties of democratic political reforms suggest the best explanation. Economic conditions and issues took a political backseat to the consolidation of parliamentary democracy during Spain's early transition years for several reasons. Initial euphoria about reform led many citizens and public servants to exaggerate, or not question, a democratic system's ability to address problems of inflation and structural unemployment. Democracy, in this respect, became to many a panacea for Spain's worsening economic conditions. Successful political reform, many believed, would naturally lead to the resolution of the country's other problems, including the economic ones.[2] And a peaceful transition to democracy was far from assured. The need for political moderation and consensus was severely challenged by a young and unstable party system, the emotions of regional politics, and central to our concern here, the economic crisis. Spain's economic problems and the end of the Franco regime appeared to have occurred simultaneously. The difficulties in pursuing at the same time both political reform and stringent economic measures were enormous. Spanish political leaders thus undertook a strategy that first called for the strengthening of the norms, rules, and procedures of democratic decision making. Then, they addressed economic and other problems. Initially at least, a majority of the Spanish electorate was not so concerned about transferring economic preferences and influences to the voting booth as it was about whether or not elections would be held at all. Democracy always came first. McDonough et al. (1981, p. 60) reported that in 1978, 78% of their survey respondents believed elections were the best method for choosing the country's government and authorities, whereas only 6% did not, and 15% did not know. Their 1979/80 responses were 78%, 5%, and 17%, respectively. Only when the tentativeness of Spanish democracy lessened did economic conditions and elections begin to be linked.

The nonrevolutionary nature of Spain's political Left greatly facilitated the country's politics of consensus and the consolidation of democracy. Spain's social and economic advances during the 1960s cooled the electorate's reception to revolutionary ideas. Likewise, the later economic downturn had a conservative political effect, moderating white-collar and worker leftist revolutionary rhetoric (Maxwell, 1983, p. 168). Spain's transition to democracy thus experienced little political extremism. Only reformist demands challenged the UCD government's timid economic and social policies. The PSOE's and the PCE's moderation in many areas, including economic policy, reflected this. At an extraordinary congress in September 1979, the PSOE formally removed its Marxist ideological label. Throughout this period, the Socialists did not promote drastic economic changes such as the nationalization of industry. Instead, they advocated economic expansion and increased employment, even at the expense of inflation. The PSOE nurtured a moderate image as a Socialist "administrator of capitalism," declaring Marxism as only one of several valid political approaches. The PCE also shed its revolutionary program. The Workers Commissions' successes in the trade union movement moderated the PCE's political rhetoric and practices. The contemporary PCE now accepts the legitimacy of Spain's social and economic system.[3] This does not imply, however, that PCE members do not remain preoccupied with economic issues. As one study revealed, in 1977 PCE supporters assigned a much higher value to ideology in comparison to program, leadership, chances of success, or capacity to govern than did members of the other major parties: 72% of PCE supporters mentioned ideology either first or second compared with PSOE's 55%, UCD's 24%, and AP's 48% (Linz, 1980). And, as suggested above, the PCE's more ideological orientation is one reason why the PSOE and not the PCE benefited electorally from Spain's economic downturn. The PCE, nevertheless, while more ideologically oriented than the PSOE, generally proposed moderate economic policy that facilitated Spain's politics of consensus during the transition to democracy.

The Left, however, disproportionately bore the cost of consensus politics. Economic agreements during this transitional period such as the Moncloa Pact and the Framework for Collective Agreements negatively affected the leftist parties, the workers' unions, and citizens' expectations in that differences in economic policy alternatives offered to the electorate were minimized (Del Aguila Tejerina, 1982, p. 115). The Spanish Left, which began the transitional period in the opposition, had in many respects to legitimate fully its own position on the Spanish political scene before it could take advantage of economic influences in its rise to power. The political Right, on the other hand, was originally in a better position to take advantage of the economic influence on citizens' voting calculus, given Spain's transition from the Franco dictatorship. The political Right often emphasizes to this day the Franco regime's economic achievements. Francoist fiscal policies, heavily reliant upon indirect taxes and easily evaded income taxes, continue to benefit disproportionately the middle and upper classes. Most democratic attempts at fiscal reform directly challenge these economic interests. One economic policy mistake of the UCD was to promote such fiscal reform. This is one reason why the Suarez government's economic policy frustrated both workers and capitalists. Suarez's desire for fiscal reform offended the Right, and his passivity in other economic policy areas aggravated the Left. Politically, defeat thus was only a matter of time.

Manuel Fraga's Popular Alliance party currently represents democratic conservatives in the contemporary Spanish political system. Now as the major opposition party, AP may well be able to exploit economic influences on future elections much better than did the UCD. The personnel overlap between the Franco and democratic regimes in both the AP's membership and party elite provides a platform for a defense against many economic reforms. Popular Alliance's control of Galicia's autonomous parliament following the September 1981 regional election also strengthens the party's current national position as the new leader of the political opposition. Economic influences on both regional and national elections in Spain are particularly important to the Center-Right and the Right since they depend heavily on independent farmers and the self-employed, whereas economic development and industrial policies are of prime concern to the political Left, particularly in Catalonia and the Basque country. The next several years may prove critical for Spain's Right in this regard. The ending of Spain's politics of consensus ushered the PSOE into power. AP, as the major voice of the opposition, will now attempt to turn the tables and benefit politically from the Spanish people's current economic frustrations.

CONCLUSIONS

Democracy has not proved the panacea for economic conditions as many in Spain previously believed. Democratically elected governmental leaders similar to those of the previous authoritarian regime have as yet been unable to rectify many of the country's severe economic problems. Spain's future difficulties reside in the fact that much of the country's unemployment is structural. The PSOE, which so eagerly pushed unemployment as a political issue while in the opposition, will continue to have many of the same problems as previous governments. Democracy in Spain, as a consequence, may encourage manipulation of other parts of the economy for political advantage. The Spanish electorate's belief, however, that the consolidation of democracy had to precede economic concerns has at least brought this parliamentary system to the point where the question is no longer *if* elections will be held but whether or not economic conditions affect election *outcomes*. The lessons Spain has learned in this regard may prove quite beneficial to other countries facing an equally difficult transition to democracy.

Acknowledgments. This essay is the first in a series of reports on the effects on economic influences on Spanish elections. Subsequent research will estimate empirical models from individual level survey data. I would like to thank the following people for helpful suggestions regarding this research: Peter McDonough, Juan J. Linz, Eusebio Mujal-Leon, Robert E. Martinez, Richard Gunther, Kenneth Maxwell, and Samuel H. Barnes.

NOTES

1. Schwartz (1976, p. 98) wrote the following about Spain and unemployment: "There will panicky action if unemployment goes beyond say 5 or 6 per cent, no matter what the repercussion on the rate of inflation: monetary leniency, special credits, import controls, incomes policy, price freezes, the whole dreary panoply will be used without compunction by whatever government is in power if prosperity is not there for the asking."
2. On the other hand, many people disposed against the democratic reforms often equated unemployment and inflation — along with many other social problems — as a consequence of democracy.
3. For example, the constitution's final draft asserts in the words "market economy" that the state must guarantee and protect free enterprise. Yet while the political Right managed this, the Left also saw that the constitution included the following: "the defence of productivity in accordance with the demands of the economy and, if necessary, of economic planning"; expropriation if compensation is paid; and the right to strike.

REFERENCES

Alt, James E., and Chrystal, K. Alec (1983). *Political Economics.* Berkeley: University of California Press.

Coverdale, John F. (1979). *The Political Transformation of Spain After Franco.* New York: Praeger.

de Miguel, Amando (1976). Spanish political attitudes, 1970. In Stanley G. Payne (ed.), *Politics and Society in Twentieth-Century Spain.* New York: New Viewpoints.

Del Aguila Tejerina, Rafael (1982). La transicion a la democracia en España: reforma, ruptura, y consenso. *Revista de Estudios Políticos* 25: 101–127.

Gunther, Richard, Sani, Giacoma, and Shabad, Goldie (1980). Party strategies and mass cleavages in the 1979 Spanish parliamentary elections. *World Affairs* 143: 163–216.

Harrison, Joseph (1978). *An Economic History of Modern Spain.* Manchester: Manchester University Press.

Kohler, Beate (1982). *Political Forces in Spain, Greece and Portugal.* Woburn, Mass.: Butterworth.

Lancaster, Thomas D. (1983). *Regime Change and Public Policy: The Political and Macro-Economic Decision-Making of Spanish Energy Policy.* Unpublished Ph.D. dissertation: Washington University.

Lieberman, Sima (1982). *The Contemporary Spanish Economy.* London: George Allen & Unwin.

Linz, Juan J. (1980). The new Spanish party system. In Richard Rose (ed.), *Electoral Participation: A Comparative Analysis.* Beverly Hills and London: Sage Publications.

Linz, Juan J., Gomez-Reino, Manuel, Orizo, Francisco A., and Vila, Dario (1982). *Informe sociológico sobre el cambio político en España 1975/1981.* IV Informe Foessa-Volumen I. Madrid: Foessa.

Lojendio, I. M. (1979). El Estado social y sus cargas. Expectativa española. In *Las experiencias del proceso político constitutional en Mexico y España.* Mexico City: UNAM.

López Pintor, Rafael (1981, July–September). Los condicionamientos socio-económicos de la acción política en la transición democrática. *Revista Española de Investigaciones Sociológicas* 15: 9–32.

López Pintor, Rafael (1983, July–August). Actitudes políticas y comportamiento electoral en España. *Revista de Estudios Políticos* 34: 9–39.

Maravall, J. M. (1979). Political cleavages in Spain and the 1979 general election. *Government and Opposition* 14: 299–317.

Maravall, J. M. (1981). Los apoyos partidistas en España: polarización, fragmentación y estabilidad. *Revista de Estudios Políticos* 23: 9–31.

Maravall, J. M. (1982). *The Transition to Democracy in Spain.* New York: St. Martin's Press.

Marcus, Jonathan (1983). The triumph of Spanish socialism: the 1982 election. *West European Politics* 6: 281–286.

McDonough, Peter, Lopez Pina, Antonio, and Barnes, Samuel H. (1981). The Spanish public in political transition. *British Journal of Political Science* 11: 49–79.

Maxwell, Kenneth (1983). The emergence of democracy in Spain and Portugal. *Orbis* 27: 151–184.

OECD (1983). *National Accounts, Main Aggregates: 1952–1981.* Paris: Organization For Economic Cooperation and Development.

Pallarés, Francesc (1981, September–October). La distorsión de la proporcionalidad en el sistema electoral español: análisis comparado e hipótesis alternatives. *Revista de Estudios Políticos* 23: 233–267.

Pollack, Benny (1983). The 1982 Spanish general election and beyond. *Parliamentary Affairs* 36: 201–17.

Schwartz, Pedro (1976). Politics first: the economy after Franco. *Government and Opposition* 11: 84–103.

Wright, Alison (1977). *The Spanish Economy 1959–1979.* New York: Holmes & Meier Publishers.

CHAPTER 7

Economic Effects on the Vote in Norway

Arthur H. Miller
Center for Political Studies, University of Michigan

Ola Listhaug
University of Trondheim, Norway

The electoral consequences of economic conditions are the subject of an increasingly voluminous literature in the United States. By comparison, research on this topic in Scandinavian countries is quite rare. However, recent years have witnessed an increasing interest in the topic among both economists and political scientists.

Most of the Scandinavian work in this area relies on aggregate indicators to determine the relationship between economics and political behavior. Frey (1979), for example, employed rate of inflation, change in unemployment, and growth in real income to predict the popularity of the incumbent party in Denmark, Norway, and Sweden over a period of 67 years. The results are at best mixed. He found significant political effects for inflation in Denmark and unemployment in Sweden. For Sweden there is also an additional effect of real income growth but only in the bivariate model. These disappointing results are explained by structural changes in society and the short-lived tradition of placing economic security within the government's domain. "It may, for instance, be argued that voters have only held the government responsible for unsatisfactory economic conditions since the Keynesian revolution, i.e., since World War II" (Frey, 1979, p. 314). This interpretation is corroborated by an analysis showing that the popularity of the Swedish government during the period 1967–73 was significantly related to all three economic indicators.

In a similar study, Jonung and Wadensjö (1979) predicted the popularity of the Swedish Social Democratic party for the period 1967–78. Their model incorporated monthly data on unemployment, consumer prices, and real income. As the Social Democrats were in power from 1967 to 1976 but not during the 1977–78 period, a test of the incumbency factor was possible.

Although the estimates were sensitive to different model specifications, the main conclusions are fairly straightforward: unemployment, inflation, and to a lesser extent, decreasing real income have negative consequences for the Social Democrats when they govern. When they are out of power the sign of the coefficients reverses for inflation and unemployment, but not for real income growth. However, only the effect of unemployment is statistically significant at the .05 level in this model.

The Swedish case has also been analyzed by Sigelman (1983) in a study that covers the period 1967–74. This study has two advantages over the previously discussed works: it includes variables from a competing model of electoral behavior, and it uses an estimation method that is more appropriate with time series data (GLS as compared to OLS). The indicators of the political economy model include the demand for unskilled labor (as reported by Swedish firms) and the consumer price index. Two other indicators from a communication model are also included; the percentage of the editorials in newspapers with comments that are critical of the government, and the percentage of editorials expressing negative evaluations, regardless of their focus. The analysis results, when predicting the popularity of the government, show fairly strong effects in the predicted direction for the unemployment indicator, and more moderate effects of the consumer price index and media criticism.

By far the most advanced aggregate study has been done by Madsen (1980), who analyzed time series data for the Scandinavian countries for the period 1920–75. Among the strengths of the study is the explicit consideration of problems in the specification of a model for multiparty systems. Since coalition governments have been more the rule than the exception in the Scandinavian countries, especially in Denmark, the question is who gets the blame or the benefit from changing economic fortunes. In Norway and Sweden, Madsen used support for the incumbent parties as the dependent variable.

But for Denmark, Madsen assumed that the party supplying the prime minister will be seen as responsible for economic conditions, and he consequently used support for this party as the dependent variable in his model. An objection to this approach, however, is that the prime minister may come from one of the smaller parties in the coalition, thus the assumption may be less valid than when the prime minister represents the largest or dominant party in the coalition.

In addition to the conventional variables like percentage increase in real gross domestic product (GDP) per capita, level of unemployment, net change in unemployment, and inflation, Madsen also attempted to include variables that capture changes in the social and political system. For example, he used a measure of increases in tax revenue to account for the growth of the public sector during the period investigated. He also took into account long-term changes in the electoral support for the parties by constructing a normal vote variable that is the average support across three previous elections.

The results of the estimation provide no support for the hypothesized economic effects in either Denmark (with the exception of inflation) or Norway. For Sweden, on the other hand, the economy is found to influence electoral outcomes as predicted: the incumbent party benefited from favorable economic conditions and was hurt by a deteriorating economy. The evidence produced by Madsen (1980) for the long-term period and the results of the analyses for the sixties and seventies thus makes the evidence in the Swedish case relatively strong. Denmark and Norway, by comparison, apparently do not fit the political economy model, at least as determined by the aggregate studies.

Madsen offered two explanations for the absence of economic effects in Norway and Denmark. He suggested that the economic conditions in these small countries are dominated by fluctuations in the international economy; thus country specific indicators fail to capture the appropriate variance (1980, p. 16). Second, he argued that the impact of class differences on the vote may be so strong as to eliminate other effects (1980, p. 26). The difficulty with these suggestions, and indeed with all the aggregate analyses, is that the additional explanatory variables are rarely included in the specified models.

Class is only one possible cleavage that may overshadow economic effects in Scandinavian countries. A weakness of the aggregate studies is that they do not take these relevant cleavages into account in the prediction of the vote. This is normally not an objection against individual-level studies based on survey data. These studies generally incorporate a number of factors from competing models of electoral behavior. In principle, such studies can include the economic items with a number of other variables; thus we can assess the relative net impact of economic perceptions.

The major study based on survey data comparing economic factors with other important elements in a model of voting was done by Pettersen (1981). Through a set of regression equations predicting the vote for each of the Norwegian parties, he included independent variables from three models of electoral behavior: the identification model, the issue proximity model, and the investment model. In the investment model, he incorporated mediated retrospective items (assessments of the government's policies and perform- ance on unemployment and inflation) and simple prospective items (expec- tations on personal finances and fear of unemployment). Pettersen's study is based on data from the Norwegian Electoral Studies and covers the elec- tions of 1965, 1969, and 1977.

The major conclusions are that party identification is the most important determinant of the vote and that issues also have some importance, especially in the 1977 election. Only for the 1965 election is the investment model of some relevance. It is important to note, however, that the 1965 study did not include the personal finances items. The effects of the investment model in that election were, therefore, attributed to mediated items only. The simple economic items were included in the 1977 study, but Pettersen did not ex- plicitly specify the relationship between the simple and the mediated items. It might be that the impact of personal concerns on the vote choice is depen- dent on the perception of how the alternative parties will handle inflation and unemployment.

A question that naturally arises is, Why have so few studies been published on the relationship between the economy and the vote in the Scandinavian countries when, at least for Norway, relevant items have been included in the surveys from 1965 on? The answer is at least twofold. First, the standard model for explaining electoral behavior in the Scandinavian countries, and probably most clearly in Norway, has been the cleavage model (Rokkan, 1967; Valen and Rokkan, 1974). This model sees the voters' position in the matrix of economic and cultural cleavages as the fundamental determinant of partisan affiliations. In more recent studies (Valen, 1981; Valen and Aardal, 1983), the ideology and issue positions of the voters have been linked to their cleavage locations to give a more complete model of how the vote is deter- mined. This model does not easily facilitate the private economic concerns of the voter.

Second, to the extent that economic attitude items have been studied, they are assumed to reflect the partisan positions of the voters and consequently are treated as dependent variables (Valen and Aardal, 1983, chap. 10). The dominant view has been that there is little room for independent economic calculation on behalf of the Norwegian voter; they more or less automatically assess the parties and government alternatives from their structural positions and ideological inclinations, and once partisan attachment is determined, this strongly colors the perceived economic relevance of the parties and the government.

In summary, a review of the relevant literature provides little evidence supporting the hypothesis that economic conditions influence voting behavior in Scandinavia. The macrolevel studies show that economic effects are consistently found only for Sweden. However, the macrolevel studies cannot be viewed as conclusive, as they are often plagued by specification and measurement problems. Nevertheless, the infrequent individual-level analyses that have been conducted also failed to discover consistent economic effects. The major theoretical thrust of the microlevel studies has been to assume that economic judgments linking politics and economics are thoroughly confounded with the predisposing effects of partisanship.

If personal economic conditions are cognitively associated with evaluations of government or connected with the vote choice at all, it is only done as an extension of social cleavages or partisan loyalty, not as an independent, rational assessment of either personal self-interest or collective benefits. Given these conclusions from the literature, we would predict that any economic effects on individual-level political behavior in Norway, the Scandinavian country we focus on in this paper, would be at best weak, inconsistent across time, and most likely a spurious reflection of partisanship and other cleavages.

PERSONAL ECONOMIC VOTING IN THE WELFARE STATE

An alternative theory that derives from work on France suggests very different expectations. Lewis-Beck (1983) reported finding a significant correlation between personal economic conditions and the vote in the French parliamentary elections of 1973 and 1978. His results are in sharp contrast to those that have been repeatedly documented for the United States. Economic effects on the vote in the United States appear to arise mainly from a concern with collective economic conditions rather than personal economic experiences (Kinder and Kiewiet, 1979). By comparison, the French data actually reveal a stronger impact of economic judgments about personal experiences rather than about collective conditions.

The difference in the findings for the two countries is so striking that Lewis-Beck invoked a "cultural" explanation for the dissimilarity. He argued that because of years of continuous growth in the centralization of economic authority in the French government, French voters are more likely than Americans to express their personal financial woes through the ballot box. Americans, in contrast, are assumed, on the basis of previous research (Feldman, 1982; Kinder and Kiewiet, 1979; Kinder and Mebane, 1983), to place blame on the individual more and to attribute their personal economic misfortunes to themselves or other proximal causes rather than to the government.

The Lewis-Beck "cultural" thesis appears to be a powerful explanation for what has plagued U.S. researchers for some time — namely, how to explain the lack of a correlation between individual economic optimism/pessimism and the vote. Unfortunately, Lewis-Beck did not provide data to test his cultural hypothesis, he merely presented it as a speculative explanation for the differences in the French and American data.

The Norwegian case provides an excellent opportunity to extend the cultural hypothesis and investigate it with available empirical evidence.[1] Similar to France, the Norwegian government plays a much more pervasive role in directing the economic fortunes of the country than is true for the United States. Moreover, the welfare state is based on the principal of equality, and equalization of individual economic rewards and conditions is an explicit goal of the society. Individualism, therefore, should be much less prevalent and less highly regarded as a value in Norway relative to the United States.

Given these cultural differences we would expect, following Lewis-Beck's thesis, to find that: (1) Norwegians are more likely than Americans to hold the government responsible for economic problems; (2) personal economic fortunes should be more strongly correlated with both evaluations of government economic performance and the vote in Norway; and (3) evaluations of which party would do a better job in dealing with inflation and unemployment should be more strongly associated with the vote in Norway than in the United States. Each of these points is investigated in turn.

Is Government Responsible?

Over the years, the Norwegian election surveys have included a set of questions asking if government policies or other causes are most responsible for inflation and unemployment. The responses to these questions reveal a surprisingly high percentage of individuals who see causes other than government actions as responsible for the country's economic ills. In each year, approximately half or more of the Norwegian respondents saw other nongovernmental sources as the cause of high prices and unemployment (see Table 1). The only exception occurred in 1981 when 36 percent attributed inflation to nongovernmental causes. By comparison, between 16% and 32% pointed unequivocally to government as the most important cause of inflation and unemployment.

Contrary to the cultural hypothesis, the Norwegian data on attributions for economic ills appear very similar to comparable evidence from the United States. In 1976, for example, three out of every ten U.S. survey respondents blamed the government rather than labor unions or big business for the economic difficulties facing the country at that time (see Table 1). Similarly, Kinder and Mebane (1983) reported that 18% of the respondents in a 1979 consumer attitudes survey mentioned government as the cause of inflation.

Of course, it could be argued, on the basis of Table 1, that the percentage

TABLE 1. Perceived Cause of Economic Problems

Perceived Cause of Problem	Data by Country and Years		
	Norway		
	1969	1977	1981
Unemployment			
Government policy	16%	16%	21%
Both	25	29	33
Other sources	59	55	47
Total	100%	100%	100%
(N)	(1,172)	(1,322)	(1,453)
Inflation			
Government policy	20%	21%	32%
Both	27	30	32
Other sources	53	49	36
Total	100%	100%	100%
(N)	(1,168)	(1,459)	(1,416)
	United States		
	1976		
Economic Problems			
Congress	19%		
President	12		
Labor unions	33		
Big business	36		
Total	100%		
(N)	(1984)		

of respondents mentioning government as the cause of economic ills was much higher in Norway than in the United States. This conclusion could be reached by combining those who said "both" with those who unambiguously blamed government. Because the "both" category is difficult to interpret, the evidence of Table 1 appears troublesome but inconclusive for the cultural thesis. Despite this lack of definitiveness the data suggest that, although government is seen as a prominent cause of economic problems, it is not the most predominant culprit in either society. While government may be faulted by many citizens for not solving economic problems, relatively few people see government as the cause of those difficulties.

Are Personal and Collective Economics Connected?

The cultural thesis also leads us to expect a relatively stronger correlation in Norway than in the United States between optimism/pessimism about one's personal economic situation and collective economic judgments. In a

TABLE 2. Correlations of Personal Economic Concerns With Assessed Economic Performance of Parties and the Vote[a]

	Inflation	Unemployment	Vote
Norway			
1969	.04	.01	.08*
1973	b	b	−.02
1977	−.08*	−.06	−.07*
1981	.19**	.20**	.30**
United States			
1976	−.15**	−.08*	.09*
1978	.07	.05	.08
1980	.07*	.06*	−.10*
1982	−.22**	−.18**	.10*

[a]Personal economic concerns was coded: 1 = personal financial situation will be better in coming year; 3 = same; 5 = worse. Party performance for Norway was coded: 1 = better by Socialists; 3 = same; 5 = better by Bourgeois. For the U.S. it was: 1 = better by Democrats; 3 = same; 5 = better by Republicans. Vote in Norway and the U.S., respectively, was coded: 1 = Socialist parties, 2 = Bourgeois parties; 1 = Republican, 2 = Democrat.
*$p < .01$; **$p < .001$.

welfare state, the government explicitly acts as the planning agent for economic stability, not just at the national level but at the individual level as well. We might, therefore, expect the average citizen to link these economic spheres cognitively. In the United States, however, there should be little or no relationship between personal and collective economic evaluations because government is "relatively fragmented and nondirective, at least with regard to people's economic life" (Lewis-Beck, 1983, p. 355).

Again we find little evidence to support the part of this cultural hypothesis that focuses on Norway. In 1969, 1973, and 1977, only weak correlations exist between judgments regarding personal economic conditions and either government economic performance or the vote (see Table 2). This pattern of relationships is similar to that found in the United States for 1976, 1978 and 1980. From those years one would conclude that assessments of personal economic conditions are not politicized in either country. The results would also clearly contradict the cultural hypothesis.

However, 1981 in Norway and 1982 in the United States provide a curious anomaly for both the cultural hypothesis and previous work on economic politics. In both countries for those years we find a stronger linkage between personal economics and political evaluations.[2] Clearly cultural differences do not explain this sharply stronger association between personal and collective economic judgments. We suggest that the issues and tenor of the political debate in those elections focused more clearly on economics and particularly

TABLE 3. **Correlations of Vote With Assessed Economic Performance of Parties**

	Inflation	Unemployment
Norway		
1969	.39[a]	.40
1977	.45	.46
1981	.49	.48
United States		
1976	.61	.52
1978	.50	.41
1980	.62	.57
1982	.48	.44

[a]All correlations are positive, indicating that people were more likely to vote for the party they thought would do a better job in dealing with the economic problem. All correlations are significant well beyond the .001 level.

on the implications of government economic policies for individual prosperity. In Norway, for example, inflation had reached 14% in 1981, and Kaare Willoch, then floor leader of the Conservatives and later prime minister, directed considerable criticism during the campaign toward the economic record of the ruling Labour party. Similarly, the 1982 U.S. congressional elections were held amid considerable discussion of Reagonomics, cuts in social welfare programs, growing unemployment, remaining fears of inflation, and a world wide recession.

In short, we speculatively suggest that an interaction between the economic nature of the times and the discussion of economic problems by the candidates and the media produced the increased politicization of the personal financial assessments. This outcome suggests two additional conclusions. First, the link between individual and collective judgments may have more to do with specific political campaigns and the transmission of political information than with cultural differences. Second, generalizations regarding the independence between personal and collective economic beliefs need to be specified more clearly.

Are Assessments of Government Economic Performance Reflected in the Vote?

One last prediction of the cultural hypothesis is that evaluations of government economic performance should be more strongly reflected in the vote of a welfare state than is true for the United States. Again the data fail to support this prediction. In fact, as the correlations in Table 3 demonstrate, the vote and performance judgments are often more strongly associated in the U.S. data. The impact of economic performance on the vote choice in Norway has, however, increased over the years.

Partly the increased correlations reflect a shift by the public away from the perception of the bourgeois parties as less capable than Labour in dealing with economic problems. In 1969 the socialist parties were perceived as more likely to deal effectively with the economy by roughly two to one over the bourgeois parties. By 1981 this had changed considerably. In that year the socialist and bourgeois parties were mentioned by nearly equal percentages as the party best able to handle unemployment and the bourgeois had surpassed Labour in the public's estimation as the party most capable of controlling inflation.

The strong correlations between the vote and these mediated economic evaluations of which party would better handle economic problems raise several other theoretically relevant questions. First, in those years when we find a significant zero-order correlation between personal economic conditions and the vote, is this relationship reduced to insignificance by controlling on the party evaluations? Second, in a more fully specified model incorporating class ideological and partisan cleavages, do either the personal or collective economic judgments continue to have any independent effect on voting behavior?

In contrast to the Lewis-Beck (1983) finding, both Fiorina (1981) and Kinder and Mebane (1983) have proposed models that argue for no independent, direct effects of the individual's personal economic situation on the vote. According to these models, personal economic distress is connected with the vote only through politicized intervening variables such as government economic performance or perceptions of how the broader economy is functioning. The Norwegian data for both 1969 and 1981 offer examples that are contrary to the U.S. models. After controlling for the inflation and unemployment party performance measures, personal finances were still significantly, albeit weakly, correlated with the vote in 1969 and rather strongly correlated in 1981 (Beta = .18).

Specifying the model more fully does reduce personal finances to an insignificant level for the 1969 data, but not in 1981 (see Table 4). In general, the Norwegian data suggest that as the more traditional cleavages associated with class and party loyalties have decayed, economic performance has come to the fore as a major determinant of the vote. Contrary to what was suggested by the earlier macrolevel studies, economic factors appear to have influenced the vote choice rather strongly in recent elections. Indeed, the fairly recent rise in the importance of the economic factor may explain the absence of economic effects in the earlier macrolevel studies of Norway, as well as the disregard for these factors in the microlevel analyses.

Of course, one might argue that part of the relationship between the vote and the economic indicators is a reflection of reciprocal causation originating in other prior predispositions or the vote choice itself. Clearly we have

TABLE 4. Regression Coefficients for a More Fully Specified Model Predicting the Vote[a]

| | Norway | | |
Predictors	1969	1977	1981
Personal finances	.01*	− .02*	.13
Party best–inflation	.14	.19	.22
Party best–unemployment	.16	.23	.20
Left/Right ideology		.28	.27
Party identification	.44	.21	.24
Class	.22	.19	.11
R	.69	.70	.72

| | United States | | | |
Predictors	1976	1978	1980	1982
Personal finances	.01*	.02*	− .08	.02*
Party best–Inflation	.26	.22	.31	.12
Party best–unemployment	.20	.09	.15	.10
Liberal/conservative	.13	.05*	.04*	.02*
Party identification	.33	.42	.41	.47
Class	.03*	.01*	.05*	.01*
R	.73	.64	.76	.63

[a]Vote in Norway was coded: 1 = Socialist, 2 = Bourgeois. In the U.S., it was coded: 1 = Republican, 2 = Democrats.
*Denotes coefficients that are *not* significant at the .05 level. All other entries are significant at the .01 level or better.

not tested for all these reciprocal relationships. Our task has been a more modest one of attempting to determine if there is any independent effect of economic considerations after controlling for all those other assumed prior predispositions. Having incorporated the major alternative explanations for the vote, we feel rather safe in concluding that in Norway there is definitely an impact of the economy which is independent of partisan ideological and social cleavages. For 1981, this economic effect appears quite similar to Lewis-Beck's French findings and contrary to the U.S. models. Nevertheless, there is little evidence to suggest that this result can be explained by a "cultural" difference.

SPECIFYING THE CONNECTION BETWEEN ECONOMICS AND POLITICS

Having dismissed the "cultural" explanation for the 1981 results, it behooves us to provide some other individual-level explanation. Following the lead of Kinder and Mebane (1983), we can search for those factors that might increase the availability of information that would facilitate the cognitive link between economics and politics. We might expect, for example, that since there was a significant rise in the proportion of the Norwegian population blaming the government for inflation in 1981 (recall Table 1), that this fostered a closer tie between personal economic worries and political behavior in that year. Similarly, we might predict that people who are better informed and intensely interested in politics may have either more fully developed political schemas or stronger partisan attachments which facilitate the connection between economic concerns and political choices.

Before turning to these psychological or cognitive factors which can influence the linkage between private economic concerns and the vote, we will also consider one social factor. Kramer (1983) has argued that observable changes in individual welfare may be caused by two unobservable components, one which is government induced, and hence politically relevant, and one which is caused by life cycle and other politically irrelevant factors. His argument suggests that issues of personal finances may be of greater relevance for individuals who are more closely linked to the government sector and be of less relevance for persons making their fortunes outside the direct reach of government economic decisions. While this latter group may be considered very small in a society like Norway, the degree to which the government is an important cause in determining personal welfare certainly varies across individuals.

We propose that persons employed in the public sector of the economy, for example, will be more influenced by the economic decisions of the government than persons employed in the private sector. Consequently, the linkage between economic concerns and voting should be stronger for the former than for the latter group. If this were true, it would also help explain the increased importance of economic factors in voting behavior during recent years, as the public sector grew rapidly between 1969 and 1981.[3]

We do, in fact, find the predicted pattern for 1969 and 1977. Among persons employed in the private sector of the economy, there was virtually no relationship between personal finances and the vote, while the correlation is moderately strong for those employed in the public sector (see Table 5). However, in 1981 the pattern reverses: the correlations for both sectors are significant, but personal economic concerns and the vote are most strongly associated among respondents employed in the private sector. The 1981 results, therefore raise serious doubts about employment in the public sector as a sufficient condition for specifying the connection between personal finances and the vote.

Of course, it may be that people employed in the private sector in 1981 were even more likely than those in the public sector to hold government responsible for their economic fortunes. Kinder and Mebane (1983) argued that how individuals explain their economic situation strongly conditions

TABLE 5. Correlation Between Personal Financial Concerns and the Vote Control-
ing for Specifying Variables – Norway

Specifying Variables[a]	Correlations		
Employment by sector:	1969	1977	1981
Private	– .01	.01	.40**
Public	.16*	– .12**	.24**
Blame government for unemployment:			
No	.02	– .02	.33**
Partly	.20**	– .03	.25**
Yes	.08*	– .09*	.17**
Blame government for inflation:			
No	.02	– .02	.27**
Partly	.13**	– .13**	.26**
Yes	.04	– .07	.19**
Strength of party identification:			
Independent	.02	– .01	.14**
Weak	.08*	– .07*	.26**
Strong	.09*	– .11**	.42**

[a]Vote was coded: 1 = Socialists, 2 = Bourgeois. Economic concerns were coded: 1 = personal
financial situation will be better in coming year; 3 = same; 5 = worse.
*$p < .01$; **$p < .001$.

the relationship between personal economic worries and presidential voting.
They predict that the relationship among those who have "collectivist" economic views and hold government responsible for the state of the economy
should be weaker than for those who are "privatistic" and attribute the cause
for economic problems to nongovernmental sources.

This theory would predict a stronger linkage between personal financial
prospects and the vote for persons who blame the government for unemployment or inflation than for those who say the causes lie elsewhere. The empirical evidence from Norway, however, is less than fully supportive of the
hypothesis for 1969 and 1977 because the correlations are slightly stronger
for those who blame the government than for those who don't (see Table 5).
But the difference between the correlations is so small as to be insignificant.
Moreover, the 1981 data clearly contradict the hypothesized pattern.

Although controlling for the perceived cause of economic problems fails
to confirm the Kinder/Mebane thesis, it may suggest an alternative theory.
Upon closer examination, the pattern of correlations obtained after controlling for the perceived cause of inflation and unemployment appears somewhat curvilinear. That is, the correlations tend to be stronger for people
saying that the government is partly to blame for economic ills than for those
who hold government entirely responsible. This difference might reflect a

greater degree of political sophistication among the former than among the latter group. Certainly a reasonable view is that the government alone can only partially control unemployment and inflation. Blindly "blaming" the government, therefore, may actually reflect somewhat less political-economic sophistication, which in turn increases the difficulty of translating personal economic experiences into voting behavior.

This suggests the possibility that the connection between personal economic conditions and political behavior may have more to do with cognitive structuring than with attributing the cause of economic woes to particular sources. The connection may simply be more dependent on how well-informed and capable the person is to abstractly conceptualize politics. The richer the person's cognitions of politics, the more likely they should be expected to connect economic conditions and political preferences.

Whereas it is difficult to provide definitive proof for this argument, we have found some rather convincing evidence. First of all, we find stronger correlations between personal finances and the vote among people who are more interested in politics. Moreover, since strength of party identification indirectly indicates both the richness of political cognitions and the ability of a person to structure political experiences, we would expect it to be the mediating variable par excellence. Previous research shows that strong identifiers are much more likely to relate their views to political parties and to politicize their experiences. We would expect, therefore, that the link between economic concerns and the vote will depend on the strength of party identification. Strong identifiers should be more likely than independents to make the connection.

Unlike the results obtained with the previous controls, those for varying levels of party strength are both supportive of the hypothesis and consistent across all the years (see Table 5). Strong identifiers, particularly in 1981, were indeed more likely than Independents to link the vote and personal economic concerns. A similar analysis performed with the U.S. data reveals the same pattern of results especially for the years 1976 and 1982.

How are we to interpret the pattern of correlations obtained with the various specifying variables? In general, all three indicators (sector of employment, blaming government, and strength of party identification) appear to reflect factors that influence a person's ability to translate personal economic concerns into political behavior. Yet the three variables give rise to somewhat different interpretations. Both employment in the public sector and strength of partisan attachment lend themselves to a more benign interpretation than the one derived from the attribution of responsibility items.

In the latter case, we assume that citizens are consciously aware of the impact that government actions have on their own economic conditions and they punish the incumbents for detrimental outcomes. In the former case,

TABLE 6. Correlation Between Personal Financial Concerns and the Vote Controlling for Strength of Partisanship and Focus of Responsibility — United States[a]

Strength of Party Identification Identification	1976	1978	1980	1982
Independent	.03	.02	− .07	.04
Weak	.11*	.07	− .08	.09
Strong	.14*	.09	− .11	.19**

	Blame Government (1976 only)	
	Yes	No
Total	.16**	.07
Independent	.12	.01
Weak	.16	.09
Strong	.19**	.12*

[a]Vote was coded: 1 = Republican, 2 = Democrat. Economic concerns were coded: 1 = personal financial situation will be better in coming year; 3 = same; 5 = worse.
*$p < .01$; **$p < .001$.

certain individuals, because of their occupational location, connection with partisan organizations, or self-interest, have available or seek out and are better prepared to utilize political-economic information. The connection between economics and partisan choices are, therefore, more readily made and used by these people in making electoral decisions. In short, their understanding of economics is more politicized regardless of whether or not they blame the government for their own *personal* economic conditions.

The Norwegian data separating these two potential connections are quite conclusive. There is no correlation between strength of partisan identification and blaming the government for inflation or unemployment. In addition, the correlation between personal finances and the vote fails to vary systematically with respect to blaming the government after having first controlled for strength of party identification. In brief, the link between personal economic assessments and the vote is enhanced by strength of partisanship and not by attributions of economic responsibility.

Data from the United States, on the other hand, suggest that both blaming the government and strength of party attachment help mediate the connection between personal economics and the vote choice (see Table 6). For Independents or those who do not hold the government responsible for economic problems, there is no linkage between personal finances and the vote, whereas quite a significant correlation is found for strong identifiers (particularly in 1976 and 1982) or for those who blame the government. Unfortunately, 1976 is the only year we can test for the effects of blaming the government as this measure was not included in other National Election Studies (NES) surveys. Nonetheless, the 1976 data demonstrate that both factors independently help facilitate the connection of everyday economics with politics. The weakest correlation occurs among Independents who do not blame the government and the largest for strong identifiers who hold the government responsible.

The difference between the U.S. and Norwegian results when controlling for both strength of party identification and blaming the government may arise from a difference in the functions of political parties in the two countries. In Norway, the party organizations are a major source of political information for the voter. But in the United States, very little political information originates directly from the political parties. Strength of party identification in the United States, therefore, is more an indicator of self-motivation, whereas in Norway it also reflects integration into a network of political communications and organizational activities. In addition, the findings reported here fit nicely with Fiorina's (1981) suggestion that partisan attachment is heavily influenced by retrospective assessments of how well the parties have performed in office. Given this argument then, we would have expected to find, as we do, a closer linkage between economic performance attitudes and the vote among stronger identifiers.

CONCLUSIONS

Contrary to the earlier macrolevel studies, we have found a strong and systematic impact of economic concerns on political behavior in Norway. As the social cleavages that traditionally dominated Norwegian politics dissipated, economic factors came to have an increasingly powerful influence on election outcomes. The absence of economic effects in the macrolevel studies may, therefore, have been an accurate representation of an earlier period in Norwegian political history, rather than the result of statistical limitations. One major problem with macrolevel studies, however, is that they are not sensitive to shifts in social and political forces as they are occurring.

The microlevel data, on the other hand, provide less than conclusive evidence as a counter to the "small nations" argument, which has been raised by the macrostudies. Economic conditions in smaller countries with open markets are subject to political decisions and economic fluctuations in other countries. Politicians in these smaller nations frequently point to fluctuations in the world economy as the culprit for economic problems at home. Voters in Norway and other small countries, therefore, might be less likely to translate economic grievances into votes against the incumbent because they might perceive the incumbent as exercising little control over economic conditions (Lewis-Beck, 1982).

The 1969 and 1977 Norwegian data showing insignificant relationships between personal economic conditions and the vote actually fit the smaller nations explanation. Likewise, the appearance of a strong relationship in 1981 may be interpreted as reflecting the influence of the worldwide recession occurring at that time rather than a public reaction to the economic policies of the Norwegian government. However, one piece of evidence that contradicts the external forces thesis is the 1969-to-1981 rise in the percentage of Norwegians blaming the government for inflation and unemployment. Another is the increasing impact on the vote found for perceptions of which party would better handle economic difficulties.

These trends seem to suggest that Norwegian politics are becoming less a reflection of the vagaries of external market conditions and more sensitive to questions of economic self-determination. This change may have been enhanced by a number of factors including the 1972 debate over membership in the European Economic Community, the discussions surrounding the development of off-shore oil, as well as the criticisms which Conservative politicians have leveled against the economic policies of the previously dominant Labour government. Now that the Conservatives have been in office since 1981, it remains to be seen how important internal economic conditions are for their reelection in 1985. But a definitive determination of whether the election outcome reflects internal or external economic forces cannot be obtained without directly exploring the assumptions of the smaller nations thesis. Future studies in Norway, therefore, should attempt to ascertain if voters are less likely to hold their government responsible for economic conditions because they attribute the cause to uncontrollable external factors.

A variation on the "cultural" hypothesis may also merit further attention. Whereas we found little support for this thesis as articulated by Lewis-Beck, the Norwegian data do suggest that differences in the political structures of various countries might influence the link between personal economics and political behavior. Namely, cross-cultural differences in the type of party structure and the party functions may help explain variation in the extent to which personal economic factors are important determinants of the vote.

Acknowledgments. This paper was prepared while the senior author, A.H.M., was on a Fulbright Fellowship at the Department of Sociology, University of Trondheim, Norway. We wish to thank Henry Valen for making the Norwegian data available. The Norwegian Election Surveys are conducted under Henry Valen's supervision.

NOTES

1. The Norwegian Election Surveys are based on personal interviews with a cross section of Norwegian adults. The sampling procedure has two stages. In the first stage a number of

geographical areas are randomly chosen. These areas are stratified by region, socioeconomic characteristics of the "kommuner," and size of population. Within each area (sampling unit) a random sample of persons are selected. In the election studies 1957–73 the lists of all voters ("manntallet") were used to select the individuals. In the two most recent studies the person register of the Bureau of Statistics has been employed. The U.S. data in each case derive from the American National Election Studies conducted by the University of Michigan, Institute for Social Research.

2. A close inspection of the sign of the correlations for the 1981 Norwegian data reveals what might initially also be regarded as an anomaly. In that year, those who expected to be worse off in the future voted more heavily for the Labour party, the ruling party at that time. Normally we would expect economic pessimists to vote against the ruling party, but in 1981 the widespread anticipation that the bourgeois parties would win the election may have increased economic optimism among their supporters. Those who thought they would be worse off logically voted for Labour, as it was under a bourgeois government that they expected to be worse off. The pattern of correlations thus fits with what we would normally expect, that is, people vote for the party that they think will promote the most beneficial economic conditions. The important difference in 1981, therefore, is not the sign but the strength of the correlation.

3. The differentiation of private and public employment is based on the self-report of the respondents. This categorization of private and public sector occupations, therefore, may be less precise than the work of others (see, for example, Kolberg, 1983) but shows the same trend. The Norwegian Election Survey data reveals 30% of the 1969 sample employed in the public sector as compared with 44% in 1981.

REFERENCES

Feldman, S. (1982). Economic self-interest and political behavior. *American Journal of Political Science* 26:446–466.

Fiorina, M. P. (1981). *Retrospective Voting in American Presidential Elections.* New Haven: Yale University Press.

Frey, B. (1979). Politometrics of government behavior in a democracy. *Scandinavian Journal of Economics* 81:308–322.

Jonung, L., and Wadensjö, E. (1979). The effect of unemployment, inflation and real income growth on government popularity in Sweden. *Scandinavian Journal of Economics* 81:343–353.

Kinder, D., and Kiewiet, D. (1979). Economic discontent and political behavior: the role of personal grievances and collective economic judgments in congressional voting. *American Journal of Political Science* 23:495–527.

Kinder, D., and Mebane, W. (1983). Politics and economics in everyday life. In K. Monroe (ed.), *The Political Process and Economic Change.* New York: Agathon Press.

Kolberg, J. (1983). Utviklingen av de Skandinaviske velferdsstater fra 1970 til 1980. Paper presented at the Nordiske Sociologkongressen, Stavanger, 19–22 August.

Kramer, G. (1983). The ecological fallacy revisited: aggregate- versus individual-level findings on economics and elections and sociotropic voting. *American Political Science Review* 77:92–111.

Lewis-Beck, M. (1982). Economics and elections in the west. A proposal submitted to the National Science Foundation.

Lewis-Beck, M. (1983). Economics and the French voter: a microanalysis. *Public Opinion Quarterly* 47:347–360.

Madsen, H. (1980). Electoral outcomes and macro-economic policies: The Scandinavian cases. In P. Whitely (ed.), *Models of Political Economy.* London: Sage Publications.

Pettersen, P. (1981). Identification, agreement and government performance; the relative impact on voting. *Scandinavian Political Studies* 4:221–252.

Rokkan, S. (1967). Geography, religion, and social class: crosscutting cleavages in Norwegian politics. In S. Lipset and S. Rokkan (eds.), *Party Systems and Voter Alignments.* New York: Free Press.

Sigelman, L. (1983). Mass political support in Sweden: retesting a political-economic model. *Scandinavian Political Studies* 6:309–315.

Valen, H. (1981). *Valg og politikk.* Oslo: NKS-Forlaget.

Valen, H., and Aardal, B. (1983). *Et valg i perspektiv.* Oslo: Statistisk Sentralbyrå.

Valen, H., and Rokkan, S. (1974). Norway: conflict structure and mass politics in a European periphery. In R. Rose (ed.), *Electoral Behavior.* New York: Free Press.

CHAPTER 8

Economic Self-Interest and the Vote: Evidence and Meaning

Stanley Feldman

Department of Political Science, University of Kentucky

Speculation about the relationship between the economy and political behavior has a long and illustrious history. Systematic empirical study of the subject can be traced back to Kramer's (1971) study of the impact of macroeconomic conditions on congressional voting (for a review of earlier studies, see Monroe, 1979). Although a number of important issues have been raised by the growing body of literature on the subject, one of the most important, and certainly most debated, issues has been the existence of personal self-interest. Put more concretely, do changes in people's personal financial well-being influence their evaluations of political leaders and institutions? The answer to this question is important for several reasons. Most basically, there is the question of the mechanism by which changes in macroeconomic conditions affect political behavior. That people act on the basis of changes in their personal ecomic well-being certainly provides a plausible (and possibly attractive) linkage mechanism. The assumption that personal self-interest is a critical component of political behavior has been a common assumption in political thought and forms the basis of a major theoretical line of political inquiry (see Downs, 1957). The extent to which people respond politically to changes in their economic well-being may also have a direct bearing on the economic policies the government may undertake while still maintaining public support. A strongly self-interested public may limit the ability of the government to manipulate public support symbolically (Edelman, 1964). Moreover, in the long run, the way in which people react to economic conditions may help determine the legitimacy of the political system (Lipset, 1960).

Do people vote their pocketbooks? Tufte (1978) provided evidence that politicians *believe* they do. As in other matters political, one suspects that where there is smoke there is fire. In order to determine if there are flames, it is first necessary to consider a more basic question: why should we expect people to act on the basis of personal economic self-interest? It should be noted to begin with that the concept of personal self-interest is vague and potentially tautological. It is possible to argue that people who ignore recent changes in their own financial well-being while acting on perceived changes in the state of the nation's economy are behaving in a way that will maximize their long-term personal economic well-being. On the other hand, people who vote against the incumbent president because their financial well-being has recently declined would not necessarily be acting in their personal self-interest if those economic problems were due to the addition of a new child or money spent playing video arcade games. Although by no means solving these problems, people will be considered as acting in their personal economic self-interest when their political evaluation or behavior is influenced by those changes in their economic status that can reasonably be attributed at least in part to the actions of the government.

There are several reasons for expecting people to act politically on the basis of their personal economic self-interest. The concept of personal self-interest has an obvious intuitive appeal. It is very easy to believe that people who feel that they are being hurt personally by the economic policies of the government will punish the incumbent administration. The self-interest argument also depends heavily on the personal experiences of people. People's knowledge of how they are being affected by economic conditions is acquired on the basis of daily experiences: buying food, clothing, and other goods; keeping track of budgets and savings; shopping for a new house, and so forth (see Popkin et al., 1976). Consequently, the information costs of acting on the basis of personal self-interest are small. On the other hand, keeping oneself informed about the state of the national economy and the likely impact of macroeconomic events on personal well-being may require more effort than many people seem to devote to politics.

EVIDENCE FOR PERSONAL ECONOMIC SELF-INTEREST

The results of aggregate level studies of the relationship between macro-economic conditions and congressional voting (or presidential popularity) provide the strongest evidence that political behavior and evaluation respond to changing economic conditions. The rate of inflation and changes in real disposable income seem to be most closely linked to political evaluation, although some studies find that unemployment also has a pronounced effect. Taken as a group, the results of the aggregate level studies provide strong evidence that the common wisdom is in fact correct: politicians' fates depend greatly on the state of the economy. A closer examination shows, however, that the aggregate level research does not yield a completely consistent picture of the impact of macroeconomic conditions. In fact, empirical results seem to be altered by almost any slight change in the specification of the model (see Stigler, 1973). The effects of unemployment come and go, the estimated lag time of the effects vary from study to study, and most annoyingly, some specifications seem to show little or no effect of economic conditions (see for example, Arcelus and Meltzer, 1975; Owens and Olson, 1980; Monroe, 1981; Norpoth and Yantek, 1983).

Clearly, more work is needed to better understand the aggregate level relationships. But that is not my purpose here. More relevant to this paper is the *interpretation* of the aggregate level findings. As has been noted (Kinder and Kiewiet, 1979; Kramer, 1983), a relationship between macroeconomic conditions and political behavior can be explained in a number of ways: people reacting to changes in their personal well-being; people blaming (or rewarding) the government for changes in the state of the economy; or even political elites altering their behavior in anticipation of a reaction by the public (Jacobson and Kernell, 1982). The basic problem is that the aggregate level studies provide evidence only of covariation between various time series; they cannot examine the mechanisms responsible for the relationships. While clearly valuable in answering questions about the overall responsiveness of the public to changing macroeconomic conditions (and other events as well), the aggregate level studies leave us groping for the individual level processes.

The aggregate level findings are thus *consistent* with the hypothesis that people evaluate the government on the basis of changes in their personal economic well-being, but are also compatible with hypotheses that people do no such thing. For more direct evidence on this question, researchers turned to survey data to examine the microlevel relationship between economic well-being and political behavior. Some of the most positive evidence of this sort came from Tufte, who found substantial relationships between reported change in personal well-being and presidential voting in CBS News exit polls (Tufte, 1978). Other researchers, using SRC/CPS National Election Study data (for the most part) were not as impressed with the size of the relationships uncovered. Studies by Fiorina (1978), Wides (1976, 1979), and Klorman (1978) found only modest effects of reported changes in economic conditions on vote choice. The size of the relationships varied over time and across types of elections: stronger for presidential voting than for congressional voting. A particularly careful attempt by Sigelman and Tsai (1981) to test various models of the relationship between economic well-being and vote choice concluded that the overall relationship was weak to nonexistent.

Although the results of this research were certainly gloomy for those hopeful of finding strong signs of personal self-interest, the evidence was not uniformly negative. Personal economic well-being was often related — modestly but significantly — with presidential vote choice. Moreover, Fiorina (1981b) demonstrated that personal well-being often has a substantial effect on what he called "mediated retrospective evaluations": evaluations of the government's handling of the economy and relative party competence on economic matters (see also Conover and Feldman, 1983). Thus, a review of the microlevel research shows some evidence for personal economic self-interest in some situations and contributing to some evaluations of the government and parties. It is clear, however, that the magnitude of the personal self-interest effect found thus far is far too small to account for the aggregate level covariation between economic conditions and voting.

Even the claims of modest relationships between personal well-being and political evaluation have recently been challenged. Based primarily on the results of a split half experiment in the 1979 National Election Pilot Study, Sears and Lau (1983) argued that the survey findings of correlations between change in economic well-being and evaluations of the president are artifactual. According to Sears and Lau, the observed correlations are induced by the proximity of the two questions on the survey instrument; where the presidential evaluation question closely precedes the economic well-being item, the latter becomes "politicized" in the survey context and responses appear to be related to the previous political evaluations. If Sears and Lau are corrected, even the slim evidence for personal self-interest may be inadmissible.

The failure to find evidence of a microlevel relationship between personal well-being and political behavior not only casts doubt on the self-interest hypothesis but further emphasizes the ambiguity of the aggregate level research. Macroeconomic conditions may influence the outcome of elections and presidential popularity, but how? Into this morass, charged Kinder and Kiewiet (1979, 1981). They began by again examining the evidence of relationships between personal well-being and political behavior and once again found that the effects are at best tiny and often nonexistent. Instead of stopping there, Kinder and Kiewiet went a step further and provided evidence that vote choice does depend on people's perceptions of economic well-being; rather than from their personal well-being, the relationship derives from perceptions of the nation's economic well-being (what they term *sociotropic voting*). They showed clearly that congressional and presidential vote choice responds to perceptions that the economy is improving or worsening and evaluations of the government's and the parties' handling of the economy. Both Fiorina (1981b) and Lau and Sears (1981) criticized the latter set of variables, since they to some extent represent partisan evaluations (Fiorina's mediated retrospective evaluations) as well as perceptions of the state of the economy. Using only simple retrospective evaluations of the nation's economy, Lau and Sears (1981), Fiorina (1981b), and Conover and Feldman (1983) found clear evidence that political evaluations are strongly influenced by perceptions of the nation's economy.

The findings on sociotropic voting are important for two reasons. First, they provide clear evidence that the economy does have an influence on political behavior. Perceptions that the economy is worsening (improving) are reflected in declining (increasing) support for political leaders. The evidence fits nicely into the retrospective voting model developed by Fiorina (1981a). Second, the results on sociotropic voting help to resolve the ambiguous nature of the aggregate level findings. The strength of the aggregate level relationships (and the methodological problems of accepting null results) left people suspecting that personal self-interest at the microlevel must be operating if only we look in the right place. Now it can be argued that such a search is not necessary. The aggregate level findings can be reconciled with the survey research results. No personal self-interest effect is required; the sociotropic model seems to be the answer.

Not everyone was convinced. In particular, Kramer (1983) has offered an argument that purports to show that all of the individual level research that finds no evidence of personal self-interest is based on a seriously misspecified model and should be disregarded. Although acknowledging that the aggregate level research cannot distinguish among the mechanisms responsible for the relationship between economic conditions and vote choice, he argued that such research at least guarantees a relatively unbiased estimate of the overall relationship; not even this can be claimed for the microlevel research.

Kramer's conclusions are based on his explorations of a simple model relating changes in personal economic conditions to vote choice. Rather than reproducing his entire analysis, it is sufficient for our purposes to highlight some of the major assumptions that direct his analysis. First, Kramer makes it clear that he is interested in a particular question: the impact of *governmentally induced* changes in personal well-being on vote choice. This alters the focus of the analysis from the political effects of changes in personal well-being to the impact of only those changes *directly caused by* government economic policy (voters should not hold the government responsible for changes in their economic well-being that are purely personal in nature, or changes resulting from macroeconomic events not under the direct control of the government). Kramer is thus interested only in accounting for the overall relationship between governmentally induced macroeconomic conditions and vote choice, and not in explaining the overall dynamics relating personal well-being to political evaluation. It is important to recognize that Kramer is defining the question to be answered in significantly narrower terms than most other researchers.

Individual level studies of the relationship between economic well-being and political evaluation typically rely on a general measure of change in personal (financial) well-being. This means that we are not directly observing that part of the change in well-being that is governmentally induced, but rather:

$$y_{it} = g_{it} + e_{it}$$

where y_{it} is the observed change in well-being, g_{it} is the governmentally induced change in well-being, and e_{it} is all other (extraneous or idiosyncratic) variation. Estimates of the effect of personal well-being rely on y_{it} when — according to Kramer's argument — the important relationship involves only g_{it}. Two important assumptions follow. First, Kramer argued that most of the variation in the general financial well-being variable, y_{it}, is due to the idiosyncratic component rather than the governmentally induced component. The general well-being variable is, therefore, substantially "contaminated" by variation irrelevant to the issue under study. Second, he argued that the observed variable, y_{it}, is likely to be correlated with partisan attitudes. Since, in his model, partisanship is absorbed into the error term, a major assumption of the regression model is violated and the estimates of the impact of personal well-being on the vote are biased. In fact, Kramer went on to show that the estimated slope coefficient from such a model will depend almost entirely on the correlation of the observed variable with partisan attitudes.

Of the two assumptions leading to this conclusion, let us consider the second assumption first. The observed change in financial well-being variable will be correlated with the error term in Kramer's regression model if two conditions hold: y_{it} is in fact correlated with partisanship, and the model is misspecified by excluding a term for partisanship. The first is certainly a plausible situation; to the extent that partisanship is related to income and variation in financial well-being is also related to income, well-being will be correlated to some degree with partisanship. On the other hand, Kramer's assumption that partisanship is excluded from the model is much more tenuous. Certainly, if there is one thing that the study of voting behavior has accomplished, it is our ability to measure partisanship satisfactorily. If any part of a model of vote choice is likely to be well specified, it is partisanship. Although Kramer wrote that it is "implausible" to expect that as much as 81% of the variance in partisanship is controlled for, I suspect that other investigators would find this level of control on partisanship not at all implausible.

If we assume, then, that it is possible to control for most of the relationship between variations in well-being and partisanship (and other relevant political variables), what is left of Kramer's conclusion? According to his model, we are still faced with a situation in which the cross-sectional estimate of the relationship between personal well-being and the vote is attenuated by 75% to 90%. From this perspective, the modest findings of economic self-interest in the microlevel data may be just the tip of the iceberg. Personal economic self-interest may be alive and well after all.

ANOTHER LOOK AT THE EFFECTS OF PERSONAL WELL-BEING

Government Economic Policies and Personal Well-Being

A key aspect of Kramer's analysis is his assumption that most of the cross-sectional variation in personal well-being is due to factors unrelated to government activity. In general terms, it is hard to argue with this. For most people, factors unrelated to government economic policy will chiefly determine how well they do financially (at least in the short run). Kramer would have us believe, however, that the major impact of government economic policy is to raise or lower only the *mean* level of the distribution of incomes. At least in some situations this is a questionable assumption.

The past 3 years of the Reagan administration provide evidence that government policy may have very significant effects on the distribution of income. Taxes, social security, food stamps, and other social programs have substantial consequences for particular classes of people. Although large-scale manipulation of programs such as these may not have been common (at least until now), it is clear that government economic policies may have profound effects on certain types of people relative to others (see Page, 1983; Thurow, 1980).

More common are downturns in the economy. Here, I would argue, recessions act to a considerable degree to redistribute income (and well-being more generally) upward. Unemployment, temporary joblessness, reduced working hours, and the like have adverse effects on very clearly identifiable groups of people. Many other people may be largely unaffected by even substantial recessions. For example, over the first 2 years of the Reagan administration, the unemployment rate among blue-collar workers rose from 9.6% to 16.3%, while the rate among white-collar workers increased only from 3.7% to 5.6%. Government workers, on the other hand, were hardly affected at all by joblessness. Moreover, it is interesting to note that per capita mean disposable income actually rose over the first 8 months of the Reagan administration. It then declined slightly ($1,070.40 to $1,052.10) by month 13 only to rebound to the previous high level by month 24; this was during a time when unemployment was running at a post–World War II record level.[1] This particular recession (and more generally other recessions) acted largely to redistribute economic well-being rather than to change the mean level of disposable income. These macrolevel economic changes are consistent with Weatherford's (1978) finding that the working class responds most intensely to recessions in punishing the incumbent party.

A more general conclusion is that the proportion of the variance in financial well-being caused by the actions of the federal government varies significantly over time and, at least during recessionary periods, may be quite substantial. This line of reasoning leads to two other interesting hypotheses. First, self-interested economic voting may be substantial only during recessionary periods when the effects of economic conditions on people's well-being are most apparent and pronounced (Mueller, 1973; Bloom and Price, 1975; Mosely, 1978). In good economic times there is reason to believe that voters may not credit the government (or even the economy) when their income rises, instead taking credit for it themselves (see Katona, 1975; Feldman, 1982). Second, in more ordinary economic times it is not clear that the *personal* impact of macroeconomic conditions is typically substantial enough to account for the aggregate level relationship between economic conditions and the vote. Are enough people sufficiently affected (personally) by macroeconomic conditions (changes in disposable income) to produce significant changes in vote totals? At a minimum, this analysis suggests that researchers should not be surprised to find that the cross-sectional relationship between personal economic well-being and political evaluations varies significantly from one election to another (see Alford and Hibbing, 1982). This is in part a result of the fact that the distributional effects of government economic policy vary to a substantial degree over time.

Indicators of Personal Economic Well-Being

The analysis to this point has implicitly assumed that the only way to assess the relationship between the personal impact of economic conditions and political evaluation is through the use of a general measure of personal economic well-being. This is clearly not the case, and consideration of other indicators reinforces the findings of little personally self-interested political behavior. The best example of this is unemployment. Although indicators of the personal impact of joblessness are also contaminated to some degree by variation independent of government activity, much of the incidence of unemployment in the years after World War II can be attributed at least in part to government policy. By Kramer's logic, we should find considerably more effect of unemployment on political evaluation than is found for the general financial well-being measure, since it is a "purer" indicator of the effects of government economic policies.

But we do not. The most comprehensive study of the political effects of unemployment—by Schlozman and Verba (1979)—found that personal experience with unemployment has virtually no effect on vote choice. In fact, Rosenstone (1982) has shown that adverse economic conditions actually depress turnout. Even if the unemployed were inclined to evaluate the incumbent administration poorly, the effect would be negligible if they fail to make it to the polls. Kiewiet (1983) has turned up slightly more evidence of the impact of unemployment, but the estimated coefficients are still small. Moving from general economic well-being to more specific economic adversities yields no more evidence of personal economic self-interest.

Before closing the books on this line of inquiry, it is worth considering if, perhaps, researchers have looked broadly enough at the personal effects not only of joblessness but also of underemployment and other adverse job situations. It is also possible that the political effects of these personal problems will be large only during recessionary periods when the unemployed can see that they are not alone in their suffering and when the role of the government is most clear. The 1978 National Election Study is a good place to examine both of these possibilities. The survey was conducted as the nation was recovering from several years of high unemployment, and the survey asked respondents not only about their current employment status but also about recent job-related problems: unemployment, temporary layoffs, having work hours reduced, having to take a job below qualifications, and having to change work shifts. These five additional variables provide a more complete set of indicators of work-related problems[2] and should provide a closer look at the consequences of personal experience with job adversity.

Several dependent variables were examined: the standard change in financial well-being question, two questions rating Carter's job performance, and a rating of the performance of Congress (all recoded on a 0–1 interval, with 1 representing improved well-being and approval of Carter and Congress). In addition to the five job variables and current unemployment, the four dependent measures were regressed on a number of other variables to hold constant partisan and ideological preferences as well as a host of social background and demographic characteristics. This should reduce the problem of misspecification and biased estimates of the effects of the work-related indicators.[3] The results of the four regression analyses are presented in Table 1.

It is first of all apparent that job-related adversity has a substantial impact on personal well-being. Taking a pay cut, taking a job below qualifications,

TABLE 1. Impact of Job Adversity 1978

Independent Variables	Financial Well-Being	Rate Carter	Carter Approval	Rate Congress
Current unemployment	− .20(.07)	.05(.04)	.07(.06)	− .01(.04)
Previous unemployment	− .06(.04)	− .03(.02)	− .02(.03)	− .02(.02)
Temporarily laid off	.06(.04)	.03(.02)	.03(.04)	− .02(.02)
Took pay cut	− .11(.04)	− .04(.02)	− .01(.04)	− .01(.02)
Work hours reduced	.00(.04)	.00(.02)	.04(.04)	.05(.02)
Job below qualifications	− .08(.04)	.04(.02)	.05(.04)	.01(.02)
Work different shift	.05(.04)	.00(.02)	− .03(.04)	− .03(.02)
Party ideology (Democrat)	.03(.04)	.22(.02)	.40(.03)	.08(.02)
Liberal	.02(.06)	.10(.03)	.16(.05)	− .02(.03)
Race (black)	.06(.04)	.03(.02)	.01(.04)	.06(.02)
Gender (female)	− .05(.02)	.02(.01)	.06(.02)	.04(.01)
Age	− .004(.001)	.000(.001)	− .002(.001)	− .001(.0004)
Education (years)	.007(.004)	.004(.002)	− .003(.004)	− .004(.002)
Income ($1,000's)	.004(.001)	.001(.001)	− .002(.001)	.000(.001)
Occupational prestige	.001(.001)	.000(.001)	.001(.001)	.000(.001)
Population (100,000's)	− .005(.002)	.000(.001)	.000(.001)	− .002(.001)
Length of residence	.000(.001)	.000(.001)	.000(.002)	.004(.002)
Rent/own	− .04(.03)	.00(.01)	.01(.02)	.00(.01)
Divorced/separated	− .08(.04)	.00(.02)	− .04(.04)	− .01(.02)
Widowed	− .05(.05)	.03(.02)	.00(.04)	.03(.02)
Never married	− .01(.03)	.01(.02)	.05(.03)	.01(.02)
Retired	− .01(.04)	.00(.02)	.01(.04)	− .03(.02)
Region				
North central	.03(.05)	− .03(.02)	− .09(.05)	− .04(.03)
Mountain states	.06(.07)	.00(.04)	− .03(.06)	− .06(.03)
Border states	.06(.06)	− .03(.03)	− .16(.06)	− .05(.03)
Pacific states	.12(.06)	− .02(.03)	− .06(.06)	− .02(.03)
Middle Atlantic	.02(.06)	− .06(.03)	− .10(.05)	− .06(.03)
Solid South	.02(.05)	− .03(.03)	− .09(.05)	− .04(.03)
R^2	.10	.15	.18	.07

Note. Entries are unstandardized regression coefficients with standard errors in parentheses.

and especially current unemployment produce large declines in financial well-being. Despite this, these indicators have very little (or no) impact on evaluations of Carter or Congress. The largest effect is registered for current unemployment on evaluations of Carter, and the direction of the coefficient is consistent with a policy-related impact rather than an incumbency effect (see Kiewiet, 1983). Yet even these effects of unemployment are small, given the quite substantial impact of joblessness on financial well-being. The coefficients for the five other job-related indicators fail to come up even to level of the unemployment effect. Thus, a closer look at job-related adversity in a period in which the collective nature of joblessness should have been fairly apparent turns up virtually no evidence of people's acting on the basis of personal self-interest. This is so despite the fact that the indicators of personal economic well-being used here are not nearly as contaminated by irrelevant, personal variation as the more general financial well-being measures.

The Attribution of Blame

Another reason not to accept Kramer's conclusion quickly is that we have findings from other nations that show clear evidence of cross-sectional relationships between personal economic well-being and political evaluation. Butler and Stokes (1969) analyzed data from several British elections in the 1960s similar to that used in the individual level research in the United States. Contrary to the American case, they reported consistently strong relationships between change in personal well-being and support for the incumbent government. More recently, Lewis-Beck (1983) used survey data from France to examine evidence of both personal self-interest and sociotropic effects. Employing a well-specified model, he found strong evidence of *both* processes on vote choice. In particular, even holding constant sociotropic evaluations, the impact of personal economic well-being is clear. According to the logic of Kramer's argument, unless government-induced changes in personal income dominate idiosyncratic sources of variation in these two countries, there should be little or no observed relationship in these cross-sectional survey data. Yet there clearly is.

These strong correlations between personal well-being and vote choice in Britain and France would be more puzzling than significant if there were no way of explaining the differences between them and the U.S. findings. Fortunately there is: what Sniderman and Brody (1977) termed "the ethic of self-reliance" or what others have labeled economic individualism. Consider the rational self-interested voter. As noted earlier, our self-interested voter should not change his/her evaluation of the government or politicians on the basis of idiosyndratically determined changes in financial status (precisely

Kramer's assumption). Political evaluations should be affected only when changes in personal well-being are perceived to be a consequence of government policy. However, in many cases the existence of a direct connection between changes in personal well-being and government policy will not be intuitively obvious (Feldman, 1982; Sniderman and Brody, 1977). Thus, a key element in the existence of a relationship between personal well-being and political evaluation will be the attribution of responsibility.

An increasing number of researchers have now shown, however, that most people do *not* attribute changes in their personal well-being to the actions of the federal government or even to the macroeconomic environment more generally (Feldman, 1982; Kinder and Mebane, 1983; Schlozman and Verba, 1979; Sniderman and Brody, 1977). When asked to explain why their economic well-being has recently changed, most people (particularly people whose well-being has increased) refer to events in their personal lives. As suggested by Kinder and Kiewiet (1979) and Schlozman and Verba (1979) and shown by Feldman (1982), the personal attribution of responsibility is strongly related to people's belief in economic individualism: the work ethic and equality of opportunity. Attributions of changing personal well-being to the wider societal context is only common among those who question both of these cultural beliefs. It is not just a matter of people's failing to see government responsibility because the government in fact has little or none. Rather, people's beliefs about success and failure, in general, appear to influence strongly their understandings of specific events.

Moreover, there is now evidence that when the government *is* seen to be at least partly responsible for changes in personal well-being people behave exactly like model self-interested actors (Feldman, 1982; Kinder and Mebane, 1983; Lau and Sears, 1981). This is a particularly important result. Kramer argued that the failure to find strong relationships between the measure of change in personal well-being and vote choice is due to fact that the well-being variable is "contaminated" by substantial amounts of purely idiosyncratic variation. The results of these studies show that the absence of strong relationships can be explained instead by the general lack of any attribution of changing well-being to government activity. Where that attribution is made, even the "contaminated" well-being measure strongly relates to political evaluation and vote choice. I am not arguing that the idiosyncratic component of personal well-being does not limit its association with political evaluation. Rather, the very low relationships apparent in the microlevel data are in large part a consequence of the way people in this country *understand* the factors that impinge upon their economic well-being.

Two additional bits of evidence are consistent with this interpretation. First, Schlozman and Verba (1979) showed that people who are unemployed also fail to see the connection between government economic policy (or even macroeconomic conditions) and their loss of jobs. Although it is clear that some unemployment is unrelated to macroeconomic conditions, in a Keynesian world a large part of the variation in unemployment rates is dependent on government economic policies. Yet, Schlozman and Verba's results show that many directly affected by government activity (the unemployed) fail to make the connection. Second, Katona et al. (1971) have shown that, compared with Americans, Western Europeans are much more likely to see their economic well-being tied to macroeconomic conditions and government economic policy. Although the research necessary to demonstrate this is yet to be done, this result is consistent with findings of stronger relationships between personal economic conditions and vote choice in Britain and France than in the United States.

Finally, it should also be noted that the results of studies of personal economic conditions and voting are largely consistent with other attempts to find evidence of personally self-interested political behavior. In particular, Sears and his colleagues (see, for example, Sears et al., 1980; Sears et al., 1979) have shown in a series of papers that evidence of personally self-interested political behavior is difficult to find. In a number of cases where people's political attitudes and evaluations should reflect aspects of their personal lives or situations, no such relationship obtains (with occasional exceptions, see Lau and Sears, 1981). The failure to find strong evidence of personally self-interested behavior in the economic realm is thus not an isolated result, but consistent with other research on the determinants of political attitudes and behavior.

ARE THERE NO PERSONAL SELF-INTEREST EFFECTS?

To this point I have argued that—Kramer's protests to the contrary—the accumulated evidence points to no strong effects of personal financial well-being on the vote. However, the failure to find *strong* self-interest effects does not imply a complete absence of personally self-interested behavior. In fact, there is evidence that personal conditions do affect political evaluation—although not to the degree that Kramer would like. Analysis by Fiorina (1978), among others, showed that personal financial well-being is more strongly related to vote choice in presidential elections than in congressional elections. Fiorina (1981a) also showed that personal economic well-being often has substantial effects on what he termed *mediated retrospective evaluations*—evaluations of government economic performance and party competence (see also Conover and Feldman, 1983). Kiewiet (1983) showed that unemployment experience has a small but consistent political effect in a policy-oriented fashion: voters who are unemployed tend to favor the Democrats over the Republicans regardless of the incumbent party. More generally, Kiewiet showed that, although the effects of personal financial well-being are fairly small, they are large enough to have an impact on an otherwise close election. More recently, Weatherford (1983) argued that self-interested voting is more likely among those who do not closely attend to the media for information about the state of the nation's economy. Along the same line, Conover et al. (1984) found that people with little information about the state of the national economy rely substantially on recent changes in their personal well-being in making retrospective judgments about the state of the national economy. Therefore, although the effects are always fairly small, there are consistent indications of some personally self-interested political behavior.

To the extent that people do behave in accord with personal economic self-interest, our previous analysis suggests that this should be most likely when the perceived connection between changes in their well-being and government policy is clearest. Thus, it is not surprising that Lau and Sears (1981) found the strongest evidence of personal self-interest when it came to the effects of taxation. Recent events provide an even better opportunity to find effects of self-interest. The first 3 years of the Reagan administration produced several situations in which the relationship between personal economic conditions and government policy should be fairly apparent. The first involves those people who lost direct government benefits as a result of budget cuts. A second area is the impact of the large income tax cuts implemented over these 3 years. Finally, if unemployment experience is ever likely to be politicized (short of a replay of the Great Depression), it should have come as a consequence of the most severe recession since World War II.

The 1982 National Election Study provides an opportunity to examine the impact of these events. Respondents were as usual asked about their current employment status. In addition, they were also asked whether they had lost any benefits from government programs and whether the income tax cuts had a significant effect on their disposable income.[4] The first column of Table 2 shows the effects of these three variables, partisanship and ideology, and a series of social background and demographic variables on change in financial well-being. As was found in 1978, current unemployment had a substantial effect on financial well-being. What is surprising is that the loss of government benefits has virtually no detrimental effect on well-being. Reports of the effects of the tax cut do little better. One other interesting finding is that Democrats report that their financial well-being declined much more than that of Republicans. Given the controls on income, race, and other such variables, it is unlikely that this is due to Democrats' actually suffering significantly more than Republicans as a result of their social and economic status. Moreover, the results in 1978 showed no effect of partisanship on personal well-being (see Table 1). It is

TABLE 2. Impact of Government Economic Programs, 1982

Independent Variables	Financial Well-Being	Approve Reagan	Approve Congress	Effects of Reagan Economic Policies	
				On Self	On Nation
Current					
unemployment	− .25(.05)	− .06(.04)	− .05(.04)	− .11(.04)	− .06(.05)
Loss of benefits	− .05(.04)	− .10(.03)	− .02(.03)	− .16(.03)	− .01(.03)
Tax cut effects	.08(.05)	.03(.03)	.04(.04)	.08(.04)	.10(.04)
Party ideology					
(Democrat)	− .15(.04)	− .50(.03)	− .04(.03)	− .16(.03)	− .30(.04)
Liberal	− .02(.06)	− .34(.05)	.14(.05)	− .13(.05)	− .15(.06)
Vote Reagan, 1980	− .05(.03)	.11(.02)	− .05(.02)	.02(.02)	.10(.03)
Race (black)	− .09(.04)	− .15(.03)	− .06(.03)	− .12(.03)	− .15(.04)
Gender (female)	.00(.02)	− .02(.02)	.03(.02)	− .04(.02)	− .05(.02)
Age	− .003(.001)	− .002(.001)	− .002(.001)	.000(.001)	− .002(.001)
Education (years)	.006(.004)	− .002(.002)	− .001(.003)	.009(.003)	.009(.003)
Income ($1,000's)	.002(.001)	.001(.001)	.000(.001)	.002(.001)	.000(.001)
Population					
(100,000's)	− .002(.001)	− .001(.001)	− .001(.001)	− .001(.001)	.001(.001)
Union member	.03(.03)	− .05(.02)	− .03(.02)	− .03(.03)	− .07(.03)
Persons in					
household	− .02(.01)	.00(.01)	− .01(.01)	.00(.01)	.00(.01)
Divorced/					
separated	− .04(.03)	.02(.03)	.00(.03)	− .02(.03)	.04(.04)
Widowed	.00(.05)	.07(.03)	.00(.04)	.04(.04)	.04(.04)
Never married	− .04(.04)	.00(.02)	.01(.03)	.07(.03)	.04(.04)
Retired	.07(.04)	.06(.03)	.01(.03)	.07(.03)	.04(.04)
Housewife	.03(.06)	− .08(.05)	− .05(.05)	.05(.05)	− .04(.06)
Region					
South	− .04(.03)	.00(.03)	− .02(.03)	− .01(.03)	.04(.03)
North central	− .07(.03)	− .05(.02)	− .05(.03)	− .06(.03)	− .07(.03)
West	− .07(.03)	− .03(.03)	− .07(.03)	− .04(.03)	.01(.03)
R^2	.10	.42	.06	.19	.23

Note. Entries are unstandardized regression coefficients with standard errors in parentheses.

likely then, that the economic situation of the nation and the policies of the Reagan administration served to "politicize" people's perceptions of their economic well-being. (Whether this politicization is a "real" phenomenon or a product of the interview cannot be determined from this.)

The impact of these same variables on approval ratings of Reagan and Congress is shown in columns 2 and 3. What is most interesting about these estimates is that people who lost government benefits are significantly more disapproving of Reagan than those who did not. This effect is larger than that of unemployment, even though unemployment had a much greater impact on personal well-being than the loss of government benefits. Compared with those who were unemployed, the people who lost government benefits seemingly knew exactly whom to blame — Reagan. This appears to be evidence that self-interested behavior is more dependent on the attribution of responsibility than on the damage done to one's budget. As shown in column 3, Congress seemed to be little affected by the cutoff of government benefits; clearly Reagan was held accountable not Congress.

The nature of people's reactions to personal consequences of government economic policy should be more evident in evaluations of the economic policies of the Reagan administration than in overall evaluations of the president. Two questions included in the 1982 Election Study allow for a much more detailed look at the nature of economic self-interest. One question asks people to evaluate the impact of Reagan administration economic policies on their own well-being and the other asks them about the impact of Reagan policies on the nation's economy. The results of regressing these two variables on the set of independent variables are shown in columns 4 and 5. The contrasts between these two sets of estimates show that people *can* distinguish between the effects of policy on their own condition and effects on the national economy. Specifically, unemployment experience, loss of government benefits, and the tax cuts strongly influence evaluations of the personal impact of Reagan administration policy. By contrast, only personal effects of the tax cut generalize to evaluations of the national impact of Reagan policies (and the tax cut variable is clearly more subjective than the other two personal economic indicators, making it more susceptible to the effects of partisanship). People who lost government benefits or who were unemployed are barely more negative on the national effects of Reagan economic poilicies than are people who escaped these hardships. It is also interesting to note that partisanship and previous votes for Reagan had much more effect on evaluations of the national impact of Reagan policies than on the personal consequences.

These results provide clear evidence that under certain situations — poor economic conditions and clear attributions of responsibility — personal economic self-interest can play a role in political evaluation. Moreover, voters seem to be able to attribute responsibility to particular branches of the government and to distinguish between the personal and societal effects of government economic policies.

Problems of Measurement

There is one last lead to pursue in the search for personal self-interest effects. Throughout virtually all of the microlevel analysis researchers have

been content to rely on a single indicator of personal economic well-being —
the trichotomous change in financial well-being question that has appeared
on a long series of National Election Studies and other survey instruments.
A recent analysis of the 1983 NES Pilot Study by Rosenstone et al. (1983)
suggested, however, that this indicator may contain substantial random
measurement error and may therefore lead to attenuated estimates of the
relationship between personal well-being and political evaluation. Rosenstone et al. constructed a four-item scale to measure a general dimension of
personal well-being and found that it is more strongly related to candidate
evaluation than is the simple trichotomous variable. This raises the distinct
possibility that previous research has significantly *underestimated* the
degree of personal economic self-interest by relying on a single unreliable
indicator.

There is one potential problem with this argument. The Sears and Lau
(1983) research discussed previously suggests that these new, larger estimates of the self-interest effect are artifacts of survey construction. This is
especially plausible when — as in the 1983 pilot study — the questions on personal well-being closely follow a pair of questions on approval of Reagan's
job performance. On the other hand, a paper by Lewis-Beck (1984) found
no relationship between the closeness of the political and economic well-
being questions on a series of election studies and the magnitude of the relationship between them. A more direct way of determining whether the
stronger relationship between personal economic well-being and evaluations
of Reagan in the pilot study is due to better measurement or rationalization
is to specify and estimate a nonrecursive model. This would make it possible
to estimate the simultaneous effects of personal well-being and Reagan evaluation on each other. According to the Sears and Lau hypothesis, with the
effects of Reagan evaluation held constant, the impact of personal well-
being should be substantially reduced or even eliminated.

To settle this question, a pair of equations was estimated; one equation
for approval of Reagan and one for financial well-being. Each appears in
the other equation, and the equations are identified by excluding certain
variables from each: positive and negative emotions toward Reagan and
feelings about his competence and integrity are assumed to directly influence only Reagan approval, whereas specific economic adversity and income
change are included only in the financial well-being equation.[5] The two
equations were estimated via full information maximum likelihood using
the LISREL program. The results are shown in Table 3.

Before considering the estimates, it is interesting to note that the simple
correlation between the financial well-being scale and approval of Reagan is
a healthy .40. The question is whether this relationship is due to the use of a
more reliable measure of financial well-being or the proximity of the Reagan

TABLE 3. Financial Well-Being and Reagan Approval Estimates

Independent Variables	Financial Well-being	Reagan Approval
Financial well-being		.25(.11)
Reagan approval	.15(.07)	
Specific economic adversity	.49(.06)	
Income change	.05(.02)	
Unemployment-respondent	− .06(.08)	− .04(.08)
Unemployment-spouse	− .10(.09)	− .07(.09)
Positive emotions-Reagan		.26(.05)
Negative emotions-Reagan		− .11(.04)
Reagan competence		.19(.08)
Reagan integrity		.38(.09)
Party ideology (Democrat)	− .06(.05)	− .15(.05)
Liberal	.05(.08)	− .17(.08)
Income ($1,000's)	.000(.001)	.001(.001)
Education (years)	.005(.004)	− .007(.005)
Age	− .002(.001)	− .002(.001)
Race (black)	− .02(.05)	− .04(.05)
Gender (female)	− .10(.03)	.00(.03)
R^2	.42	.62

Note. The coefficients were obtained using full information maximum likelihood estimation via the LISREL program. Entries are unstandardized coefficients with standard errors in parentheses.

and well-being questions on the pilot study instrument. The estimates indicate that Sears and Lau are both right and wrong. Approval of Reagan does influence reports of financial well-being. Those who thought Reagan was doing a good job were more likely to report an improved financial status compared with people who disapproved of Reagan. Although Sears and Lau seem to be correct about the potential for surveys politicizing reports of well-being, this process does not eliminate the effect of well-being on approval of Reagan. In fact, in unstandardized units (both variables scaled on the 0–1 interval) the effect of financial well-being on approval of Reagan is significantly larger than the reverse relationship (the standardized coefficients are almost exactly equal, .19). Furthermore, since the Reagan approval question preceded all the financial well-being items, there is no way that the effect of financial well-being on approval could be a survey artifact: responses to the financial questions could not have influenced (personalized) previous responses to the Reagan question.

Thus, it appears as if previous estimates of the relationship between political evaluations and personal well-being may have been inflated by question proximity. On the other hand, the results obtained here show that such survey effects do not necessarily produce all of the observed relationship. Moreover, the results of the new items in the pilot study suggest that previous estimates of the relationship between political evaluation and personal well-being may have been *underestimated* because of measurement error. In these estimates, the impact of financial well-being on approval of Reagan rivals the effects of factors such as party identification and traits. It is important to remember, however, that the impact of financial well-being found here (as of summer 1983) may *not* be generalizable to other time periods. The magnitude of the recession, the tax cuts and budget cuts, and the general salience of economic concerns may have combined to boost the impact of financial well-being on attitudes toward the president to unusually high levels. Certainly, the summer of 1983 fits almost perfectly the scenario that has been developed in this paper for maximizing the potential for self-interest effects. Until much better specified models are developed, the strongest statement that one should make about the findings of economic self-interest from one point in time is that they should be generalized to other points in time only with the utmost of care.

SOME CONCLUDING THOUGHTS

The reader may be somewhat puzzled at this point. In one part of this paper, I argue that the evidence does not support the conclusion that personal economic self-interest is a major influence on political evaluation and vote choice, and elsewhere I provide evidence that self-interest effects are clearly observable. Before it is charged that I am alternately arguing opposite positions, let me show why the analysis developed here is quite consistent.

Within the space of 3 months two significant articles were published dealing with the issue of economic self-interest and the use of survey research. Gerald Kramer argued that many people may be acting politically in their personal economic self-interest regardless of the results from survey analyses that show no such effect. David Sears and Richard Lau argued that survey research findings that show some personally self-interested behavior are beset by methodological problems and that there is even *less* evidence of self-interest than previously thought. What has been missing from all of this is an analysis of *when* and *why* people are likely to base their evaluations of politics on their economic well-being.

This paper has looked closely at such research on the political effects of economic self-interest and has tried to sort out the results in terms that might make the conflicting findings more understandable. Two critical questions emerge from the analysis: (1) Under what conditions and to what extent is people's economic well-being affected by the actions of the government? (2) When and under what conditions will people relate their financial hardships and successes to the actions of the government? We will not adequately understand the relationship between people's personal situations and their political behavior until both of these questions are answered. More simply, we need to look more at the *process* underlying self-interested behavior, and less at the observable *magnitude* of the relationship. The more research deals with the latter instead of the former, the more conclusions will tend to be inconsistent, puzzling, and noncumulative.

Despite protests to the contrary, the accumulated evidence very strongly suggests that vote choice and presidential evaluations are at best modestly influenced by *personal* economic considerations. This is not because people are incapable of acting in their own self-interest. When government policies have a direct impact on them *and* they attribute responsibility to the government, people do alter their evaluations accordingly. Much evidence now shows that these conditions are often not met. The result is that personal self-interest is typically not a major element in studies of political behavior. The important issues research now needs to deal with involve the ways in which people are affected by general economic conditions and the explanations they develop to explain their financial status and well-being.

Acknowledgments. The data used in this paper were collected by the National Election Studies and made available through the Inter-University Consortium for Political and Social Research, neither of which bears any responsibility for the analysis or interpretation reported here. I would like to thank Lee Sigelman for his close reading of an earlier version of the paper.

NOTES

1. I would like to thank David Lowery for providing these statistics and for helpful discussions of some of these issues. He should not be blamed for any errors I may have made.
2. Respondents were asked whether they had faced any of these problems in the preceding 2 years. It is likely that their reports underestimate the actual occurrence of job-related adversity (see Rosenstone et al., 1983). The questions used in this analysis refer to the specific experiences of the respondent. Reestimation of the model, substituting job adversity faced by the respondent or by a family member, produced almost identical coefficients.
3. With a few exceptions, all the variables used in this and the other analyses in this paper have been recoded so that high scores = 1 and low scores = 0. For multicategory variables, values between 0 and 1 were assigned to create equal distances between the categories. This permits a ready interpretation of the unstandardized regression coefficients and makes possible comparisons of the coefficients within and between equations. The exceptions to this coding are: income (in thousands of dollars), education and age (years), and population of place of residence (100,000's). This model and the following ones were also estimated using

a pair of dummy variables for party identification, since some of the impact of the economic well-being variables may be through changes to the seven-category variable. This specification did not produce any larger coefficients for the economic variables.

4. Respondents were asked about the loss of the following government benefits: social security, food stamps, Medicaid and Medicare, unemployment benefits, Aid to Families with Dependent Children, student loans, aid to the handicapped, veteran's benefits, and government retirement pension benefits. Analysis of each individually is not possible because of the small N's involved. For the effects of the tax cuts, respondents were asked how much of a difference the tax cuts made in the money they had left after taxes: a great deal of difference, some difference, or barely any.

5. The general financial well-being measure was constructed from three questions: people's perceived change in financial well-being, change in income, and whether they watch their budget more closely. The measure of specific economic adversity measure has four components: putting off buying things, putting off medical treatment, changes in borrowing, and looking for new jobs or more working hours. The pilot study was a reinterview in the summer of 1983 with people originally interviewed as part of the 1982 National Election Study. As a result, the analysis employed lagged versions of party identification and liberal-conservative self-placement. The positive emotions used asked whether Reagan made them feel "hopeful" or "proud." The negative emotion scale utilized "angry" and "afraid." The goodness-of-fit statistics from LISREL were very good; there was no evidence of significant model misspecification.

REFERENCES

Alford, J. R., and J. R. Hibbing (1982). "Pocketbook Voting: When and Where It Occurs." Paper presented at the 1982 Annual Meeting of the American Political Science Association, Denver.

Arcelus, F., and A. H. Meltzer (1975). "The Effect of Aggregate Economic Variables on Congressional Elections." *American Political Science Review* 69:1232–1239.

Bloom, H., and H. D. Price (1975). "Voter Response to Short-run Economic Conditions: The Asymmetric Effect of Prosperity and Recession." *American Political Science Review* 69:1240–1254.

Butler, D., and D. Stokes (1969). *Political Change in Britain.* London: Macmillan.

Conover, P. J., and S. Feldman (1983). "Emotional Reactions to the Economy." Paper presented at the 1983 meeting of the American Political Science Association.

Conover, P. J., S. Feldman, and K. Knight (1984). "Looking Forward and Backward: Retrospective and Prospective Evaluations of the Economy." Paper to be presented at the 1984 meeting of the Midwest Political Science Association.

Downs, A. (1957). *An Economic Theory of Democracy.* New York: Harper & Row.

Edelman, M. (1964). *The Symbolic Uses of Politics.* Urbana, Ill.: University of Illinois Press.

Feldman, S. (1982). "Economic Self-interest and and Political Behavior." *American Journal of Political Science* 26:446–466.

Fiorina, M. P. (1978). "Economic Retrospective Voting in American Elections." *American Journal of Political Science* 22:426–443.

Fiorina, M. P. (1981). *Retrospective Voting in American National Elections.* New Haven: Yale University Press. (a)

Fiorina, M. P. (1981). "Short- and Long-term Effects of Economic Conditions on Individual Voting Decisions." In D. A. Hibbs and H. Fassbender (eds.), *Contemporary Political Economy*. Amsterdam: North-Holland Publishing Co. (b)

Jacobson, G., and S. Kernell (1982). *The Structure of Choice: A Theory of Congressional Elections*. New Haven: Yale University Press.

Katona, G. (1975). *Psychological Economics*. New York: Elsevier.

Katona, G., B. Strumpel, and E. Zahn (1971). *Aspirations and Affluence*. New York: McGraw-Hill.

Kiewiet, D. R. (1983). *Macroeconomics and Micropolitics*. Chicago: University of Chicago Press.

Kinder, D. R., and D. R. Kiewiet (1979). "Economic Grievances and Political Behavior: The Role of Personal Discontents and Collective Judgments in Congressional Voting." *American Journal of Political Science* 23:495–527.

Kinder, D. R., and D. R. Kiewiet (1981). "Sociotropic Politics: The American Case." *British Journal of Political Science* 11:129–162.

Kinder, D. R., and W. R. Mebane (1983). "Politics and Economics in Everyday Life." In K. Monroe (ed.), *The Political Process and Economic Change*. New York: Agathon.

Klorman, R. (1978). "Trends in Personal Finances and the Vote." *Public Opinion Quarterly* 42:31–48.

Kramer, G. (1971). "Short-term Fluctuations in U.S. Voting Behavior, 1896–1964." *American Political Science Review* 65:131–143.

Kramer, G. (1983). "The Ecological Fallacy Revisited: Aggregate versus Individual-Level Findings on Economics and Elections, and Sociotropic Voting." *American Political Science Review* 77:92–111.

Lau, R. R., and D. D. Sears (1981). "Cognitive Links between Economic Grievances and Political Responses." *Political Behavior* 3:279–302.

Lewis-Beck, M. S. (1983). "Economics and the French Voter: A Microanalysis." *Public Opinion Quarterly* 47:347–360.

Lipset, S. M. (1960). *Political Man*. New York: Doubleday.

Monroe, K. R. (1979). "Econometric Analyses of Electoral Behavior: A Critical Review." *Political Behavior* 1:137–174.

Monroe, K. R. (1981). "Presidential Popularity: An Almon Distributed-lag Model." *Political Methodology* 8:43–69.

Mosely, P. (1978). "Images of the Floating Voter, or the 'Political Business Cycle' Revisited." *Political Studies* 26:375–394.

Mueller, J. (1973). *War, Presidents, and Public Opinion*. New York: John Wiley.

Norpoth, H., and T. Yantek (1983). "Macroeconomic Conditions and Fluctuations of Presidential Popularity: The Question of Lagged Effects." *American Journal of Political Science* 27:785–807.

Owens, J. R., and E. C. Olson (1980). "Economic Fluctuations and Congressional Elections." *American Journal of Political Science* 24:469–493.

Page, Benjamin I. (1983). *Who Gets What from Government*. Berkeley: University of California Press.

Popkin, S., J. W. Gorman, C. Phillips, and J. A. Smith (1976). "Comment: What Have You Done for Me Lately: Toward an Investment Theory of Voting." *American Political Science Review* 70:779–805.

Rosenstone, S. J. (1982). "Economic Adversity and Voter Turnout." *American Journal of Political Science* 26:25–46.

Rosenstone, S. J., J. M. Hansen, and D. R. Kinder (1983). "Measuring Personal Economic Well-Being." Report submitted to The Board of Overseers, National Election Study, and the 1984 National Election Study Planning Committee.

Schlozman, K. L., and S. Verba (1979). *Injury to Insult.* Cambridge, Mass.: Harvard University Press.

Sears, D. O., and R. R. Lau (1983). "Inducing Apparently Self-Interested Political Preferences." *American Political Science Review* 27:223–253.

Sears, D. O., C. P. Hensler, and L. K. Speer (1979). "Whites' Opposition to Busing": Self-Interest or Symbolic Politics." *American Political Science Review* 73: 369–384.

Sears, D. O., R. R. Lau, T. R. Tyler, and H. M. Allen (1980). "Self-Interest vs. Symbolic Politics in Policy Attitudes and Presidential Voting." *American Political Science Review* 74:670–684.

Sigelman, L., and Y. Tsai (1981). "A Reanalysis of the Linkage between Personal Finances and Voting Behavior." *American Politics Quarterly* 9:371–399.

Sniderman, P. M., and R. A. Brody (1977). "Coping: The Ethic of Self-Reliance." *American Journal of Political Science* 21:501–523.

Stigler, G. (1973). "General Economic Conditions and National Elections." *American Economic Review* 63:160–167.

Thurow, Lester C. (1980). *The Zero-Sum Society.* New York: Basic Books.

Tufte, E. R. (1978). *Political Control of the Economy.* Princeton, N.J.: Princeton University Press.

Weatherford, M. S. (1978). "Economic Conditions and Electoral Outcomes: Class Differences in the Political Response to Recession." *American Journal of Political Science* 22:917–938.

Weatherford, M. S. (1983). "Economic Voting and the 'Symbolic Politics' Argument: A Reinterpretation and Synthesis." *American Political Science Review* 77:158–174.

Wides, J. W. (1976). "Self-perceived Economic Change and Political Orientations: A Preliminary Exploration." *American Politics Quarterly* 4:394–411.

Wides, J. M. (1979). "Perceived Economic Competency and the Ford/Carter Election." *Public Opinion Quarterly* 43:349–373.

CHAPTER 9

Economics, Politics, and the Cycle of Presidential Popularity

Helmut Norpoth
Department of Political Science,
State University of New York, Stony Brook

Economics is the fate of politicians, as the saying goes. It is an article of faith that success or failure of governments in dealing with the economy decides whether or not they survive politically. The humiliating defeat of Jimmy Carter by Ronald Reagan in 1980, following his tough renomination fight, comes to mind as a telling case; to which might be added the similar experience of Prime Minister Callaghan in the British election of 1979, President Giscard d'Estaing in the French elections of 1981, and Chancellor Schmidt and the SPD in West Germany in 1982–1983. The economic adversity suffered by all these countries in the late 1970s proved extremely hazardous to the political health of the "ins," the incumbent governments, that is (Lipset, 1982). More generally, between elections the ups and downs of economic indicators seem to go hand in hand with the ups and downs of public approval of governing parties or leaders. Ronald Reagan's approval rating, for example, hit bottom in late 1982 just when the economic recession bottomed out and soared to a high level in the wake of a brisk economic recovery in late 1983 (Smith, 1984).

Research on presidential popularity for the most part has substantiated the impact of macroeconomic conditions, although this case is by no means open and shut.[1] Largely following Kramer's (1971) lead, Kiewiet and Rivers in this issue describe the dominant model of economic effects as being:

> (1) retrospective, (2) incumbency-oriented, and (3) based upon the results of economic policies, and not upon the actual policies themselves.

It is fair to say that time-series studies have made a stronger case for this model than have cross-sectional studies. Whatever the discrepancy between the two types of findings, Kramer (1983) has affirmed, in principle, the primacy of aggregate time-series evidence. Even so, the matter is far from settled within the time-series domain. Questions continue to be asked, for one, about the proper lag structure with which economic performance influences government popularity (Monroe, 1978; Hibbs, 1982; Kernell, 1980; Golden and Poterba, 1980). Second, what share of the often dazzling explanatory power of popularity models belongs to the economic side, how much to noneconomic factors such as foreign policy crises, domestic scandal, war, presidential personality, and the like (Mueller, 1973; Kernell, 1978)? Third, how much of the variation in government popularity ought to be attributed to a surge-and-decline cycle that appears to repeat itself with the inauguration of each new president (Mueller, 1973; Stimson, 1976)?

The answers to these questions are important for our understanding of the political process, especially the responsiveness of mass opinion to economic performance, and the extent to which governments are held responsible for that performance. From a policy perspective, the answers are important for what they tell us about the incentives of governments to steer the economy in a certain direction; and what mix of unemployment and inflation to strive for. At the same time, estimates for noneconomic factors may help put the economic incentive in perspective. How much should a government concerned with political survival preoccupy itself with the economy as opposed to other issues? To what extent can foreign policy triumphs or even unforced crises neutralize or overshadow the economic fallout? To strike a fatalistic note, how many of the ups and downs of government popularity are simply beyond the power of any government to manipulate to its benefit?

These questions are addressed below with the help of models specifically tailored for time-series data (Box and Jenkins, 1976). The chief virtue of these stochastic models is that they enable the analyst to assess the dependence of one time series on another while holding constant the dependence of each series upon itself. The use of those models, I admit, is not foolproof, especially when what we wish to observe is buried in noise. In order to muffle this noise, the analysis below relies on aggregated quarterly observations rather than monthly ones. The time frame extends from the first quarter of the Kennedy administration to the last one of Carter's.

PITFALLS OF TIME SERIES STUDIES

Time-series studies of macroeconomic effects have been dogged by methodological troubles. As we all know, curious things can and do happen over time. We encounter exceedingly high correlations between two kinds of events observed across time that defy any reasonable explanation. Even worse, such correlations may be as high as those between plausibly related kinds of events. From 1952 to 1976, for example, whenever the American League team won the World Series in a presidential election year the Republican candidate subsequently won the presidency; and the Democratic candidate did so when the National League team had won it. Is there an economic indicator that would predict the outcome of those presidential elections equally well?

Given the ease with which variables observed over time rhyme, regardless of reason, one must be far more wary in evaluating time-series evidence than is the case with cross-sectional data. The chief reason for this special caution is that time-series observations are dependent. A president winning election once may win reelection, and a World Series winner may repeat. This month's unemployment rate is pretty much the same as last month's, and so is the president's approval rating.

There is nothing surprising about this dependency. Nevertheless, many time-series studies employ statistical models that are designed for data where independence can be safely assumed. To the extent that the violation of the independence assumption is recognized in time-series studies, corrective attempts concentrate on the residuals. These corrections, moreover, are limited to fairly simple types of dependence. It would seem far more compelling to face the issue of dependence head-on in analyzing time series of government popularity. Box-Jenkins ARIMA models are employed below for that purpose.

With time-series observations being as dependent as they are, correlations between one series of interest (say, popularity) and lagged values of another (say, inflation) can easily be documented, up to a considerable number of lags. Whether or not that proves that the public has a long memory is debatable. Several distributed-lag schemes have been tried: from the rather flexible polynomial model (Almon, 1965; Monroe, 1978; Golden and Poterba, 1980) to the highly restrictive geometric-decline mode (Koyck, 1954; Rivers, 1980; Kernell, 1980; Hibbs, 1982). Unfortunately, the resulting lag estimates diverge considerably from one another and fail to agree on which particular side of economic performance matters significantly. Whereas some of these findings offer strong incentives for government action — with ominous warnings in case of poor economic performance — others seem to give policymakers little reason for either fear or hope in connection with economic performance.

What is needed, apparently, is some better empirical footing for identifying lag structures independently of the actual estimate of lag weights. Transfer function analysis proposed by Box and Jenkins (1976) in the context of ARIMA modeling promises some welcome guidance for this endeavor. This type of analysis implies a notion of causality similar to Granger causality (Granger, 1969; Granger and Newbold, 1974), although the "direct Granger estimations" take a different analytical route (Freeman, 1983; Kirchgassner, 1983).

The Box-Jenkins strategy, it must be noted, has not been greeted everywhere with enthusiasm. The main concern is that it poses too grave a risk of "throwing out the baby with the bathwater." That is to say, this strategy seems to favor the null hypothesis of no effects. Indeed, many users of Box-Jenkins models have experienced the thrill or disappointment, depending on what they hoped to find, of coming up empty-handed. Although it is not without merit to debunk what may ultimately prove to be wrong theory, the ease with which the lack of significant effects can be shown with the Box-Jenkins method should raise a caution flag. As so often, then, we are threatened by a trap on one side — falling victim to the built-in dependence of time series — and a pitfall on the other — tossing away the wheat with the chaff, to adopt another metaphor. If nothing else, the study of popularity functions has a bit of suspense left.

CROSS-CORRELATIONS BETWEEN ECONOMIC AND POLITICAL SERIES

Anyone curious whether or not economic conditions influence presidential popularity, with what lag and lag structure, might begin by looking at correlations between the values of the popularity series and lagged values for the economic series. Let us designate the values a particular economic series lagged by k time units as X_{t-k}, and let Y_t represent the unlagged values of the popularity series. A correlation between Y_t and X_{t-1}, for example, would tell us how strongly popularity at any given time correlates with the economic series at the immediately previous time point. Let us obtain a string of such "cross-correlations" between Y_t and the increasingly lagged X_{t-k}, and call this string a cross-correlation function (CCF). A single significant value exhibited by this CCF at lag 5, for example, would suggest that the economic indicator influences popularity with a delay of 5 time units, be they months, quarters, or whatever. A pattern of significant values at, say, lags 3, 4, 5, and 6 would point to a dynamic relationship. Say, moreover, that these values turned out to be .5, .25, .125, and .06. In that event they would form a geometrically declining sequence of the sort postulated by Hibbs (1982), Kernell (1980), and Rivers (1980).

Most CCFs between observed time series, unfortunately, are not so revealing. More likely, they will shower the analyst with significant values everywhere, including values on the other side of the CCF, where popularity is lagged, and values have the wrong sign. The reason for this indiscriminate flood is quite simple: autocorrelation *within* both series. Readily interpretable are CCFs only when the supposed input series, the economy here, is "white noise," i.e., purely and utterly random (Box and Jenkins, 1976, p. 379). At the very least, the input series should be stationary, that is, free of trend or drift. When, as will be invariably the case, the observed input series is not white noise, "prewhitening" is recommended by Box and Jenkins.

Prewhitening entails removing the nonstationary features, the autoregression components, and the moving-average components, if present, from the observed time series (for method, see, besides Box and Jenkins, 1976; Pierce, 1977; Pindyck and Rubinfeld, 1976; McCleary and Hay, 1980; McDowall et al., 1980). The values of a time series thus transformed have the advantage of being uncorrelated with each other, and not just at the first lag, but at *any* lag. Now correlations between such a variable, say the unemployment series, and another one treated in the same fashion, say the popularity series, can tell us something about the relationships *between* the variables of interest. No longer does the suspicion of autocorrelation cloud the interpretation of cross-correlations.

Studies by Norpoth and Yantek (1983a, 1983b) applied ARIMA prewhitening to monthly series of economic indicators and presidential popularity. Unlike the cross-correlations between untransformed series—which presented a cluttered picture—the cross-correlations based on the prewhitened series made them reach for the magnifying glass. To be sure, a few scattered values can be spotted but as often with the wrong sign as with the right. The conclusion of Norpoth and Yantek (1983a) was:

> the evidence produced by the cross-correlations is too mixed to support a lag structure for either inflation or unemployment. The cross-correlations are not consistently negative. Neither are the negative values substantial, nor do they suggest a pattern. (p. 796)

These findings raise some troublesome questions, although some would argue less about the impact of economic conditions than about Box Jenkins models, or the use of those models. Warnings have been sounded by Geweke et al. (1979), Nelson and Schwert (1982), Freeman (1983), and

Kirchgassner (1983). These studies make the point that prewhitening impedes detection of true effects. The analyst is misled to "accept" a false null hypothesis of no effects. To repeat a familiar metaphor, the baby is being thrown out with the bathwater.

No doubt this danger is acute when something like monthly readings of presidential popularity is analyzed. Each monthly popularity value represents a sample estimate with a typical error margin of roughly plus or minus three percentage points. That is not much relative to the true popularity value of say 50% or 60% and may cause little worry, unless the aim is to make a forecast. But when one takes the change in popularity between this month and last month, the resulting difference may prove no larger, in absolute terms, than the typical margin of error. Since such changes are usually calculated as part of the prewhitening procedure, significant cross-correlations between prewhitened monthly economic series and the accordingly transformed popularity may have been hard to obtain. That this is not impossible, however, even with monthly data, was demonstrated for government popularity in Britain by Whiteley (1984). His findings of economic effects, even after prewhitening, should discourage defeatism. We see no reason to forego ARIMA modeling in general or prewhitening in particular, but in order to minimize the threat posed by measurement error, we will aggregate the monthly observations by quarters. This step can be expected to produce sample estimates of presidential popularity based on roughly three times as many respondents. The error component, relative to true scores, will be sharply reduced, and first differences will be more reliable.

ARIMA MODELS FOR QUARTERLY ECONOMIC SERIES

The two economic problems that are most often cited by respondents in public opinion polls are unemployment and inflation. The percentage unemployed and the change in the consumer price index are items of news eagerly awaited each month. They receive front-page attention in the media and fuel the debate among politicians over the economic health or sickness of the nation. Few other economic indicators command such a steady attention in the mass public.

The period from 1960 to 1980 witnessed wide fluctuations of both unemployment and inflation. Each of these series, but especially inflation, pushed upward. Neither of them displayed a behavior that could be considered "stationary." That is to say, neither fluctuated around a constant mean level. Hence it is advisable to take the first differences for each series of quarterly observations from 1961 to 1980:

$$\nabla UE_t = UE_t - UE_{t-1}$$
$$\nabla INF_t = INF_t - INF_{t-1}$$

The differenced series no longer admit of nonstationary behavior and can be diagnosed as a simple AR(1) process. For unemployment, the estimates, with t-ratios and chi-square for residuals, are:

$$\nabla UE_t = \quad .453\nabla UE_{t-1} + a_t$$
$$(4.52)$$

$$\chi^2 = 25 \qquad DF = 19 \qquad p > .10$$

For inflation,[2] the respective estimates are:

$$\nabla INF_t = \; - .460\nabla INF_{t-2} + a_t$$
$$(-4.02)$$

$$\chi^2 = 31 \qquad DF = 19 \qquad p = .05$$

To be sure, the quality of these estimates is nothing to brag about, but the autocorrelations of residuals (a_t) up to a lag of 20 quarters, that is, 5 years, hint at no particular defect. In any event, the fitting of univariate ARIMA models to the economic series should only be considered a preliminary step in an analysis that aims at estimating the effects of these economic conditions on presidential popularity.[3] With the ARIMA results in hand, we can proceed to prewhiten each economic series and obtain some hint as to the lag structure of economic effects and whether or not any effects can be spotted.

For cross-correlations between unemployment and popularity, the following transformations are involved:

$$\alpha_t = (1 - .453B)\nabla UE_t$$
$$\beta_t = (1 - .453B)\nabla POP_t$$

We designate the "prewhitened" series, here unemployment, as α_t and the "prefiltered" series, here popularity, as β_t. The estimated cross-correlations between them are displayed in Figure 1. While the value for lag 0 exceeds the 95% limits (marked by +), no lagged effects, not to mention a lag structure, can be identified for the quarterly unemployment series. The significant value at lag 0, nevertheless, represents a reassuring finding compared with the utterly bleak results derived from monthly series.

FIG. 1. **Plot of Cross-correlations between prewhitened unemployment and prefiltered presidential popularity, 1961-1980.**

```
          -1.0 -.8 -.6 -.4 -.2  .0  .2  .4  .6  .8 1.0
 LAG  CORR. +----+----+----+----+----+----+----+----+----+
                                  I
 -20  .126                   +    IXXX +
 -19 -.011                   +    I    +
 -18 -.007                   +    I    +
 -17  .070                   +    IXX  +
 -16 -.144                   + XXXXI   +
 -15  .051                   +    IX   +
 -14  .068                   +    IXX  +
 -13 -.050                   +    XI   +
 -12 -.033                   +    XI   +
 -11  .139                   +    IXXX +
 -10  .000                   +    I    +
  -9  .105                   +    IXXX +
  -8  .025                   +    IX   +
  -7 -.082                   +   XXI   +
  -6 -.101                   +  XXXI   +
  -5 -.084                   +   XXI   +
  -4  .016                   +    I    +
  -3 -.178                   + XXXXI   +
  -2  .189                   +    IXXXXX+
  -1  .045                   +    IX   +
   0 -.243                   X+XXXXI    +
   1  .122                   +    IXXX +
   2  .098                   +    IXX  +
   3  .027                   +    IX   +
   4 -.098                   +   XXI   +
   5  .182                   +    IXXXXX+
   6  .077                   +    IXX  +
   7  .014                   +    I    +
   8  .068                   +    IXX  +
   9  .173                   +    IXXXX +
  10 -.128                   +  XXXI   +
  11 -.178                   + XXXXI   +
  12 -.029                   +    XI   +
  13 -.114                   +  XXXI   +
  14  .072                   +    IXX  +
  15 -.108                   +  XXXI   +
  16 -.016                   +    I    +
  17 -.071                   +   XXI   +
  18 -.103                   +  XXXI   +
  19  .272                   +    IXXXXX+X
  20  .083                   +    IXX  +
```

FIG. 2. Plot of Cross-correlations between prewhitened inflation and prefiltered presidential popularity, 1961–1980.

```
            -1.0  -.8  -.6  -.4  -.2   .0   .2   .4   .6   .8  1.0
   LAG  CORR.  +----+----+----+----+----+----+----+----+----+----+
                                       I
   -20  -.040                      +   XI   +
   -19   .082                      +   IXX  +
   -18  -.051                      +   XI   +
   -17   .081                      +   IXX  +
   -16   .059                      +   IX   +
   -15  -.111                      +  XXXI  +
   -14  -.024                      +   XI   +
   -13  -.074                      +  XXI   +
   -12  -.051                      +   XI   +
   -11  -.035                      +   XI   +
   -10   .104                      +   IXXX +
    -9   .068                      +   IXX  +
    -8   .084                      +   IXX  +
    -7   .052                      +   IX   +
    -6   .138                      +   IXXX +
    -5   .189                      +   IXXXXX+
    -4   .064                      +   IXX  +
    -3   .023                      +   IX   +
    -2  -.240                  XXXXXXI      +
    -1   .057                      +   IX   +
     0  -.120                    + XXXI     +
     1  -.311                XX+XXXXXI      +
     2  -.039                      +   XI   +
     3  -.140                      +  XXXI  +
     4  -.173                      +  XXXXI +
     5  -.175                      + XXXXI  +
     6   .099                      +   IXX  +
     7   .034                      +   IX   +
     8   .029                      +   IX   +
     9   .102                      +   IXXX +
    10   .150                      +   IXXXX +
    11   .232                      +   IXXXXXX
    12   .220                      +   IXXXXXX
    13   .114                      +   IXXX +
    14   .123                      +   IXXX +
    15  -.053                      +   XI   +
    16  -.050                      +   XI   +
    17  -.069                      +  XXI   +
    18  -.014                      +    I   +
    19  -.172                      + XXXXI  +
    20  -.127                      +  XXXI  +
```

For inflation, the result is similar. After appropriate transformations,

$$\alpha_t = (1 + .460B^2)\nabla \text{INF}_t$$
$$\beta_t = (1 + .460B^2)\nabla \text{POP}_t$$

we obtain estimated cross-correlations between α_t and β_t, which are displayed in Figure 2. This time it is lag 1 where the cross-correlation estimate exceeds the 95% limit. That would suggest that inflation may affect popularity, in the expected way, with a delay of 3 to 5 months. There is also a vague hint that some of inflation's effect may be contemporaneous ($-.12$ at lag 0) and another part be delayed by a year ($-.17$ at lag 4). Since, in fact, the CCF between unemployment and popularity suggests an effect at lag 0, and since unemployment and inflation correlate negatively with each other, it is advisable to keep a lag 0 effect in mind for inflation as well. Hence, our tentative specification of the influence of economic performance on presidential popularity includes a contemporaneous effect for both unemployment and inflation, as well as a one-quarter lagged effect for inflation. Before estimating these effects, let us spell out the noneconomic variables of our popularity model. Their omission would severely bias the estimates for the economic variables included in the model and distort the policy implications that might be derived from them.

NONECONOMIC VARIABLES

Rally

It is quite apparent even to the casual peruser of opinion polls that presidential approval ratings strongly react to certain events in world politics. An international crisis, threats to the nation's international security, presidential decisions of high salience pertaining to a matter of foreign policy all seem to elicit what Mueller (1970) dubbed the "rally 'round the flag" phenomenon. The use of this variable has become a staple of the cottage industry dealing with presidential popularity (e.g., Kernell, 1978; Rivers, 1980; Hibbs, 1982). Like Kernell (1978), we think it wise to set aside the "early term" effect. In scoring rally points, we follow a simple rule: a rally boosts presidential popularity in the quarter in which it occurs but the effect wears off in the immediately subsequent quarter. Rallies are not considered to give a permanent boost to presidential popularity. Hence in a quarter where a rally event occurs, the "rally" variable is scored $+1$, whereas a -1 is entered for the immediately following quarter unless a fresh rally event occurred there, in which case a score of 0 is entered, as in quarters without a rally event.[5] A quick check shows that a president gained 3.4 percentage points, on average, in a quarter with a rally event whereas he lost 2.8 points in the immediately following quarter.

Vietnam

The effect of the Vietnam War on presidential popularity, especially that of Lyndon Johnson, has been a matter of some dispute. Mueller (1970, 1973) failed to turn up a significant effect, whereas Kernell (1978), Hibbs (1982), and Yantek (1982) demonstrated robust effects. Johnson himself, as quoted by Mueller (1973, p. 196), attributed 20% of the slide of his approval ratings to the Vietnam War. It seems most likely, as suggested by Kernell (1978, p. 510), that in Mueller's model the impact of the war is picked up by the trend variable specific to Johnson's second term—what Mueller called the "coalition-of-minorities" effect and what is specified separately for each presidential term.

In coming to grips with the supposed effect of the Vietnam War, we must bear in mind that the ratings of two presidents may have been affected by that war in quite opposite ways. Nobody would argue that it helped Johnson's approval rating in any way; the only plausible effect, if any, would be the one lamented by Johnson himself. This is not necessarily the case for Nixon, who could and did claim to have inherited the sorry war. He pursued a policy of winding down the American troop commitment without winding up losing the war. In the 1972 election the Vietnam War was an item that seems to have added "2 percentage points to Nixon's margin of victory" (Kelley, 1983, p. 108). Among his core supporters as well as marginal voters, according to Kelley's study, the war issue had a pro-Nixon pull second only to the issue of competence. This lends some credence to supposing that Nixon's handling of the Vietnam War benefited his presidential popularity instead of hurting it. We shall try to test this hypothesis by scoring the Vietnam War -1 for Johnson, $+1$ for Nixon, and 0 elsewhere. Since our dependent variable consists of first differences of presidential approval ratings

$$\nabla POP_t = POP_t - POP_{t-1}$$

this scoring implies an erosion of approval levels for Johnson and a gain for Nixon.[6] Given the similar length of time each of them dealt with the war, that makes it a zero-sum game: it cost Johnson in popularity what it gained Nixon.

Watergate

Fortunately, there are not enough Watergates to require a genuine variable called "scandal" to be included in a time-series analysis of presidential popularity. In a sense, the Watergate scandal, being unique as it is, qualifies as a random shock and should be considered under that rubric. By taking note of it, however, we help reduce the share of random variation in the popularity series and probably capture the catastrophic drop in Nixon's approval rating in his last year of office. Given that little is known *a priori* about the dynamics with which scandals affect presidential popularity we treat Watergate as a dummy variable, with quarters 1973/2–1974/2 scored 1, all others 0.

Inauguration and Erosion

The inauguration of a president has all the trappings of a coronation in a monarchy. A newly elected president can count on widespread approval going far beyond the share of the vote received in the election. Most studies of presidential popularity recognize this early term, honeymoon, euphoria effect, whether separately or as part of the "rally 'round the flag" phenomenon.

Like the "rally" effect, the "early term" effect is bound to wear off. Long before opinion charts and statistical estimates drove home the point, Thomas Jefferson noted that "no man will ever bring out of the Presidency the reputation which carries him into it" (as cited by Kenski, 1980, p. 68). Present-day studies typically treat this loss in a deterministic fashion, that is, as a linear function of time. But that is a rather procrustean way, cutting off the end and squeezing the rest. We do not know over what time span to expect the "early term" effect to decline and in what fashion. It would seem preferable not to constrain this process, and instead model it as follows:

$$POP_t = \theta + \omega I_t \qquad \theta < 0, \ \omega > 0$$

$$I_t = \begin{array}{l} 1 \text{ in first quarter of} \\ \quad \text{president's term} \\ 0 \text{ elsewhere} \end{array}$$

The ω parameter represents the early term effect, here called "inauguration" effect, since it is expected to occur in the first quarter of a new president's term. From the second quarter on, the erosion of this effect sets in and continues until the incumbent president leaves office. This "erosion" is captured by the θ parameter, whose sign is predicted to be negative.

Attempts to capture and explain what appears to be the inevitable cycle of surge and decline of presidential popularity are common in longitudinal studies of presidential popularity. Mueller (1970, 1973) sought to explain it by a "coalition-of-minorities" phenomenon, Stimson (1976) by "disillusionment," whereas others were content to capture the downward trend (Lewis-Beck, 1980; Yantek, 1982). In all these studies, time enters as an explicit variable into the model. Kernell (1978) has waged a strong campaign against this use of time. He has argued that time is a slippery concept whose substantive meaning is the stuff of speculation; we should let time measure, well, just time.

By ignoring time, however, Kernell leaves whatever time trends may be present in the variables of his model. That is a risky step, for it may lead to estimates of economic and noneconomic effects that are confounded with trends. Differencing and prewhitening help us avoid this pitfall while allowing us to capture, through the θ parameter, whatever decline occurs in the popularity series. That decline is closely tied to the "inauguration" effect, in fact, one could say, precipitated by it. Hence, it represents the erosion of an advantage bestowed on a president at the beginning of his tenure. It is part and parcel of a cycle.

ESTIMATES OF EFFECTS

With all the explanatory variables assembled now, our model of presidential popularity includes the following explanatory variables: inflation (contemporary and lagged by one quarter), unemployment; the Vietnam War, Watergate, and rally 'round the flag; inauguration and erosion. In addition, the error term of the model is estimated as a moving-average process. It was

TABLE 1. Estimates for Presidential Popularity Models: 1961/1-1980/4

	Model I		Model II	
Variable	Estimate	t-ratio	Estimate	t-ratio
Inflation	− 139.33	− 1.26		
Inflation lagged	− 306.42	− 2.91	− 277.21	− 2.70
Unemployment	− .93	− .87		
Vietnam	.97	1.78	.92	1.73
Watergate	− 2.96	− 2.01	− 3.61	− 2.56
Rally	2.54	3.96	2.53	3.94
Inauguration	19.95	11.43	19.86	11.40
Erosion (constant)	− 1.32	− 4.30	− 1.33	− 4.29
Random: MA(2)	.37	3.15	.35	3.13
χ^2/DF	17/11		16/13	
$\bar{R}^2$	.69		.69	
N	80		80	

Note. ARIMA Transfer Function estimates performed with BMDP2T (Box-Jenkins time series program, Department of Mathematics, UCLA, June 1981 version). Dependent variable is the differenced popularity series; inflation, inflation lagged (one quarter), and unemployment are also differenced.

so identified after an initial model estimation with error assumed to be "white noise" was rejected.

There can be little doubt that the economy matters for presidential popularity. Our estimates presented in Table 1 largely point to the influence of lagged inflation. Contemporary inflation and unemployment also have estimates with the proper (negative) signs, but their significance falls short of the mark. Given the complications involved in our inflation index – differencing and logging – the estimate for inflation (– 306.42) does not lend itself to a straightforward interpretation. To illustrate its effect, consider a rise of the CPI from 185.3 in quarter one, to 188.5 in quarter two, to 193.4 in quarter three. These changes in the CPI – which roughly correspond to an annualized inflation rate of 8% and were recorded in 1977-1978 – should be expected, according to the model I estimate for lagged inflation to precipitate a decline of 2.6 percentage points in the presidential approval rating in quarter four.

Presidents Nixon, Johnson, and Carter suffered considerable losses in their popularity as a result of the performance of the economy. For Nixon, the model I estimates translate into a loss of almost 7 percentage points because of inflation and 1.5 points because of unemployment. Most of the inflation-induced loss, however, occurred during his last year in office when Watergate dominated the political agenda. Johnson's loss because of inflation is estimated to be 4.5 percentage points. In his case, however, a net gain of 2.0% because of shorter unemployment lines served to limit somewhat the economic damage to his popularity. Similarly, Carter's loss because of inflation comes to 4.4 percentage points, reduced only slightly by a gain of four-tenths of a percentage point because of declining unemployment.

Ford seems to be the only president in the 1961-1980 period whose popularity benefited from economic performance: the falling inflation rate netted him 6.6 percentage points, compared with a loss of 2.6 points because of rising unemployment. Kennedy's popularity apparently was neither harmed nor helped a great deal by economic performance, what with a net gain of just one percentage point because of the combined record of inflation and unemployment.

When only lagged inflation, the single clearly significant economic indicator, is used to represent economic performance (model II), the economic effect on presidential popularity looks less dramatic. Still, Nixon, Johnson, and Carter suffered net losses in their popularity as a result of worsening inflation, whereas Ford gained considerably from a slowdown of the inflation rate, and Kennedy came out essentially even.

Economic performance, nevertheless, cannot match in impact some of the noneconomic items of the model. The "inauguration" effect towers over all the others. A new president should be expected to take office with an approval rating roughly 20 percentage points higher than what his predecessor is leaving with. This initial bonus contributes more to the dynamics of presidential popularity than anything else. Next most significant is the loss of this bonus as a president serves his term: 1.3 percentage points per quarter. This inauguration-erosion cycle, according to our account, affords a remarkable justice: over a full 4-year term, or 16 quarters, the cumulative loss of 21.1% (1.32×16) almost exactly equals the size of the inauguration bonus. In other words, what the inauguration giveth, the term taketh away.

Rally events temporarily reverse this course. They boost a president's rating, we estimate, by about 2.5 percentage points in the quarter where they occur, only to be succeeded by a commensurate drop in the immediately following quarter, unless a new rally event occurs. The statistical significance of this pattern is beyond doubt. Watergate, not surprisingly, proves its wrath for Nixon's popularity. Its stronger and more significant showing in model II owes to the fact that during the Watergate quarters inflation shot up at a fast clip, a colinearity that is reduced in model II by the exclusion of contemporary inflation.

The estimate for the Vietnam War supports our directional hypothesis: hurting Johnson's popularity while benefiting Nixon's. Johnson, so the estimate shows, suffered a loss of roughly one percentage point for each quarter that he prosecuted the war. Nixon, on the other hand, gained a percentage point per quarter. An estimated cumulative loss from model I, for Johnson comes to 11.6 percentage points, or roughly half of what he figured himself. That is still a substantial drop that testifies to the destructive effect of the Vietnam War on the public standing of a president.

While the finding of a Vietnam-inflicted drop of Johnson's popularity squares with common sense, Nixon's apparent gain, coming to a cumulative total of 12.6 percentage points, may seem puzzling. After all, everyone knows that Nixon's popularity curve did *not* rise. That is true, but it did not fall in the expected fashion either. Nixon's popularity held quite steady until Watergate did him in. His curve avoided the normal erosion by 1.3 percentage points a quarter. Our explanation is that his handling of the Vietnam War — getting out without getting defeated — earned him sufficient public credit to offset in large part, though not completely, the normal erosion (Kelley, 1983).

Overall, with the specification of a moving-average noise process, model I passes the crucial test of white noise residuals. No autocorrelations of residuals up to lag 20 are statistically significant. The explanatory fit of the model, as provided by the adjusted R^2, reaches .69, a value that might strike readers used to time-series results as disappointing. It must not be forgotten, however, that our dependent variable consists of first differences. That is to say, our model explains the quarterly *changes* in presidential popularity.

With such a variable, it becomes quite difficult to reach respectable R^2-heights. Once we "integrate" our model and treat the popularity rating in any given quarter, and not the change from the previous quarter, as our *explanandum,* the R^2 soars to .92.

DISCUSSION

The findings reported in this paper should help settle several points raised by previous studies of presidential popularity. For one thing, they add to the list one more piece of evidence that the economy does matter for presidential popularity. Inflation, with a delay of one quarter, certainly influences presidential approval ratings, although unemployment leaves less of an imprint.

The fact that this particular analysis was able to demonstrate an impact of the economy goes to show that Box-Jenkins ARIMA models do not suppress what others have long recognized as true relationships. ARIMA models make the task harder for the analyst, but not an impossible one. To be sure, correction for nonstationary behavior and prewhitening, as done by ARIMA modeling, may derail the research effort in certain circumstances. The threat that the baby is thrown out with the bathwater looms large. Monthly data pose an especially grave risk of this sort (Norpoth and Yantek, 1983), because first differences of monthly observations are easily dominated by noise. Quarterly observations, being less vulnerable to this threat, are found to yield more robust results.

Our estimates for economic effects accord with findings reported by several other studies. For inflation, no effects were detected by this analysis beyond two quarters, or 6 months, as was essentially true for the study by Kernell (1980). Monroe's (1978) estimate of a peak effect for inflation at lags of 4 to 5 months may also be consistent with our result. Some type of distributed lag model for the short term, with a peak effect a few months removed from the present, could be reconciled with our findings. The estimates presented by Hibbs (1982) and Golden and Poterba (1980), on the other hand, suggest more extended effects.

The more significant effect of inflation as compared to unemployment also puts our results alongside those reported by Monroe (1978) and, in this instance, Golden and Poterba (1980), too. They all confirm that inflation preoccupied the public to a higher degree than did unemployment. For the 1961–1980 period that should not be surprising since except for the recessions of 1975 and 1980, unemployment rarely reached or exceeded the 7% mark. Inflation, on the other hand, dogged Johnson, Nixon, and Carter. Whereas the two Democrats resorted to wage-price guidelines to stem inflation, Nixon, in an act highly uncharacteristic of the GOP free-enterprise spirit, imposed wage-price controls in 1971. The concern of these leaders with the inflation side of macroeconomic performance seems justified in view of the vulnerability of presidential popularity to inflation.

Presidents, nevertheless, are not at the mercy of the economy. Whereas Johnson may have suffered a loss because of inflation of 4.6 percentage points, he fell roughly 11 points, according to our estimates, as the result of the Vietnam War. The war, far more than inflation, put Johnson's popularity curve into a nose dive, clouded his reelection prospects in early 1968, and made him forego seeking another term. Likewise, the war as handled by his successor earned the latter a credit of roughly 12 percentage points in the approval ratings, more than enough to balance the 7% debit accrued from inflation.

Big international events, moreover, allow a president to regain considerable ground in the short run, although they cannot help him in the long run. But a few quick rallies may put a president in a more comfortable position in the popularity chart than the cumulative effect of a whole term's inflation could damage him. Nothing illustrates this point better than Carter's extraordinary jump from a 31% approval rating to almost twice that level in the wake of the seizure of the American embassy in Iran in late 1979. However much inflation had chipped away Carter's popularity, this rally more than restored it instantly, enough perhaps to beat back Kennedy's challenge for the Democratic nomination. By the same token, the unfolding of the Watergate scandal, which our estimates suggest cost Nixon a total of 15 percentage points, more than doubled his inflation-induced loss of 7 points. No doubt, economic performance matters significantly for presidential popularity, but the way a president handles a war, international crises, or scandals of Watergate dimensions makes an even stronger impression on his popularity. No president should feel secure in his approval standing just because the economy is performing well; at the same time, no president should take too much comfort from quick boosts stemming from international crises, since these boosts most often prove short-lived.

The economy, rally events, the Vietnam War, and Watergate go a long way toward accounting for the fluctuations of presidential popularity. For the most part, economic performance as measured by inflation has played a part in deflating the popularity of presidents; so has the Vietnam War under Lyndon Johnson and Watergate under Richard Nixon. These variables, however, fall short of fully accounting for the downward drift of popularity curves. Popularity still erodes at a pace of 1.3 percentage points a quarter, even with inflation (contemporary and lagged), unemployment, Vietnam, Watergate, and rally events included in the model. Could something still be missing that might make the downward trend vanish? We think that is unlikely.

Instead, the reason for the erosion appears to lie in the inflated sense of approval with which every president takes office. So long as there is an "inauguration" effect close to 20 percentage points, elevating a new president way above the level of support received in the election, losses are impossible to avoid. Our findings on this matter square with Mueller's (1970, 1973) and Stimson's (1976), although our interpretation differs somewhat from theirs. Over the average tenure of a president, which from 1961 to 1980 happened to be exactly 4 years, or 16 quarters, erosion takes away almost exactly what inauguration bestows. There is some justice and consolation in this balance; justice because the inauguration effect is nothing but a gift, something unearned; consolation because the expected cumulative erosion still should leave most presidents at comfortable levels in the poll standings. Erosion does not spell defeat. Only if poor economic performance, an unpopular war, or a scandal compound the erosion does electoral defeat become likely. By the same token, an economy in good health, the winding down of an unpopular war, the avoidance of scandal, and an international rally at the right moment will counteract and may even offset the erosion that otherwise would occur.

NOTES

1. For recent reviews of the voluminous literature on this topic, see the articles by Schneider and Kiewiet and Rivers in this volume; also the discussion in Norpoth and Yantek (1983, pp. 787–789).
2. Our measure of inflation consists of quarter-to-quarter changes of the logged consumer price index; the logging was necessary to stabilize the variance of the series. The resulting index of inflation produces values quite similar to what would be obtained by computing, as is often done, the percentage change for any given quarter. Data for the CPI and unemployment were obtained from *Business Statistics* (U.S. Department of Commerce) and the *Monthly Labor Review* (U.S. Department of Labor).
3. The popularity series is based on the percentage "approve" of monthly Gallup surveys ("Do you approve or disapprove of the way . . . is handling his job as president?"). See *The Gallup Opinion Index,* Report No. 182, October–November, 1980. The monthly figures, sometimes more than one a month, were averaged by quarters. For the fourth quarter of 1963 and the third quarter of 1974, when the presidency changed hands in the middle of a term, only values for the new president were used each time. Popularity values were interpolated for the third quarters of the election years 1964, 1972, and 1976.
4. The estimation of CCFs for the whole period 1961–1980 might be criticized on the grounds that in so doing we make one administration pay the price or reap the benefit for economic performance under the previous administration. To guard against this threat, we estimated separate CCFs for the Kennedy-Johnson, Nixon-Ford, and Carter administrations. The result was that none of these CCFs suggested any more extended lagged effects or structures than did the overall CCFs, neither for unemployment nor inflation.
5. For the years from 1961 to 1980, we used the rallies included in Mueller's list (1973, p. 211). For the 1969–1980 period, the following rallies were selected: Cambodia invasion (1970/2), Laos invasion (1971/1), China trip (1972/1), Mining of Haiphong, Moscow Summit (1972/2), Vietnam Peace Treaty (1973/1), Brezhnev Visit (1973/2), Vladivostok Summit (1974/4), Mayaguez incident (1975/2), Panama Canal Treaty (1978/1), Camp David Accord (1978/4), Deng visit (1979/1), SALT-II signed (1979/3), Iranian Embassy seized

(1979/4). The Iranian rally was also scored for 1980/1 since this event was only partly registered in 1979/4 polls. As a result, 1980/2 and 1980/3 were coded in a way to accommodate the wearing-off of the Iranian rally.

6. The presence of the Vietnam War was scored (-1) from 1965/2 to 1968/1, immediately after which Johnson announced that he would not seek reelection and initiated steps to negotiate with North Vietnam. For Nixon the war was scored ($+1$) from 1969/2 to 1972/2; no further quarters were scored since the popularity value for 1972/3 is interpolated anyway and the presidential election took place in 1972/4.

REFERENCES

Almon, Shirley (1965). "The Distributed Lag between Capital Appropriations and Expenditures." *Econometrica* 33:178–196.

Box, George E. P., and Gwilym M. Jenkins (1976). *Time Series Analysis: Revised Edition*. San Francisco: Holden-Day.

Freeman, John R. (1983). "Granger Causality and the Time Series Analysis of Political Relationships." *American Journal of Political Research* 27:325–355.

Geweke, J., R. Meese, and W. Dent (1979). "Comparing Alternative Tests of Causality in Temporal Systems: Analytic Results and Experimental Evidence." Social Systems Research Institute Workshop Paper No. 7928. University of Wisconsin, Madison.

Golden, David G., and James M. Poterba (1980). "The Price of Popularity: The Political Business Cycle Reexamined." *American Journal of Political Science* 24:696–714.

Granger, Clive W. J. (1969). "Investigating Causal Relations by Econometric Models and Cross-spectral Methods." *Econometrica* 37:424–438.

Granger, Clive W. J., and Paul Newbold (1974). "Spurious Regressions in Econometrics." *Journal of Econometrics* 2:111–120.

Hibbs, Douglas A., Jr., with R. Douglas Rivers and Nicholas Vasilatos (1982). "On the Demand for Economic Outcomes: Macroeconomic Performance and Mass Political Support in the United States, Great Britain, and Germany." *Journal of Politics* 43:426–462.

Kelley, Stanley, Jr. (1983). *Interpreting Elections*. Princeton University Press.

Kenski, Henry (1980). "Economic Perception and Presidential Popularity." *The Journal of Politics* 42:68–75.

Kernell, Samuel (1978). "Explaining Presidential Popularity." *The American Political Science Review* 72:506–522.

Kernell, Samuel (1980). "Strategy and Ideology: The Politics of Unemployment and Inflation in Modern Capitalist Democracies." Paper presented at the annual meeting of the American Political Science Association, Washington, D.C.

Kiewiet, D. Roderick, and Douglas Rivers (1984). "A Retrospective on Retrospective Voting." *Political Behavior,* 6:369–392 (and this volume).

Kirchgassner, Gebhard (1983). "Welche Art der Beziehung herrscht zwischen der objektiven wirtschaftlichen Entwicklung..? "In Max Kaase and Hans-Dieter Kingemann (eds.), *Wahlen und Politisches System*. Opladen: Westdeutscher Verlag, pp. 222–256.

Koyck, L. M. (1954). *Distributed Lags and Investment Analysis*. Amsterdam: North-Holland Publishing Company.

Kramer, Gerald H. (1971). "Short-term Fluctuations in U.S. Voting Behavior, 1896-1964." *The American Political Science Review* 5:131-143.

Kramer, Gerald H. (1983). The Ecological Fallacy Revisited: Aggregate- versus Individual-Level Findings on Economics and Elections and Sociotropic Voting." *American Political Science Review* 77:92-111.

Lewis-Beck, Michael S. (1980). "Economic Conditions and Executive Popularity: The French Experience." *American Journal of Political Science* 24:306-323.

Lipset, Seymour Martin (1982). "No Room for The Ins: Elections around the World." *Public Opinion* 5:41-43.

McCleary, Richard, and Richard A. Hay, Jr. (1980). *Applied Time Series Analysis.* London: Sage.

McDowall, David, Richard McCleary, Errol E. Meidinger, and Richard A. Hay, Jr. (1980). *Interrupted Time Series Analysis.* London: Sage.

Monroe, Kristen R. (1978). "Economic Influences on Presidential Popularity." *Public Opinion Quarterly* 42:360-369.

Mueller, John E. (1970). "Presidential Popularity from Truman to Johnson." *American Political Science Review* 64:18-34.

Mueller, John E. (1973). *War, Presidents, and Public Opinion.* New York: Wiley.

Nelson, Charles R., and G. Schwert (1982). "Tests for Predictive Relationships between Time Series Variables: A Monte Carlo Investigation." *Journal of the American Statistical Association* 77:11-17.

Norpoth, Helmut, and Thom Yantek (1983). "Macroeconomic Conditions and Fluctuations of Presidential Popularity: The Question of Lagged Effects." *American Journal of Political Science* 27:785-807. (a)

Norpoth, Helmut, and Thom Yantek (1983). "Von Adenauer bis Schmidt: Wirtschaftslage und Kanslerpopularitat." In Max Kaase and Hans-Dieter Klingemann (eds.), *Wahlen und Politisches System.* Opladen: Westdeutscher Verlag, pp. 198-221. (b)

Pierce, David A. (1977). "Relationships—and the Lack Thereof—between Economic Time Series, with Special Reference to Money and Interest Rates." *Journal of the American Statistical Association* 72:11-26.

Pindyck, Robert S., and Donald L. Rubinfeld (1976). *Econometric Models and Economic Forecasts.* New York: McGraw-Hill.

Rivers, Douglas (1980). "Distributed-lag Models in Political Research." Paper presented at the annual meeting of the Midwest Political Science Association, Chicago, Ill.

Schneider, Friedrich (1984). "Public Attitudes Toward Economic Conditions and Their Impact on Government Behavior." *Political Behavior* 6:211-217 (and this volume).

Smith, Hedrick (1984). "Times/CBS Poll Shows President in Strong Position as Glenn Fades." *The New York Times,* 25 January 1984, p. 1.

Stimson, James A. (1976). "Public Support for American Presidents: A Cyclical Model." *Public Opinion Quarterly* 40:1-21.

Whiteley, Paul (1984). "Economic Performance and Government Popularity in Britain." *Political Behavior,* 6:395-410 (and this volume).

Yantek, Thom (1982). "Public Support for Presidential Performance: A Study of Macroeconomic Effects." *Polity* 15:268-278.

CHAPTER 10

The Voter as Juror:
Attributing Responsibility
for Economic Conditions

Mark Peffley
Department of Political Science, Drake University

Over the past decade, the literature exploring the connection between economic conditions and political behavior has grown at a staggering pace. Analysts have employed a variety of different types of data, statistical techniques, and model specifications to uncover evidence for the political importance of economic conditions. Especially fruitful have been the efforts of survey analysts, who have made great strides in putting together seemingly incongruous pieces of evidence to construct a portrait of economic voting in U.S. national elections.

One rough indicator of progress at the individual level is the number of revisions made to the "traditional reward-punishment theory" of economic voting that motivated earlier studies.[1] In various passages of *The Responsible Electorate*, V. O. Key, Jr. (1966) first articulated many of the working assumptions of the theory, suggesting that citizens primarily react to the *past performances* of the incumbent administration when choosing candidates for national office. Retrospective voting is thus a referendum on the incumbent party, where citizens are oriented toward past performance rather than the future promises of the candidates.

Recent research, however, indicates that a strict adherence to the assumptions of Key's theory led investigators to underestimate the political importance of economic problems. Many citizens do not simply rely on the most accessible information about past economic performance to guide their vote decision. Rather, economic voters are found to be more oriented toward the *future* performance of the economy (Kuklinski and West, 1981; Fiorina, 1981), and they are more "policy oriented" (Kiewiet, 1981, 1983; Fiorina, 1981) than the reward-punishment theory postulates. The overall image of the economic voter that emerges from recent research is of an individual who uses more information and more complex decision rules than earlier studies indicated (e.g., Weatherford, 1983).

Very few scholars, however, have questioned another assumption of the reward-punishment theory—that voters hold the incumbent party responsible for all manner of economic fluctuations. Key viewed the voter's decision rule as an act of sanctioning: the individual either "rewards" the president's party for economic improvements or "punishes" it for deteriorations. Prior to sanctioning, however, voters presumably decide on the extent to which incumbents are in fact *responsible* for those conditions. That is, citizens must first reach the conclusion that the president's party is liable for "hard times" before throwing it out of office. This necessary precondition for sanctioning is ignored by adherents of Key's theory because responsibility judgments are assumed to be automatic; the citizen "simply takes past performance as a *prima facie* indicator of the government's competence (or lack thereof)" (Fiorina, 1981, p. 12). Complex questions of responsibility are reduced to a simple rule of inference: if economic conditions are good, give the president and his party credit for it; if conditions are poor, blame them for that.

Some analysts have expressed skepticism about the sensibility of such a decision rule. In his criticism of Kramer's (1971) seminal article, economist George Stigler (1973) made the following argument:

> Per capita income falls over a year or two—should the voter abandon or punish the party in power? Such a reaction seems premature: the decline may be due to developments (e.g., a foreign recession) beyond the powers or the responsibilities of the party. (p. 165)

But while such *post hoc, propter hoc* reasoning by voters may appear shallow and even simpleminded, it has been justified on practical as well as normative grounds. Economic affairs are extremely complicated, it is argued, and tracing complex connections between the polity and the economy to decide who is responsible would entail astronomical information costs and decision-making costs (see Fiorina's [1978] general arguments in favor of retrospective voting). Automatic attributions of responsibility are therefore a practical necessity. In his treatment of reward-punishment theory, Page (1978) articulated a normative argument for blaming politicians for any and all economic discontents, since this provides an incentive for their accountability and responsiveness in office:

> Indeed the theory could work even though voters knew nothing about the causes of bliss and misfortune, and simply attributed everything to incumbents. . . . Even if the crop failures of the 1970's resulted from bad weather, and oil prices were due to OPEC, why not blame the American president and his party? To err on the side of forgiveness would leave voters vulnerable to tricky explanations and rationalizations; but to err on the draconian side would only push politicians to greater energy and imagination in problem solving. (p. 222)

While both arguments have an obvious intuitive appeal, the assumption of automatic political blame, like the assumptions of performance and past-orientation, has simply not been supported by the evidence. A review of the survey literature indicates that under just those conditions where the assumption is least defensible, the evidence has been particularly thin. One good example is the literature investigating the political importance of personal economic discontents — being unemployed, affected by a recession, or experiencing a worsening financial situation. In their wide-ranging survey studies, Kinder and Kiewiet (1979; 1981) found personal discontents to be only marginally helpful in explaining presidential and congressional (House) voting. Their research indicates that it is perceptions of *national* economic conditions and the government's performance in that area that have more weighty political consequences.

Subsequent research by Feldman (1982) clearly demonstrates that the failure of personal grievances to become politicized rests on questions of responsibility. In his analysis of 1972 CPS survey data, Feldman found that most people tend to attribute their economic misfortunes to personal and proximate forces rather than to systemic forces like the government or the national economy. Only for the small minority of the sample that furnished systemic reasons for their economic misfortunes were personal conditions a significant (indeed, a powerful) determinant of presidential and congressional voting. Why do most Americans fail to hold the government responsible for their personal economic well-being? Feldman found one answer in the widespread adherence to the belief in hard work and equal opportunity — what Schlozman and Verba (1979) referred to as the American Dream.

In their study of cognitive links between economic conditions and presidential popularity, Lau and Sears (1981) found a similar interactive pattern. People suffering from personal economic problems were more likely to withdraw support from Jimmy Carter if they blamed him for their hardships.[2] Thus, one reason why national conditions carry more political force than personal experiences is because national politicians are held more accountable for the country's economic welfare. Not only are lines of causation between national economic trends and politics easier to trace, but representatives of the government in Washington are expected to ensure prosperity for the nation as a whole, if not for each individual.

Survey results have also been disappointing and confusing in studies of congressional elections. The relationships uncovered are often erratic and fail to achieve conventional levels of statistical significance. Once again, these patterns are more explicable when responsibility judgments are taken into account. In a study of House elections, Hibbing and Alford (1981) showed that these slight relationships are due to the fact that not all congressional candidates affiliated with the president's party are held responsible for economic conditions. They marshaled an impressive array of aggregate data (House election data since World War II and survey data (1978 CPS House election data) to support their argument that only certain members of the president's party are punished for declines in personal finances — those "who were in the best position to take credit or receive blame for those conditions — that is . . . *incumbents* of the in-party," especially the more senior members (p. 435, emphasis added).

Of course, even for these incumbents, the magnitude of the relationship pales in comparison with the results obtained in presidential elections. All of the forms of economic voting considered thus far — performance as well as policy-oriented judgments, retrospective and prospective judgments, and personal as well as national economic perceptions — are more important in presidential elections (Kinder and Kiewiet, 1981; Kiewiet, 1983; Fiorina, 1978, 1981). Quite understandably, the chief executive, as the most prominent representative of the federal government, is held more directly accountable for national economic conditions than are his party's congressional candidates.

But even where lines of responsibility are more clear-cut, the tendency for Americans to vote against the president because of an ailing national economy is not particularly strong. In their more recent study of economic voting, for example, Kinder and Kiewiet (1981) reported estimates of regression coefficients that range from .06 to .11 for national business conditions and .11 to .27 for evaluations of the government's economic performance. It may be that many voters simply do not hold the president responsible for *all* the ups and downs of the national economy. One telling contemporary example is the persistent finding of national opinion polls that less than half of the American public viewed the 1981–1982 recession as the fault of the Reagan administration.[3]

The public's reluctance to adhere to Key's assumption of automatic blame may, under a number of conditions, be perfectly reasonable. Controlling the forces of inflation, for example, may be viewed by some citizens as an impossibly hard task that would be met with failure by anyone unfortunate enough to be president these days. Or the causes of stagflation might be attributed to forces over which the president is seen to have little control, such as a foreign recession, OPEC, or the Federal Reserve Board. Finally, citizens may think that economic problems such as unemployment are caused by personal failings or that putting people back to work is not the responsibility of the federal government.

Taking Stock

From this brief review of the survey literature, several observations concerning the role of responsibility judgments in economic voting are in order. First, there appears to be little support for a central assumption of reward-punishment theory, that voters hold the incumbent party accountable for all manner of economic fluctuations. In fact, many of the apparent inconsistencies in the empirical findings of various survey studies are resolved once it is recognized that the public often assigns responsibility more conditionally than Key's theory postulates. Economic voting is much less prevalent under those conditions where incumbents are less likely to be blamed for economic downturns. Thus, the relationship between economic discontents and political behavior is greatly attenuated when the focus of investigation shifts from presidential to congressional elections or from national conditions to personal economic well-being. Moreover, though we have no direct evidence at this point, there appears to be several reasonable conditions under which presidents would be spared public retributions for national downturns.

Second, while the evidence is less conclusive on this score, it appears that the process by which citizens attribute political responsibility for economic conditions is considerably more involved than the superficial snap judgments posited by Key's theory. Not only are responsibility judgments more conditional than Key's automatic attributions, but they appear to be based on a great deal more information than that which is most readily available to voters — rough-and-ready appraisals of good times and bad times. These observations are only the beginning of a much more involved decision process in which a variety of other kinds of information are also utilized, such as the incumbents' proximity to the policymaking process (Hibbing and Alford, 1981) and the individual's beliefs of economic individualism (Feldman, 1982). Naturally, any attempt to characterize the attribution process at this point must remain tentative, since our conjectures are based primarily upon indirect evidence — the pattern of voting behavior under various conditions — instead of a direct investigation of responsibility judgments *per se.*

Even from this vantage point, however, it is fair to conclude that the attribution of responsibility is a crucial step in the decision-making process of economic voting. Before economic discontents take on political significance, people must believe either that the government produced them or that it is the government's job to remedy them. These beliefs revolve around issues of responsibility. The attribution of blame thus comes close to constituting a necessary condition for the subsequent politicization of economic events, in that the impact of economic perceptions on political behavior is mediated by judgments of accountability.

Despite the gains made by these studies, they are not without their problems. First, it is evident that responsibility judgments need to be analyzed more directly in future studies. Once it is conceded that these attitudes play a crucial role in guiding an individual's response to economic conditions, it becomes imperative that they be explicitly incorporated into models of economic voting. Analysts routinely interpret their results in terms of the public's tendency to "blame" or "credit" incumbents for the economy, but these judgments are rarely measured directly. Consequently, only an indirect test of any hypothesis concerning responsibility is possible, thus making it difficult for investigators to rule out confounding explanations for their findings. For example, in Hibbing and Alford's (1982) study of congressional elections, the finding that people are more likely to punish the senior members of the incumbent party may be due, in part, to the increased efforts of strategic elites of the opposition party in these races. Thus, the relationship between economic voting and seniority may be due to the greater availability of incriminating information in these races instead of a tendency for voters selectively to punish incumbents who are more deserving of blame (see Jacobson and Kernell, 1981; Weatherford, 1983).

While explicitly probing citizen's judgments is definitely a step in the right direction, it is also one fraught with uncharted hazards. Studies by Lau and Sears (1981) and Tyler (1982) revealed a few of the difficulties of capturing a ubiquitous concept like "responsibility" within the rigors of survey research. From these studies, it is clear that the extent to which citizens are found to hold incumbents responsible critically depends upon the way the concept is measured. Lau and Sears, for example, concluded that holding the president responsible for national economic problems is a relatively rare phenomenon. When asked in an open-ended question "Who should take care of the problem of rising prices (unemployment)?" only 26% (7%) of their respondents explicitly named President Carter. By contrast, when Tyler's respondents were asked simply whether or not Carter was responsible for economic problems, they were almost unanimous in their "guilty" verdict: 87% felt that Carter was responsible for inflation, and 78% thought he was responsible for unemployment. Such different results can be traced to the tendency for particular items to tap different aspects of responsibility.[4] The question used by Lau and Sears measures responsibility in one narrow sense of the term: who has the principal role for dealing with particular economic problems? Tyler's more general measure, on the other hand, asks only whether the president is at all responsible for these problems, in any sense of the term.

Underlying difficulties with particular indicators is an annoying lack of conceptual clarity. It is not entirely clear what responsibility means to the investigators or to the respondents in most of the studies reviewed here. As several scholars in the fields of legal philosophy (Hart and Honore, 1959; Hart, 1968) and social psychology (Fincham and Jaspars, 1980; Hamilton, 1978, 1980) have pointed out, the term *responsibility* has many meanings. One may be held responsible for the effects of his or her actions in a causal, legal, moral, or role sense of the term. More than mere semantics separates the different usages. As will be made clear below, depending on the type of responsibility that citizens have in mind, they are likely to base their judgments on a particular set of criteria that may or may not overlap with those used for other types of responsibility. Apparently unaware of the problem, researchers tend to vacillate between different usages. In Tyler's (1982) study, for example, he combined his general measures of Carter's responsibility with items measuring the extent to which presidents are able to control each problem to form a single measure of "presidential responsibility."

This conceptual confusion is symptomatic of a more fundamental problem: most researchers make little effort to articulate a *theory* of the way citizens infer responsibility. Again, the literature in psychology is useful for suggesting various perspectives and for evaluating their potential for political applications. Psychologists have investigated two classes of explanations for the attribution of responsibility, one motivational and the other cognitive.[5] A cognitive model will be outlined later; for now, it is worth exploring the many liabilities associated with the motivational approach, the focus of most empirical work in psychology. Motivational research in psychology and political science has been narrowly preoccupied with the phenomena of "defensive attributions," described by Tyler (1982) as the tendency for people to avoid the perception that personally threatening events can happen by chance. In the political realm, Tyler hypothesized that people who are personally threatened by economic hardship are motivated to hold the president responsible to assure themselves that political and economic events are controllable.

Tyler's inability to uncover any consistent empirical support for his thesis is not at all surprising.[6] Despite a long tradition of research, the defensive attribution thesis has not faired well in psychology either. In their comprehensive review of the literature, Fincham and Jaspars (1980) concluded that defensive attributions are extremely difficult to replicate and occur only under a complex and little understood set of interactive conditions. Moreover, as Fishbein and Ajzen (1975) suggested, these contradictory and inconclusive results stem from the tendency for this research to be based less on systematic theoretical analyses of attributional processes than on intuitive hypotheses and speculations. Finally, much of the limited evidence for defensive attributions can be accounted for by the operation of relatively "passionless" cognitive processes (cf., Schneider et al., 1979; Tyler and Devintz, 1981).

To avoid this empirical morass, the perspective outlined below follows the recent emphasis on cognitive models in political science and psychology.[7] Weatherford's (1983) recent analysis of economic voting offers a much richer theoretical conceptualization of the voter as a "rational processor of information." Of the myriad judgments the voter must make to arrive at a final decision, Weatherford argued that many of "these questions can be considered together as a problem in the acquisition and the processing of information" (p. 161). Once the problem of responsibility attribution is cast in terms of political reasoning or the processing of political information, analysts have at their disposal an embarrassment of riches in the wealth of studies on the subject by social psychologists.

THE ATTRIBUTION OF RESPONSIBILITY

The model of responsibility attribution formulated here is tailored to the study of how citizens blame presidents for national economic problems (e.g., inflation and unemployment), although with minor modifications it may be generalized to other incumbents and other, noneconomic problems. Many of the principles that social psychologists have found to be useful in explaining responsibility attribution in people's everyday lives should be well suited to the investigation of presidential responsibility. Not only is the presidency one of the most personalized institutions of American government, but a great deal of public attention is focused upon the man and the office (DiClerico, 1983).

As indicated above, the term *responsibility* has many meanings. When we say that a president is responsible for a declining economy, we can mean any or all of the following: the president *caused* the conditions to occur, he is *morally* or *legally* responsible for them, or that it is his *role* to correct them. For each type of responsibility a similar process of data acquisition and evaluation is involved. Viewed from the perspective of the legal setting, the citizen-juror has two related tasks before him or her. The first is to acquire the relevant evidence bearing on the problem, which may include information on the state of the economy, knowledge of the president's economic program, and so forth. The second task is to evaluate the evidence according to a particular decision rule to determine the president's liability for economic conditions. Decision rules are generally cast as if-then propositions: if the evidence meets certain criteria, then the president is held responsible and is liable to sanctions by the voter.

This overview of the attribution process is similar to Hamilton's (1978) description of responsibility attribution in the legal system, where jurors must determine whether or not a defendant is responsible according to a particular set of legal rules. She noted that different types of legal liability rely on different sets of rules and evidence. In the same way, a given type of presidential responsibility may be distinguished by the form of evidence and the decision rule that is used to infer culpability.

Causal Responsibility

Cognitive models of responsibility tend to focus on the concept of *causal* responsibility (cf., Fincham and Jaspars, 1980). This emphasis can be traced to Heider's (1958) seminal work in which he argued that observers can be likened to "intuitive psychologists" who engage in a naive causal analysis of action to assess an actor's liability for certain events or outcomes. According to Heider, one very general decision rule that people may employ to determine causal responsibility is to assess the degree to which the outcome was determined by personal versus environmental forces. The more environmental forces are felt to influence the outcome, the less the person is held responsible. In his discussion of causal inference, Heider suggested that to analyze an actor's task performance, observers weight the causal impact of three stable factors: the actor's ability, his or her intentions, and the difficulty of the task.[8]

The application of Heider's conceptual framework to the problem at hand is fairly straightforward. The more unemployment and inflation are thought to be caused by the president's incompetence or his misguided policies, the more he will be held personally responsible. On the other hand, the more the problems are perceived to be caused by external forces—Congress, OPEC, past administrations, or the sheer difficulty of the task—the less he will be held responsible.

Moral-Legal Responsibility

The works of Hart and Honore (1959, 1961), Hamilton (1980), and Fincham and Jaspars (1980) underlie the conceptualization of *moral-legal* responsibility. The view of the perceiver that emerges here is that of an "intuitive lawyer" who is intent upon tracing causes of a particular sort — those that relate to the actor's control over his or her behavior or its outcomes. For this type of responsibility, the general inference rule is, Could the actor have done otherwise? That is, if the actor's behavior is under his or her control, he or she is responsible for the outcome. In assessing presidential blame in moral-legal terms, citizens will take into account the amount of control they feel the president has over the economy. Those who feel that the president has complete control over economic fluctuations are expected to hold the president accountable for economic problems he must have caused or could have prevented.

Based on the work of presidential scholar Thomas Cronin (1980), we may expect the public to hold rather idealized perceptions of presidential power and control over economic events, because these beliefs are part of the myth of the "textbook presidency" to which many Americans are assumed to subscribe. If so, presidents may be held responsible for failing to produce economic miracles because they lack the will and the skill necessary to exploit the inherent powers of the office.[9]

Role Responsibility

Presidential blame may be assigned not only for what the president did — causal responsibility — but also for what he is supposed to do — *role* responsibility. Hamilton (1978) argued that it is possible to be responsible for an event without either having caused the event or having any control over the outcome. Both the decision rule and the evidence used to assess Hamilton's notion of role responsibility are quite simple, imposing minimal decision costs on the voter. The only new information that is required is some knowledge of the state of the economy: are conditions good or bad? are they improving or worsening? The incumbent's performance is thus matched with citizens' expectations for what presidents should achieve, and any shortfall carries a liability to negative sanctions.

This simple procedure most closely approximates current models of economic voting, where presidents are punished for any downswing that occurs during their administration. Of course, the crucial difference between Key's decision rule and Hamilton's is that in the latter case a judgment of responsibility still mediates the impact of economic perceptions on presidential support, while in Key's model they are absent. The two decision rules lead to a similar response *only* among voters who have extremely high expectations for presidential performance.

Operationalizing role responsibility from this perspective is also quite simple. Is the level of economic voting greater among citizens with higher

expectations for a president's economic performance?[10] A far more interesting line of inquiry, however, is one that attempts to uncover the beliefs and
perceptions that underlie these general expectations. As the most visible
symbol of the federal government, the president may be held liable for economic problems that people feel the *government* ought to solve. The central
question here is, Who is responsible for solving the economic problems of
others—the government or the affected individuals? The work of social psychologists Phil Brickman and associates (1982) suggested that the criteria
employed to evaluate governmental responsibility are similar to those used
to assess causal and moral responsibility, discussed above. The authors presented a general framework to examine how people decide whether to help
others cope with their problems and what form their assistance should take.
They argued that the decision to help someone suffering from a problem
rests on two related questions about the victim's responsibility: (1) did he or
she create (cause) the problem? and (2) does the victim have control over its
future solution? According to Brickman et al. (1982),

> Responsibility for the origin of a problem, generally responsibility for a past
> event, clearly involves the question of deserving blame. Responsibility for the
> solution to a problem, generally responsibility for future events, clearly involves
> an assessment of who might be able to control events. (p. 369)

The authors noted that whereas the answers to these questions are often correlated, the dimensions are nonetheless distinct. For example, even if the
problems of others are seen to be created by the social environment (they
are not responsible in a causal sense), they are responsible for finding a
solution if it is seen to be within their control (they *are* responsible in a
moral-legal sense).

Political scientists have focused on this notion of role responsibility to
account for the conditions under which Americans turn to government for
help in solving their economic problems. The implicit question being asked
is whether one's problems are one's own responsibility or the responsibility
of the government. A brief review of these studies is instructive, for many
of the same beliefs and perceptions found to mediate the political impact of
personal discontents should affect an individual's tendency to favor governmental support for *others* in coping with their hardships. In addition, as will
be seen, these considerations fall roughly into the two categories of causal
and moral-legal criteria.

One central question in determining governmental responsibility discussed by these authors is the extent to which economic problems are felt to
be caused by personal or systemic forces. In their general study of personal
problems, for example, Brody and Sniderman (1977) pointed out that problems can be placed upon a continuum of "locus of concern," running to the

"self" at one end to "society" at the other. Socially located problems such as inflation should be more likely to stimulate demands for governmental assistance than self-located concerns like the breakup of a marriage. Similarly, in their more focused study of the politicization of unemployment in the United States, Schlozman and Verba (1979) argued that "those who see the problem [of unemployment] as a function of system rather than personal failure [should] be more likely to look to government for help" (p. 191).

A second consideration is the extent to which the problem is seen to be beyond the individual's *control*. Brody and Sniderman (1977) made the following argument:

> Citizens are likely to think the government has some responsibility to help only if the type of problem . . . is beyond the capacity of any one person to deal with all by himself. (p. 339)

How do individuals decide whether the disadvantaged have control over their economic fates? Schlozman and Verba (1979) argued that the unemployed are less likely to see their problem as being the government's responsibility if they subscribe to the American Dream, i.e., the belief that hard work is rewarded with economic advancement and that opportunities for advancement are accessible to everyone. In their words:

> If those who are disadvantaged economically . . . espouse the individualistic beliefs associated with the American Dream, they would become more likely to view self-help, rather than government intervention, as the appropriate mode for dealing with their economic problems. (p. 104)

These two criteria fit nicely into the framework developed above. People are expected to view questions of governmental versus individual responsibility in terms of causality and control. Is the problem caused by external (systemic) forces or by internal (personal) ones? Is the remedy of the problem within the individual's control? In addition, these considerations should be more relevant for explaining an individual's tendency to endorse governmental solutions for more traditional economic problems like poverty and unemployment than for inflation, since the latter problem should be uniformly viewed as being caused by social forces (e.g., the government) and beyond any single individual's ability to control.[11] Unemployment, on the other hand, may be seen to be the responsibility of the government *or* the individual, depending upon one's perception of the cause of the problem and one's beliefs in people's ability to cope with it without assistance from the government.

Presidential responsibility for unemployment should thus be influenced by perceptions of the causes of joblessness and beliefs about how much control individuals have over their economic well-being. For those Americans

who feel that people are out of work simply because they lack the initiative
to find a job, then governmental solutions will be viewed as inappropriate
and the president will be held less responsible for joblessness. If, on the
other hand, unemployment is believed to be due to forces beyond the individual's control, then government (i.e., the president) should be held
responsible for the problem.

Information Costs

One might argue that the framework outlined above is essentially a
"thinking person's" version of responsibility attribution, one which would
overwhelm the average citizen with astronomical decision costs involved in
collecting and evaluating information in a world of uncertainty. Certainly
much of the evidence needed to make a judicious decision is ambiguous and
fragmentary, the product of a confusing political debate between the
administration and its critics over who is responsible for economic failures.
Yet, even under these conditions, decision costs may be minimized in at
least two ways. First, citizens are assumed to employ the same criteria to
determine the president's responsibility that they use in everyday life to
judge others. Decision strategies, therefore, are expected to be well rehearsed
and to proceed in a routine, efficient manner.[12]

Decision costs may also be reduced if we can assume that people overcome uncertainty by relying on their prior beliefs to interpret or to "fill in"
ambiguous or missing information. Thus, because it may be costly for
voters to acquire information about the *incumbent's* control over the economy, they are likely to rely on their expectations of the extent of control
exercised by *most* presidents. By the same token, judgments of governmental role responsibility are most likely based on people's "intuitive
theories" of the causes of economic problems as well as their more general
values of economic self-reliance. Hence, by using generic information
already at their disposal, citizens can make inferences about presidential
responsibility without being encumbered with unreasonable information
costs.[13]

IMPLICATIONS

Generalizing the Framework

The value of studying the dynamics of the attribution process is not
restricted to economics or to the presidency. Any time citizens base their
evaluations of public officials on their perceptions of the government's performance, questions of responsibility should play a central role in mediating

a political response. Whether citizens punish incumbents for the quality of the air they breathe, gas shortages, or foreign policy fiascoes, judging political accountability should be a necessary step in the sanctioning process. These attributions should be influenced by criteria similar to those outlined above: did the government cause the problem? does it have control over it? and what role is the government expected to play in remedying the situation?

Some important modifications may be necessary before applying the framework to congressional elections. Citizens might have enough knowledge of the president or the presidency to determine questions of causality and control, but the paucity of policy information in congressional contests should make governmental role responsibility more important. In addition, the model may also help to account for cross-national variation in the level of economic voting found in various Western democracies. Lewis-Beck (1983), for example, suggested that French and British voters are more likely than Americans to express their personal economic grievances at the ballot box because both Western European countries have a weaker individualistic tradition and a stronger central government than the U.S. These conditions make it all the more likely that Western European voters will find the government responsible in all three senses of the term. Future comparative studies must put these hypotheses to a test by measuring citizens' judgments and the reasoning behind them.

At a more general level, attributions of responsibility should be incorporated into other theories of retrospective voting, in addition to Key's. In this paper, we have focused on the reward-punishment model only because its assumptions concerning responsibility are fairly explicit and because it conceptualizes voting as an act of sanctioning, where judgments of responsibility are of paramount importance. But responsibility should play an important role in any theory of retrospective voting where observations of economic conditions are assumed to influence political judgments. Thus, in each of the theories outlined by Fiorina (1981), retrospective voting should be affected in no small measure by perceptions of whether the incumbent party is responsible for economic conditions. In Downs's (1957) version of retrospective voting, citizens use performance information to predict what policies the incumbent party would pursue if reelected. And in Fiorina's own "pyramidal" model, performance information influences partisan affiliations and judgments of the competence of the incumbent party in handling particular problems. Attributions of responsibility affect the *weight* that is assigned to performance information in making these other judgments. If a person feels that the incumbent party is not at all responsible for prevailing economic conditions, then this information tells her or him nothing about the competence of the party or the party's future policy intentions.

Directions for Future Research

What other factors should analysts consider in future studies of responsibility attribution? For one, more attention needs to be paid to the way elites (e.g., party spokespersons and the media) shape the political debate over who is responsible for economic fluctuations. Citizen judgments do not occur in a vacuum, but in a political context that is shaped as much by the actions of strategic elites as by objective material conditions. Most voters are highly dependent upon elites for distilling the complex machinations of the macroeconomy to more accessible interpretations. In fact, the judgments of many citizens may be little more than ready-made verdicts, adopted *in toto* from political elites, without any appreciation for the reasoning behind them.[14] Even for those people who weigh the evidence for themselves, much of the available information will be "prepackaged" by elite discourse. The oft-noted skill of national politicians in taking credit for anything that goes right and blaming others for anything that goes wrong (Fenno, 1978) is finely honed in dealing with economic matters. Analysts thus need to pay close attention to the way incumbents play what Norpoth and Yantek (1983) dubbed the "blame game."

Throughout our description of the average citizen as a "rational" processor of information we have avoided any questions about the accuracy of his or her final judgments. Naturally, the evidence at hand is usually so ambiguous that even the "experts" can be expected to disagree, so any normative standard of accuracy is hard to come by. Nevertheless, by employing more intensive analyses of the way people process information, analysts could investigate possible sources of "bias" (i.e., systematic errors) in the attribution process.

Social psychologists have catalogued a long list of cognitive biases that affect the several stages of the judgment process (see Nisbett and Ross, 1980; Kahneman et al., 1982). A few such errors are likely to exaggerate attributions of presidential responsibility. People are found to assign more causal weight to salient factors when observing social behavior (Taylor and Fiske, 1978), as well as to more concrete and vivid images (Nisbett and Borgida, 1975; Nisbett and Ross, 1980). There is no question that in the conduct of economic affairs presidents are much more visible than other influential actors, such as Congress and the Federal Reserve Board. This focus is especially evident in the media's coverage of politics, which, in its need to simplify and personalize events, tends to "fix on a president and make him the prime symbolic agent of government" (Cronin, 1980, p. 96).

A series of studies by Langer (1983) indicated that people often fall prey to what she termed the "illusion of control," or the belief that individuals have control over events that are objectively determined by chance. This bias is especially pervasive when skill-related factors, such as competition or choice, are present in a situation. Since presidential politics is usually viewed as a perpetual test of an incumbent's abilities and is normally rife with competition, people may tend to attribute economic dislocations to a president's incompetence rather than to random "shocks" beyond his control. When this bias is coupled with the exaggerated view of presidential power one normally gains from hyperbolic campaign pledges, the media, and early political learning, some culpability may be impossible to avoid.

In closing, this paper has recommended that analysts pursue a more theoretical approach to the study of responsibility attribution, one that borrows from models of information processing in psychology. This theoretical orientation, however, must also be accompanied by a different approach to research design if investigators are to build a cumulative body of empirical knowledge. While survey analysts are quick to point out the pitfalls of aggregate-level studies of economic voting, they often fail to recognize that their studies suffer from a similar problem—an inability to rule out an infinite number of individual-level models that are consistent with their results. To contribute to future theory building, therefore, researchers should rely less on extensive cross-sectional, correlational studies and more on intensive panel survey data and experimental designs.

NOTES

1. While Kinder and Kiewiet (1979), in their analysis of personal grievances, and Fiorina (1978) may not have had Key's theory in mind when conducting their analyses, economic voting was operationalized by these authors much like reward-punishment theory.
2. It should be noted, however, that in their analysis of data from the 1979 CPS Pilot Study, the coefficients associated with Lau and Sears's indicators of personal discontents (unemployed or laid off, underemployed, financial well-being, subjective impact of inflation) were not statistically significant, regardless of whether the respondent blamed Carter or not. Nevertheless, for people who blame Carter, the size of the coefficients do increase and their signs are more often in the appropriate direction. It is difficult for any effects to reach conventional levels of statistical significance when the regression analysis is based on such a small sample ($N = 177$).
3. See J. Stacks, America's Fretful Mood," *Time*, December 28, 1981, p. 23.
4. The time and location of the studies differed also. Lau and Sears analyzed data from a national sample of individuals interviewed in the spring of 1980, whereas Tyler's sample was drawn from the conservative 10th district of Illinois a few days after the election. These factors may have accentuated the differences produced by the two measures.
5. See Fincham and Jaspars (1980) for a comprehensive review of the literature.
6. People who expected their personal finances to worsen were slightly more likely to hold Carter responsible for inflation, but the relationship does not hold for past financial misfortunes or for Carter's responsibility for unemployment. Even this relationship could be explained by a much simpler emotional response than defensive attribution. People may be angry about their discontents and search for a convenient scapegoat (see Conover and Feldman, 1983).

7. This is not to argue that motivational factors, in general, do not influence attributions of responsibility. As Nisbett and Ross (1980) pointed out, motivational and cognitive factors, taken by themselves, are rarely sufficient explanations of social behavior—they operate in *collusion* rather than independently. In the attribution of political responsibility, one's choice of news, party information, friends, and occupations undoubtedly influences our sample of information of the political world. Thus, motives and affections may influence an individual's receptivity and exposure to the evidence bearing on presidential blame. But this is hardly the whole story, since cognitive factors such as political beliefs or intuitive political theories then come to influence the acquisition and evaluation of the information that is available. Thereafter, these same cognitive factors often influence political behavior and exposure to further evidence and information.

8. Experimental studies in attribution research find that individuals do use these factors and Heider's decision rule to explain an actor's performance on an ability-related task (Weiner et al., 1972; Meyer, 1980; Frieze and Weiner, 1971; Elig and Frieze, 1979).

9. The dimensions of causality and control overlap to some degree. Personal causes of performance are typically under the control of the president. On the other hand, for external forces to mitigate presidential responsibility, they must also be beyond the president's control. Incumbents presiding over a failing economy, for example, are usually careful to blame their economic ills on scapegoats that lie beyond the control of the White House, such as OPEC and the Federal Reserve Board.

10. This seems to be the approach of Kinder et al. (1980) in their study of presidential prototypes. They found economic voting higher among people who select "solving economic problems" as an important part of their conception of an "ideal" president.

11. Evidence for this view can be found in several studies. In his review of survey data on consumer finances, Peretz (1981) noted that "75 percent of the population is unable to think of any way to protect itself against inflation" (p. 14). Also, when subjects interviewed in the 1979 CPS Pilot Study were asked in an open-ended format what they thought caused inflation, the overwhelming majority mentioned societal forces such as government, the cost of oil, and the activities of businesses and unions. If something is to be done about these causes, the government must play a key role.

12. See Schneider and Shiffrin's (1977) distinction between automatic and controlled processing of information.

13. For a more rigorous conceptualization of the way prior beliefs guide the processing of information under conditions of uncertainty, see Taylor and Crocker's (1980) discussion of social schemata.

14. See Converse's (1975) notion of "social constraint" for a similar process by which mass political attitudes are assumed to be transmitted from elites.

REFERENCES

Brickman, P., et al. (1982). "Models of Helping and Coping." *Amegican Pyychologist* 37(4):368–384.

Brody, R., and P. Sniderman (1977). "From Life Space to Polling Place." *British Journal of Political Science* 7:337–360.

Conover, P. J., and S. Feldman (1983). "Emotional Reactions to the Economy: I'm Mad as Hell and I'm Not Going to Take It Anymore." Paper presented at the annual meeting of the American Political Science Association.

Converse, P. E. (1975). "Public Opinion and Voting Behavior." In F. Greenstein and

N. Polsby (eds.), *Handbook of Political Science* (Volume 4). Reading, Mass.: Addison-Wesley, 75–169.

Cronin, T. E. (1980). *The State of the Presidency* (2nd ed.). Boston: Little, Brown.

DiClerico, R. E. (1983). *The American Presidency* (2nd ed.). Englewood Cliffs, N.J. Prentice-Hall.

Downs, A. (1975). *An Economic Theory of Democracy.* New York: Harper & Row.

Elig, T. W., and I. H. Frieze (1979). "Measuring Causal Attribution for Success and Failure." *Journal of Personality and Social Psychology* 37(4):621–634.

Feldman, S. (1982). "Economic Self-interest and Political Behavior." *American Journal of Political Behavior* 26(3):446- 466.

Fenno, R., Jr. (1978). *Home Style.* Boston: Little-Brown.

Fincham, F. D., and J. M. Jaspars (1980). "Attribution of Responsibility: From Man the Scientist to Man as Lawyer." In L. Berkowitz (ed.), *Advances in Experimental Social Psychology* (Vol. 13). New York: Academic Press.

Fiorina, M. (1978). "Economic Retrospective Voting in American National Elections: A Micro-analysis." *American Journal of Political Science* 22(2):426–443.

Fiorina, M. (1981). *Retrospective Voting in American National Elections.* New Haven: Yale University Press.

Fishbein, M., and I. Ajzen (1975). *Belief, Attitude, Intention, and Behavior: An Introduction to Theory and Research.* Reading, Mass.: Addison-Wesley.

Frieze, I., and B. Weiner (1971). "Cue Utilization and Attribution Judgment for Success and Failure." *Journal of Personality* 39:591–605.

Hamilton, V. L. (1978). "Who Is Responsible? Toward a Social Psychology of Responsibility Attribution." *Social Psychology* 41(4):316–328.

Hamilton, W. L. (1980). "Intuitive Psychologist or Intuitive Lawyer? Alternative Model of the Attribution Process." *Journal of Personality and Social Psychology* 39(5):767–772.

Hart, H. L. A. (1968). *Punishment and Responsibility.* London: Oxford University Press.

Hart, H. L. A., and A. M. Honore (1959). *Causation in the Law.* London: Oxford University Press.

Hart, H. L. A., and A. M. Honore (1961). "Causation in the Law." In H. Morris (ed.), *Freedom and Responsibility.* Stanford, Calif.: Stanford University Press.

Heider, F. (1958). *The Psychology of Interpersonal Relations.* New York: Wiley.

Hibbing, J. R., and J. R. Alford (1981). "The Electoral Impact of Economic Conditions: Who Is Held Responsible?" *American Journal of Political Science* 25(3): 423–439.

Jacobson, G. C., and S. Kernell (1981). *Strategy and Choice in Congressional Elections.* New Haven: Yale University Press.

Kahneman, D., P. Slovic, and A. Tversky (1982). *Judgment Under Uncertainty: Heuristics and Biases.* Cambridge: Cambridge University Press.

Key, V. O., Jr. (1966). *The Responsible Electorate.* New York: Vintage.

Kiewiet, D. R. (1981). "Policy-oriented Voting in Response to Economic Issues." *American Political Science Review* 75(2):448–459.

Kiewiet, D. (1983). *Macroeconomics and Micropolitics.* Chicago: University of Chicago Press.

Kinder, R. (1981). "Presidents, Popularity, and Public Opinion. *Public Opinion Quarterly* 45(1):1–21.

Kinder, R., and D. R. Kiewiet (1979). "Economic Discontent and Political Behavior: The Role of Personal Grievances and Collective Economic Judgements in Congressional Voting." *American Journal of Political Science* 23(3):495–527.

Kinder, R., and D. R. Kiewiet (1981). "Sociotropic Politics: The American Case." *British Journal of American Politics* 11:129–161.

Kinder, R., et al. (1980). "Presidential Prototypes." *Political Behavior* 2(4):315–338.

Kramer, G. D. (1971). "Short-term Fluctuations in U.S. Voting Behavior, 1896–1964." *American Political Science Review* 65(1):131–143.

Kuklinski, H., and M. West (1981). "Economic Expectations in United States House and Senate Elections." *American Political Science Review* 75(2):436–447.

Langer, E. (1983). *The Psychology of Control.* Beverly Hills, Calif.: Sage Publications.

Lau, R., and D. Sears (1981). "Cognitive Links between Economic Grievances and Political Responses." *Political Behavior* 3(4):279–302.

Lewis-Beck, M. S. (1983). "Economics and the French Voter: A Microanalysis." *Public Opinion Quarterly* 47:347–360.

Meyer, J. P. (1980). "Causal Attribution for Success and Failure: A Multivariate Investigation of Dimensionality, Formation, and Consequences." *Journal of Personality and Social Psychology* 38(5):719–726.

Nisbett, R., and E. Borgida (1975). "Attribution and the Psychology of Prediction." *Journal of Personality and Social Psychology* 32:932–942.

Nisbett, R., and L. Ross (1980). *Human Inference: Strategies and Shortcomings of Social Judgments.* Englewood Cliffs, N.J.: Prentice-Hall.

Norpoth, H., and T. Yantek (1983). "Macroeconomic Conditions and Fluctuations of Presidential Popularity: The Question of Lagged Effects." *American Journal of Political Science* 27(4):785–807.

Page, B. I. (1978). *Choices and Echoes in Presidential Elections.* Chicago: Chicago University Press.

Peretz, P. (1981). "Why Is Inflation Seen as a Problem?" Paper presented at the annual meeting of the American Political Science Association.

Schlozman, K., and S. Verba (1979). *Insult to Injury.* Cambridge, Mass.: Harvard University Press.

Schneider, D. J., A. H. Hastorf, and P. C. Ellsworth (1979). *Person Perception* (2nd ed.). Reading, Mass.: Addison-Wesley.

Schneider, W., and R. Shiffrin (1977). "Controlled and Automatic Information Processing." *Psychological Review* 84:1–66.

Stacks, J. (1981). "America's Fretful Mood." *Time,* December 28, 1981, pp. 22–23.

Stigler, G. J. (1973). "General Economic Conditions and National Elections." *American Economic Review* 63:160–167.

Taylor, S. E., and J. Crocker (1980). "Schematic Bases of Social Information Processing." In E. T. Higgins, C. P. Herman, and M. P. Zanne (eds.), *Social Cognitions: The Ontario Symposium* (Vol. 1). Hillsdale, N.J.: Lawrence Earlbaum Associates.

Taylor, S. E., and S. Fiske (1978). "Salience, Attention, and Attribution: Top of the

Head Phenomena." In L. Berkowitz (ed.), *Advances in Experimental Social Psychology,* Vol. 11. New York: Academic Press.

Tyler, T. (1982). "Personalization in Attributing Responsibility for National Problems to the President." *Political Behavior* 4(4):379–399.

Tyler, T., and V. Devintz (1981). "Self-Serving Bias in Attribution of Responsibility: Cognitive Versus Motivational Explanation." *Journal of Experimental Social Psychology* 17:408–416.

Weatherford, S. M. (1983). "Economic Voting and the 'Symbolic Politics' Argument: A Reinterpretation and Synthesis." *American Political Science Review* 77(1):158–174.

Weiner, B., et al. (1972). "Perceiving the Causes of Success and Failure." In E. E. Jones et al. (eds.), *Attribution: Perceiving the Causes of Social Behavior.* Morristown, N.J.: General Learning Press.

CHAPTER 11

A Retrospective on
Retrospective Voting

D. Roderick Kiewiet and Douglas Rivers
California Institute of Technology

And the whole congregation of the children of Israel murmured against Moses and Aaron in the wilderness: And the children of Israel said unto them, Would to God we had died by the hand of the Lord in the land of Egypt, when we sat by the flesh pots, and when we did eat bread to the full; for ye have brought us forth into this wilderness, to kill this whole assembly of people with hunger (Exodus 16: 2-3).

The idea that a leader's political fate turns upon the material well-being of the people he or she leads is, as this passage from the Old Testament indicates, an old one. To be sure, few economies have fluctuated as extremely as that of the Israelites in the wilderness, and few political figures have experienced as many large swings in their popularity as Moses. More recently, though, historians have traced the origin of the French Revolution to a series of bad harvests followed by increasing prices, falling wages, and mass unemployment (Doyle, 1980). In Britain, following the expansion of the franchise in the early part of the nineteenth century, electoral fluctuations were regularly attributed to grain prices and other economic factors (Olney, 1973; Nossiter, 1974).

Political observers in the United States have also long believed that prevailing economic conditions exert a strong influence upon the choice voters make in national elections. Research in this area makes up for one of the oldest quantitative traditions in political science (for reviews of this early literature see Kramer, 1971, and Monroe, 1979). These studies examined several different conjectures: prosperity aids the Republicans; farm sector depressions lead to support for the populists; and conservative candidates fare better during good times. In short, the vague notion that economic conditions influence voting admits to a wide range of specific hypotheses.

The focus of research in this area narrowed considerably, however, following publication of Gerald Kramer's seminal article, "Short-Term Fluctuations in U.S. Voting Behavior, 1896–1964," in 1971. Following Kramer's lead, most subsequent studies have concentrated on a few interrelated hypotheses: that voting in response to economic concerns is (1) retrospective, (2) incumbency-oriented, and (3) based upon the results of economic policies, and not upon the actual policies themselves. Taken together, these imply that voters give greater support to candidates of the incumbent party when the election is preceded by a period of prosperity than when times have been poor. We will henceforth refer to these interlocking hypotheses as the *retrospective voting model.*

In some respects the subsequent concentration of work on this one model is unfortunate, given that there are other plausible ways different types of economic concerns might influence voters' decisions. On the whole, however, the narrowing of attention to a few potentially testable propositions has been beneficial. Retrospective voting is probably the simplest and most straightforward model of those that have been posited (perhaps also, as suggested above, the oldest as well), and it makes good sense to examine simple hypotheses before entertaining more complicated theories about political-economic relationships. Combined with the fact that most studies in this area have utilized much the same data, this concentration on retrospective voting has made it much more feasible than in other areas of political research to compare the results of different studies, and thus to identify the particular features of models and methods that lead to differences in findings.

In the next section of this paper we review the many time series analyses that followed the publication of Kramer's original article. We then turn to an examination of the other major body of research in retrospective voting — analyses of individual-level survey data. In both cases we identify the more robust findings that have emerged from the various strands of research, those findings that have not been strongly substantiated, and those subjects about which we continue to know virtually nothing. (Although much of this research has concerned European and other Western-style democracies, our discussion will be confined to studies of American national elections.) In the final section, we consider pooling cross-section and time series data as a possible solution to the data problems encountered in previous studies.

TIME SERIES ANALYSES OF RETROSPECTIVE VOTING

As indicated earlier, the retrospective voting model that has informed most of the work in this field can actually be analyzed as three separate hypotheses: voting on the basis of economic concerns is in response to actual policy outcomes, is retrospective, and is incumbency-oriented. Thus it is useful to analyze these studies taking into account the evidence they bring to bear on the following three sets of questions:

1. What exactly are the economic outcomes to which voters respond?
2. If voters judge retrospectively, what is the nature of the dynamic relation between policy outcomes and electoral responses?
3. What is the proper incumbency concept? Is it the incumbent president, congressional candidates of his party, or some other concept of incumbency.

Retrospective voting can occur on noneconomic issues, but most of the literature focuses on economic performance. Employment, inflation, and real income are neither perfectly well defined nor measured without error, but their meaning and measurement are better understood and less controversial than that of any noneconomic issues. So far as possible, we also limit our attention here to economic performance, though this can cause difficulties since wars — even unpopular ones — stimulate the economy without benefiting the incumbent administration.

Kramer found that the share of the total national vote for congressional candidates of the incumbent president's party was influenced more strongly and consistently by changes in real per capita income than by several other economic variables. Aggregate time series analyses of retrospective voting which followed Kramer's study corroborated and extended his findings. First, electoral support for the incumbent party is best predicted by one of a set of highly correlated measures of change in real output. Although most studies followed Kramer's lead and specified change in real per capita income (Bloom and Price, 1975; Tufte, 1975, 1978; Hibbing and Alford, 1981), unemployment or change in per capita real GNP appear to work nearly as well (Fair, 1978). Evidence from this class of studies on how voters react to price inflation is mixed and appears to be sensitive to small changes in data and in specification.

Another study that examined pooled cross-section time series data — state-level vote totals for president from approximately a half dozen presidential elections — reported similar findings. Although Meltzer and Vellrath (1975) were not impressed by the strength of their findings, their analysis indicated that national unemployment and price inflation often influenced presidential vote totals. The economic data analyzed in all these studies, of course, are national-level figures. In sharp contrast to the pattern of evidence that has emerged here, a study which estimated the effect of price and income changes at the level of the individual congressional district found these variables to have virtually no impact upon district vote totals (Owens and Olsen, 1980).

Second, voters appear to base their decisions primarily upon the economic conditions of the recent past. Again, most studies simply followed Kramer's lead and used the year of the election as the time frame for their economic measures (this is obviously a bit crude; because elections are held in early November, approximately one-sixth of the data summarized by such measures comes from after the election). Fair's (1978) study, however, experimented with several different lags. Although there were not enough observations in his time series to permit any firm conclusions, his evidence suggested that votes for president were best predicted by per capita change in GNP in the second quarter of the election year. It is also clear that averaging the performance indicators over a longer period improves the prospects for maintaining the null hypothesis. Stigler (1973), for instance, observed much weaker relationships between per capita income change and congressional vote totals when he adopted a 2-year retrospective time frame.

One problem with the aggregate presidential or congressional voting data is that one either has a very short time series (in the case of Tufte's 1975 analysis of post–1946 midterm elections, only eight observations) or the data extend over a period so long that the assumed stability of the regression function becomes questionable. Over the past century there has been vast change in the structure of the economy, in the size and scope of the federal government, in information and communications technology, as well as in the nature of party competition that certainly must have affected the way voters hold political leaders accountable for economic performance. Even though we gain an additional electoral observation every 2 or 4 years, we also gain a lot of history along with it.

An alternative approach that allows estimation of more complex models is to use the monthly or quarterly Gallup presidential popularity series. In keeping with the aggregate voting studies, these studies have found that approval ratings of the incumbent president are adversely affected by declines in real output (Kernell, 1978; Rivers, 1980; Golden and Poterba, 1980; Hibbs, Rivers, and Vasilatos, 1982) and by price inflation (Monroe, 1978; Norpoth, 1984).

At the risk of oversimplification, the typical presidential popularity study models voters' "memories" as a distributed lag of past performance indicators. Specifications of the lag function vary from study to study. Hibbs et al. (1982) employed a fairly complicated geometric structure that involves interadministration and interparty comparisons. Golden and Poterba (1980) and Monroe (1978) used a polynomial distributed lag, whereas Norpoth (1984) tried short, unconstrained forms. Although each of these studies has found lagged effects, none, unfortunately, has been particularly informative about the nature of the dynamic relation between government performance and political evaluations. Part of the problem is in the data: fitting two or three different distributed lags to 80 or quarterly observations is guaranteed to produce unsatisfactory estimates. The solution, of course, is to impose some *a priori* constraints on the retrospective model. Smoothness priors, of which geometric and polynomial lags are very strong forms, are one possibility, but we should insist that these have a sound theoretical basis (see Nerlove, 1972, for a good discussion of theoretically derived lag structures). Symptomatic of the theoretical sloppiness that characterizes much of this field is that many analyses ignore changes in administrations altogether, with the result that poor performance by the previous administration hurts the popularity of its successor.

It appears that we are still a long way from answering important practical questions, such as how close to an election must an economic recovery occur to help the incumbent party. Certainly the lags that have been found are not long enough to make political business cycle manipulations entirely pointless (a rectangular lag over the entire term of office would of course eliminate any advantage to timing recoveries to coincide with elections). On the other hand, most findings in this area indicate that an incumbent would be well advised to have a recovery started before the election quarter. Whether the optimal timing is two quarters in advance, three quarters, or even earlier remains an open question.

Consideration of the third major aspect of the retrospective voting model—defining who the incumbents are—may seem a bit pedantic; the studies discussed above have concerned either the incumbent president or congressional candidates of his party, and this would seem like the obvious way to proceed. There are, however, several variations on the incumbency theme that are worth noting. First, Tufte (1975, 1978) found that change in per capita income consistently influenced the electoral fortunes of incumbent party congressional candidates in midterm elections. His findings thus refute the notion that midterm elections are no more than a regression toward the mean, or a return to the "normal vote" following the "surge" toward the party of the winning candidate in the preceding presidential election (Campbell, 1966).

Second, Hibbing and Alford (1981) argued that all congressional incumbents are not created equal; their analysis of aggregate time series data suggests that congressional candidates of the incumbent president's party who are also incumbent members of Congress (incumbent incumbents, if you will) are more strongly affected by economic fluctuations than are candidates of his party running in open seats. Because incumbent incumbents have a very high probability of winning reelection, this implies, as Hibbing and Alford noted, that "the political effects of economic fluctuations, so clear when mean vote levels are examined, may lose a good deal of their force when the focus is shifted to actual seats won and lost" (p. 438). Although the robustness of their findings have been questioned (Fiorina, 1983), this remains an important point; for it is the subsequent composition of Congress, not national vote percentages, which is presumably of more interest as far as public policy is concerned.[1]

What we have learned from time series analyses of retrospective voting is that the electoral fortunes of the incumbent president and congressional candidates of his party, as well as the president's approval ratings, are influenced by fluctuations in employment, prices, and real output. To a skeptic, it might seem that this research has revealed nothing beyond what common sense should have told us in the first place. Perhaps, but propositions derived from common sense and political folk wisdom are often incorrect or contradictory.

Beyond documenting common sense, however, we now have a rough sense, at least, of the magnitude of effects of real income fluctuations on voting. Kramer (1971) initially estimated approximately that a 0.5% ($\pm 0.2\%$) decline in the incumbent party's congressional vote share would follow a 1% loss of real income.[2] Bloom and Price (1975) found a slightly larger effect for income declines, approximately 0.7% ($\pm 0.2\%$), but no evidence of any effect for income gains. Tufte (1975), controlling for presidential popularity which also depends on real income changes, estimated a 0.35% ($\pm 0.1\%$) vote loss for every 1% of real income lost. Somewhat larger effects are found on presidential votes. Fair (1978) estimated roughly point for point, 1.2% ($\pm 0.4\%$), changes in presidential vote shares and percentage real income growth rates. With stable prices, Frey and Schneider found that a 1% increase in real income raises presidential popularity about 0.85% ($\pm 0.3\%$), whereas Hibbs et al. (1982), controlling for unemployment, found that a 1% loss in real income eventually costs the incumbent about 0.8% in popularity. Of course, Stigler (1973) and Arcelus and Meltzer (1975) have demonstrated that enough tampering with the specification (period dummies, time trends, adding and deleting variables without rhyme or reason) and odd choice of variables can destroy these findings. In our view, however, a judicious summary of the empirical literature might run: *A 1% decline in real income will cost the incumbent party between 0.5% and 1% of its vote share in the last election.*

We lack, at present, any clear sense of how particular aspects of economic performance—unemployment and inflation, for example—contribute to electoral outcomes. The aggregate studies offer conflicting evidence on their effects. Some find unemployment, others inflation, some both, others neither, as significant determinants of election outcomes and popular support for political leaders. In part, this reflects heterogeneity in the population, as Hibbs (1977, 1979) has stressed, over the relative importance of full employment and price stability. Moreover, public attitudes on unemployment and inflation appear to shift over time, so there is little hope of resolving these issues with the aggregate time series data.

The time series models have not been perfected to the point necessary to produce useful and reliable forecasts. High R^2s—in the .7 or .8 range—tend to impress those nurtured on survey research, but they often provide vote forecasts with standard errors of 5% or more, which do not make them very helpful in predicting election outcomes. This problem is confounded by the fact that time series analyses of retrospective voting have estimated the impact of economic conditions upon changes in vote totals and not seat totals. (For a discussion of the shortcomings of forecasting on the basis of these sorts of models, especially those which involve calculation of swing ratios, see Rivers, 1984). One task for future work in this area is to model rigorously those factors (e.g., the nature of party competition within individual congressional districts) that determine how performance at the national level is translated into seat changes at the district level. The subsequent composition of Congress, after all, is of more direct consequence for public policy than the national vote total.

SURVEY ANALYSES OF RETROSPECTIVE VOTING

Time series analyses of aggregate voting and popularity data constitute only one part of the large body of research instigated by Kramer's 1971 paper. Dozens of other researchers turned instead to survey data for evidence on how economic concerns influence the choices made by individual voters in national elections with the intention of explaining the aggregate level time series findings. Implicit in most of these analyses was the assumption that survey data could resolve questions that the aggregate data could not, that the effects found in survey data were somehow more real than those in aggregate data since they were not subject to the "ecological fallacy," and that, equipped with the right survey questions, we could uncover the psychological motivations underlying electoral behavior. In fact, for the most part, survey analyses have provided very limited and partial answers to the questions posed. Interesting hypotheses have been proposed, but theoretical progress has been slow.

Since 1956, the American National Election studies have included an item which has frequently been used as a microlevel measure of real income change:

> We are interested in how people are getting along financially these days. Would you say that you (and your family) are better off or worse off financially than you were a year ago, or about the same?

Most survey-based investigations have proceeded on the basis that evidence of retrospective voting at the individual level would consist of voters in the "better off" category exhibiting greater support for incumbents than those in the "worse off" category and with those in the "same" category falling somewhere in between. Aggregate changes in real income are the sum of individual household changes which should be reflected by responses to this item. Incumbents' loss of electoral support during recessions would result from the fact that larger numbers of people were suffering financial hardships (and ending up in the "worse off" category).

What we have here is, in its simplest form, a linear aggregation problem. Suppose v_{it} is the measure of the ith vother's support for the incumbent administration at time t (which we will refer to, for convenience, as his or her vote, though the measure will be treated as continuous rather than discrete) and let x_{it} denote the change in the voter's income (usually real disposable income) in the period prior to the election. The assumed micromodel for retrospective voting is:

$$v_{it} = \beta x_{it} + u_{it} \tag{1}$$

where u_{it} captures the effects of all other variables on voting. Let v_t, x_t, and u_t denote the averages of v_{it}, x_{it} and u_{it} over all voters in election t. Then it follows directly from (1) that:

$$v_t = \beta x_t + u_t \tag{2}$$

If u_{it} and x_{it} are uncorrelated during election t, then the cross-sectional estimate of β obtained from (1) will be consistent. If u_t and x_t are uncorrelated over a certain time period, then the time series estimate of β from (2) will also be consistent. That is, under these conditions, the cross-sectional (micro) estimates and the time-series (macro) estimates should not conflict.

There are, however, several reasons why the micro- and macroestimates might differ. The most obvious reason, which we will return to later, is that either (1) or (2) is misspecified in the sense that x and u are correlated. We temporarily ignore this possibility and proceed on the assumption that (1) is the correct microspecification.

The survey evidence on the effect of personal financial conditions on voting is mixed. Votes for president do appear to reflect people's recent financial fortunes. With only a few exceptions, those who reported being better off financially were found to be more likely to vote for the incumbent party in presidential elections than those who reported being worse off or the same (Wides, 1976; Fiorina, 1978, 1981; Klorman, 1978; Tufte, 1978; Kinder and Kiewiet, 1979, 1981; Kiewiet, 1983). Similarly, the more favorable recent trends in family finances have been, the higher the marks individuals give to the president for his handling of the economy (Fiorina, 1981) and for the overall job he is doing as president (Wides, 1976; Kinder, 1981). Much weaker effects or even no effects at all were found in election for other offices. Although a few studies found evidence for personal financial effects in the 1950s, few congressional elections after 1960 registered this effect (Ben-Gera, 1977; Fiorina, 1978; Kinder and Kiewiet, 1979, 1981; Weatherford, 1978). Nor was the evidence more supportive in either senatorial or gubernatorial elections (Ben-Gera, 1977; Klorman, 1978).

Several problems of interpretation plague most cross-sectional analyses. First, a tendency to "control" for other attitudinal variables which may also depend on economic conditions leads to an underestimate of economic effects. Second, beyond reporting that the coefficient of the family finances item was statistically significant or not, most studies have paid little attention to the meaning of the estimated coefficients. Estimates of, for example, the effect of a percent change in real income have not been computed, so although the cross-sectional estimates have generally been viewed as inconsistent with the aggregate time series estimates, no serious systematic attempt has been made to compare the two.

The use of the survey personal finances item, of course, does not permit direct comparisons of cross-sectional estimates with the time-series estimates discussed in the previous section. In fact, the meaning of the personal finances item is a matter of considerable controversy. Rosenstone et al. (1983) reported correlations ranging from 0.16 to 0.57 between it and other more specific personal financial items, so, despite the question's rather vague wording, it does appear to measure concrete aspects of the respondent's financial situation.[3] It is also the case that high rates of real income growth are associated with larger fractions of the population reporting themselves to be "better off" financially as illustrated by the scatterplot in Figure 1. Regressing the percentages responding "better," "same," and

**FIG. 1. Survey reports of personal financial situation and
real income growth rates.**

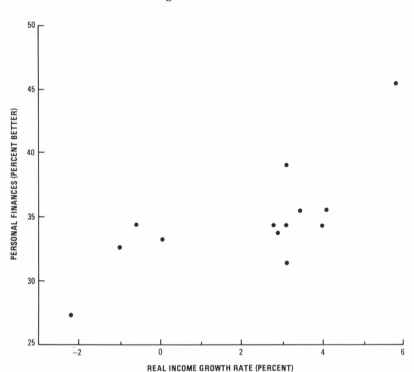

"worse" on the quarterly percentage rate of growth of real personal disposable income per capita (annualized), we obtain:

$$\text{BETTER} = 31.9 + \underset{(0.4)}{1.3} \quad \Delta\text{INC} \quad R^2 = 0.51$$

$$\text{SAME} = 37.8 + \underset{(0.9)}{0.5} \quad \Delta\text{INC} \quad R^2 = 0.03$$

$$\text{WORSE} = 30.2 - 1.8 \quad \Delta\text{INC} \quad R^2 = 0.21$$

$$T = 13 \; (1956-1980) \qquad \text{(standard errors in parentheses)}$$

The responses to the personal finances item vary over a relatively narrow
range for the most part, and when the two extreme observations (1964 and
1974) are deleted, only a tenuous correlation remains between it and the real

income growth rate. This suggests that only when times are bad enough to become a topic of general conversation will declines in real income be reflected in the survey item and that it is a rather crude instrument for measuring smaller income fluctuations. Clearly the personal finances item measures real income change rather imprecisely, which means that survey-based estimates of retrospective voting models are biased. In the simple case of Equation 1, the direction of the bias is toward zero with the degree of attenuation proportional to the squared correlation between the personal finances item and the microlevel changes in real income.

Neglecting the unreliability of the personal financial situation item as a measure of real income change, Table 1 reports an estimate of the effect of a 1% change in real income based on the regression reported above and

TABLE 1. Cross-Sectional Estimates of the Effects of Personal Finances on Voting

Year	Personal Finances			Real Personal Disposable Income Growth Rate	Incumbent Vote Loss for 1% Real Income Decline[a]
	Better	Same	Worse		
1956	39	42	18	3.0	0.34
1960	33	47	20	0.0	0.09
1964	46	40	15	5.6	0.08
1968	34	47	20	2.8	0.19
1972	36	42	23	3.3	0.25
1976	34	35	31	3.0	0.20
1980	32	25	42	-1.0	0.18

[a]See note 4 for explanation.

Kiewiet's (1983) presidential vote equations.[4] The income effects range from a 0.08 loss in the incumbent party vote share to a 0.34 loss for every percentage point decline in real income. On average the estimated vote loss for a 1% real income decline is about 0.2%. Not only are the estimated effects small relative to those found in the aggregate time-series studies, but the estimates are unstable. (Similar calculations could be made for congressional elections, but the estimates are frequently perversely signed so that the exercise would be pointless.)

Various explanations have been proposed to account for the discrepancies between the cross-sectional and time-series estimates. One approach employed to find a microlevel foundation for the aggregate relationship between economic conditions and voting was to identify subsets of voters whose political behavior was more sensitive to their personal economic situation. Weatherford (1978) found that working-class voters who had just experienced the hardship of a recession composed just such a group. In a study discussed earlier, Hibbing and Alford (1981) argued that incumbent congressmen of the president's party are more easily credited or blamed by voters in their districts for fluctuations in their personal economic conditions. Finally, according to Feldman (1982), voters' decisions in presidential elections reflect the state of their families' finances only to the extent "there is a perception of social (economic, governmental) responsibility for financial well-being" (p. 449). Most of these studies are based on data from one or two elections, so there is some doubt about the generalizability of their findings (Fiorina, 1983). In any event, even if these findings are to be believed, in no way do they resolve the discrepancy between the cross-sectional and time-series estimates. That they have identified groups of voters for whom personal economic considerations are relatively more important in deciding how to vote has to be balanced against the fact that each of these groups of voters constitute a distinct minority of the electorate.

Probably the most interesting feature of these studies, however, is that they all share the same key assumption that economic conditions influence voting decisions only to the extent that voters attribute responsibility for these conditions to incumbent politicians. In each of these studies the pattern of evidence which is reported is interpreted in terms of the differential attribution of responsibility. Thus, voters' decisions in presidential elections are influenced much more strongly by trends in family finances because the president is assigned the lion's share of credit or blame. Kiewiet (1983) found the following:

> It is the president who is primarily responsible for the general thrust of macroeconomic policy, whether it be the "guns and butter" policies of Lyndon Johnson or the "Reaganomics" of the current administration. It is also the president who shoulders most of the credit or blame for the ultimate success or failure of the policies pursued by his administration. Consequently, any sort of economic problem which voters might be concerned about will exert a larger influence upon their choice between presidential candidates than upon that between the candidates for Congress. (p. 126)

Hibbing and Alford (1981) also pointed to differential attributions of responsibility to account for the greater influence of economic concerns in elections involving incumbent incumbents:

> If anyone is held responsible for current financial conditions, it should be those who are in the best position to take credit or receive blame for these conditions — that is senior incumbents of the in-party incumbents, those gradations should be related in some positive fashion to tenure. (p. 435)

Feldman (1982) invoked the same line of reasoning:

Personal economic conditions will influence voting behavior only when there is a perception of social (economic, governmental) responsibility for financial well-being. (p. 449)

In short, the assumption that economic conditions influence voting decisions only to the extent that voters attribute responsibility for these conditions to incumbent politicians is ubiquitous in this literature. That this is so, however, raises the crucial question of exactly how such attributions should be modeled.

More precisely, do voters, having experienced a stream of economic outcomes, attempt to discriminate between that part of it which is properly attributable to the actions of incumbent policymakers and that part of it which is not? Or do they simply take this stream of outcomes at face value and evaluate the incumbents more or less favorably on the basis of it? Strict notions of voter rationality would certainly suggest that they would attempt to differentiate between income change which is "government-induced" and that which is not; after all, why should an individual choose between competing candidates on the basis of things that neither could possibly control? On the other hand, this task may well place large information costs and unreasonable demands on the inferential powers of the typical voter. The avoidance of these costs was one of the major features of Downs's (1957) model of retrospective voting. Similarly, Butler and Stokes (1969) argued that "the technical difficulties of assigning responsibility for past government action or inaction" force voters to adopt a satisficing strategy:

Modern electorates tend to "solve" this problem of causal reasoning by assuming that certain causal relationships must exist rather than by discerning what they are. Electors focus their attention primarily on certain conditions which they value positively or negatively and simply assume that past or future governments affect them. The public can call for a government's dismissal in economic hard times just as it calls for a team manager's dismissal in a losing season, in each case concluding that causal relationships must exist without knowing in detail what they are. (p. 25)

But are such distinctions really so difficult to make? There are many predictable changes in a person's financial situation over the life cycle which voters understand and anticipate. Some are favorable and improve one's financial state (e.g., finishing graduate school and taking a full-time teaching position), whereas others decrease one's income (e.g., having a child enter college or retiring). It seems farfetched that voters would credit the incumbent party with changes of this kind. Or to give a more extreme example: suppose a distant relative dies, leaving a substantial inheritance. Does the lucky recipient attribute his or her good fortune to whoever happens to be in the White House at that moment?

Moreover, there is a good deal of evidence that voters rarely associate changes in their personal financial situation with government policy. When asked *why* their family financial situation had changed, Kinder and Mebane (1983) reported that "virtually no one sees government policy contributing to their family's economic achievements or setbacks. In any single national survey, no more than 1% of those interviewed point directly to government." This is not to say that voters place *no* responsibility on government for their personal economic fortunes, but only that not *all* changes in a family finances have political effects. Schlozman and Verba's (1979) interviews with several hundred unemployed individuals yielded very similar findings, as did the studies of Brody and Sniderman (1977; and Sniderman and Brody, 1977) on "coping" and the ethic of self-reliance.

The question of whether or not voters hold government responsible for *all* changes in their personal financial situation concerns the specification of Equation 1. Kramer (1983) argued that voters respond not to changes in their real income, but instead to government-induced changes in real income. He partitioned the change in a voter's real income x_{it} into a component g_{it} which can be attributed to the actions of the incumbent government and an idiosyncratic component e_{it}:

$$x_{it} = g_{it} + e_{it} \qquad (3)$$

Kramer did not claim that voters are able to distinguish precisely which fraction of their income change is actually government induced, but only that some substantial part of the change in a family's financial situation is caused by forces clearly outside the government's control.

Replacing x_{it} by g_{it} in (1) yields:

$$v_{it} = \beta g_{it} + u_{it} \qquad (4)$$

If (4) is the correct specification for the vote equation (i.e., if g_{it} and u_{it} are uncorrelated), then the cross-sectional estimate of β obtained by regressing vote on change in family income will (under the conditions of White, 1982) converge to

$$\beta^* = \beta \; \frac{\text{var}(g_{it}) + \text{cov}(g_{it}, e_{it})}{\text{var}(x_{it})} \; + \; \frac{\text{cov}(u_{it}, e_{it})}{\text{var}(x_{it})} \qquad (5)$$

with probability one as sample size increases.

From (5) there are several obvious sources of bias in the cross-sectional estimates:

1. If the government is responsible for a relatively small fraction of the cross-sectional variation in family finances, then $\text{var}(g_{it}) < \text{var}(x_{it})$.
2. If government-induced income changes tend to compensate for non-government-induced income changes, then $\text{cov}(g_{it}, e_{it}) < 0$.
3. If u_{it} includes party or other effects on voting which are correlated with non-government-induced income changes, then the sign of $\text{cov}(u_{it}, e_{it})$ will vary from sample to sample, depending on, among other things, which party is in power at the time of the sample.

The first two effects discussed above will bias the cross-sectional estimates downward (i.e, toward zero). The third effect can bias the cross-sectional estimates either upward or downward, but, in any event, will make the estimates vary from one cross section to another. Kramer argued that these biases account for the findings of the cross-sectional studies reviewed above: unstable coefficient estimates that, on average, are somewhat smaller than those found in aggregate time-series studies.

Whether retrospective voting should be specified as a function of total income change (x_{it}) or government-induced income change (g_{it}) is seen to be a question of central importance. If the latter specification is the correct one, then absence of income effects found in many cross-sectional studies is no more than a statistical artifact. It will be difficult to resolve this issue with current survey measures. Nor is posing a question to survey respondents such as "What percentage of the increase or decrease in your income over the past year do you attribute to the effects of government policy?" likely to be very informative. Such calculations, if they occur at all, are probably subconscious and the survey responses may be tainted by rationalization. The most promising strategy in our view would be to identify—as objectively as possible—different sources of income change and then to estimate the separate effect of each type of income change on voting.

In view of the poor results obtained with the personal finances item, attention has shifted to other forms of economic effects that might provide a link between micro- and macrolevel findings. The sociotropic voting hypothesis of Kinder and Kiewiet (1979, 1981) is one effort in this direction. They argued that it is difficult for individuals in this country to disentangle the effect of current government policies upon their own economic fortunes from a whole host of other factors which affect the demand for their labor and the value of their assets. According to Kiewiet (1983), the state of the nation's economy, however, reflects upon the performance of the incumbent party in a far more direct fashion:

> Conditions in the national economy, of course, are probably not as personally salient to most individuals as their own financial situation. But national economic

assessments are, by definition, of general, widespread phenomena. Consequently, in most people's minds national economic conditions reflect upon the performance and policies of the incumbent administration much more directly than the conditions of their own lives. . . . [What national economic assessments lack in personal relevance, they make up for by being of more obvious political relevance. (p. 130)

Their hypothesis is that perceptions of national economic conditions and events determine the degree to which voters support incumbent candidates. In other words, the aggregate level time-series findings were generated not so much by voters responding to their own individual economic circumstances, but rather by their response to the aggregate level economic data themselves. Kinder and Kiewiet's analyses (1979, 1981) were based primarily upon responses to a question which closely resembled the family finances item:

> Now turning to business conditions in the country as a whole, would you say that at the present time business conditions are better or worse than they were a year ago, or about the same?

Employing a fairly simple model, they found that the more favorably voters viewed recent trends in national business conditions, the higher the probability of their voting for incumbent candidates. As with the family finances measure, however, the influence of this variable upon voting decisions was considerably stronger in presidential elections than in congressional races.

It is also the case that the distribution of responses to the national business conditions item swings much more sharply between good and bad years than the distribution of responses to the family finances item. Furthermore, the results of Kiewiet's (1983) simulations indicated that voting on the basis of recent trends in national business conditions could account for roughly twice as much variation in the level of support received by incumbent presidential and congressional candidates than voting in response to shifting family financial fortunes. He calculated that the effects of both variables taken together accounted for about half of the aggregate change in votes implied by Kramer's and Fair's findings.

Analyses of sociotropic voting are also, as Kramer (1983) has pointed out, subject to serious problems of evidence and interpretation. If a strict interpretation of the sociotropic hypothesis is taken, then the relevant variable is either the average income change (x_t) or its government-induced counterpart (denoted G_t in Kramer's analysis). Neither of these variables varies in a cross section, so it is hopeless to obtain any evidence about this form of sociotropic voting from a cross-sectional analysis. Any observed cross-sectional variation, according to Kramer, will reflect either measurement error in the survey instrument or differences in voter perceptions.

We suspect that cross-sectional variation in perceptions of national economic trends arises from many sources. Some of it will just be partisan rationalization, but some of it may reflect different sources of information available to voters. For example, in depressed areas voters may perceive national conditions to be worse than do voters in booming areas.[5] Other variation may depend on the specific form of voters' utility functions. Different individuals may focus on different economic indicators, weight the same indicators differently, or exhibit different rates of time preference. Having acknowledged that survey measures of national economic conditions may be more than an amalgamation of rationalization and measurement error, we should caution that we have very little understanding of precisely what they do measure (see Kiewiet, 1983, chap. 6).

The second major difficulty with analyzing sociotropic voting is one of interpretation. Kiewiet (1983) pointed out that

> voting in response to national economic assessments could reflect very different motivations. It could have its basis in a purely patriotic or altruistic concern for the interests of all Americans. Alternatively, it could be entirely motivated by a self-interested concern for one's economic well-being; in this case voters simply use information about national economic conditions as an indicator of how well the incumbent administration has promoted their own (and their fellow citizens') welfare. (p. 131)

In fact, if voters wish to evaluate incumbent performance on the basis of government-induced changes in their own income, the national average real income change provides a reasonable basis to distinguish idiosyncratic income changes from those which are government induced. Voters' responses to the national economic conditions question may therefore be a better indicator of their estimate of government-induced income change in their personal income than is the personal finances item.

POOLING CROSS SECTIONS AND TIME SERIES

The data problems that trouble cross-sectional analyses of retrospective voting are not solely statistical in nature. Inasmuch as the performance indicators used to estimate retrospective voting models are subject to error, the nature of this error is very different in the cross section than in the time series. More specifically, government policy will cause different kinds of income change in cross sections and time series. Depending upon where researchers learned their macroeconomics, national output and employment levels are either viewed as quite sensitive to fiscal and monetary policies (Kramer, having spent some time at the Cowles Commission, attributes roughly half the variance in the rate of real income growth to government policy) or as completely irrelevant (as is believed in some sectors of Chicago and Minneapolis).

However one stands on the new classical macroeconomics, all can agree that the government redistributes income among citizens in myriad ways: taxes, transfers, regulation, inflation, and so forth. In the cross section, all of the government-induced income *variation* is of the redistributive variety. As indicated earlier, Kramer argued that this variation makes up a relatively small fraction of the change in incomes for individuals in any period. Moreover, knowing that an individual is the beneficiary of a particular government redistributive policy will also indicate the likely partisanship of that individual. This relationship will not be stable over time or across party administrations (more Democrats receive welfare benefits than oil depreciation allowances, so changing one policy affects Democrats and Republicans differently), and as a consequence, little systematic can be learned from the personal finances item in a cross section. By aggregating, Kramer argued, it is possible to average out most idiosyncratic and redistributive incoime effects.

One hypothesis that has not been investigated here is that voting on aggregate performance and individual redistribution are of a different character.[6] It seems quite plausible that voting based on aggregate performance might be incumbency oriented; that is, voters could ignore the policies used to achieve macroeconomic goals, support any ones that seem to work, and oppose any that fail. After all, both parties claim to have the secret to macroeconomic success and if economists cannot agree on who is right, why should voters try? On redistributional issues, however, the parties do take different positions, and voters have little difficulty determining which policies benefit them. It would be unwise for the recipients of government benefits indiscriminately to credit the incumbent party — which may be trying to cut those benefits — for its supposed largesse. Aggregate performance levels would indicate the skill of the incumbent party, while redistributional effects would represent the policy position taken by the incumbent party. A purely self-interested voter might prefer a less-skilled party that was willing to redistribute income in his or her direction (see Rivers, 1983, for analysis of a model of this type).

Combining cross-sectional and time-series data permits, in principle, investigation of these and other interesting hypotheses. Rosenstone (1983), for example, has improved on aggregate electoral forecasts by disaggregating to the state level in a pooled cross-sectional analysis. Markus (1984) has tried pooling seven of the Michigan surveys to test the so-called self-interest and sociotropic voting hypotheses, and before long, many others will probably turn to pooling cross sections in the face of the Kramer critique. While panel data[7] are potentially quite useful for some questions, it is important to understand what it possibly can or cannot tell us. It is shown in the Appendix to this paper that the pooled cross-sectional regression estimate is a weighted average of the relevant cross-sectional estimates and the aggregate time-series estimate. Since, under Kramer's assumptions, *both* the cross-sectional and time-series estimates are biased toward the origin, the pooled cross-sectional estimate will also be biased, since it lies in the convex hull of these estimates. In fact, if (as is the case) the typical cross-sectional variation in real income growth is larger than the average time-series variation, the pooled cross-sectional estimate will lie closer to the average cross-sectional estimate than to the time-series estimate. Hence, no progress has been made toward alleviating the errors-in-variables problem by pooling, nor as yet do we have a feasible way of attacking cross-sectional and time-series issues simultaneously. Pooling, as Hausman and Taylor (1981) have shown, can provide a natural solution to the errors-in-variables problem, but this requires an explicit treatment of measurement errors that has not yet been attempted in retrospective voting models.

WHAT IS TO BE DONE?

The cautionary tone of our survey should not be taken as unduly pessimistic. The retrospective voting literature has raised, we think, a large number of interesting questions about the relationship between elections and public policy. If the answers that have been obtained are partial and limited, there is nonetheless an identifiable body of findings contained in this literature. The growth of knowledge about retrospective voting has been facilitated by the existence of a simple, clearly specified model. Difficulties have arisen when some concepts have not been clearly defined or when the relationship between empirical measures (particularly survey measures) and theoretical concepts have been treated too casually.

Further progress is unlikely to come by continued mining of the same types of data in traditional ways. More promising, in our view, will be efforts to identify new sources and types of data that are potentially informative about outstanding theoretical issues. If a variable of interest, for example, national economic conditions, does not vary in a particular sample (in a cross section for example), one must resort to another source of data (such as panel data). The new source of data will not be automatically free of the problems of the old data (such as measurement error, as discussed in the previous section), and it may entail new problems (e.g., sample selection bias) that could be ignored before. While we do not believe that attempts to solve these problems are guaranteed to be successful, the continued vitality of research in this area depends on the attempts being made.

The other major problem facing those interested in retrospective voting is one of interpretation. By now the proposition that voters will punish incumbents for poor performance should not be controversial. Attempts to elaborate upon this relationship may, however, raise interpretive issues that will require reformulation of the simple retrospective voting model or its extension to behaviors other than voting. For example, partisan voting was frequently viewed as a competitor of the retrospective voting hypothesis until Fiorina (1981) showed how partisanship naturally fitted within the retrospective voting framework. This makes the interpretation of party effects within these models as problematic, particularly in a field where it has been routine practice to "control" for party identification. Similarly, we have argued that the existence of aggregate economic effects on individual political behavior are consistent with either self-interested or sociotropic voting. In this case, it may be necessary to examine behavior on other issues where different decision processes can be more easily distinguished.[8] Here, too, we believe the issues raised in the retrospective voting literature are important and worthy of further attention.

Acknowledgments. Though we alone bear responsibility for the contents of this paper, we have benefited from conversations over the past few years on this topic with Morris Fiorina, Douglas Hibbs, Donald Kinder, and Gerald Kramer. The National Science Foundation provided research support under grant SES-8309994.

NOTES

1. Fiorina (1983) performed a test of equality for the coefficients of the "Better," "Same," and "Worse" dummies in Democratic, open, and Republican seats. Apart from problems with the survey data covered later, Fiorina's test lacks power since it involves open seats and voters whose financial position is unchanged, which are peripheral to the Hibbing-Alford hypothesis. In fact, Fiorina's estimates provide some support for the different treatment of incumbents in midterm but not in presidential election years.
2. Approximately 95% confidence intervals listed in parentheses. Most articles cited below report a variety of specifications with a corresponding range of estimates. The estimates reported here are selected to be representative of the results reported. Readers are encouraged to refer to the original papers rather than rely on our somewhat subjective summary.
3. The variable most highly correlated with the personal finances item is the reported direction of income change relative to the cost of living. For reasons not apparent to us, political scientists tend to prefer questions with better/worse response categories to, for example, reported dollar amounts of income change. Even if respondents do not know exactly how much their income has changed, it is difficult to see how forcing them into vague response categories will reduce measurement error.
4. Kiewiet (1983) reported probit estimates of the form:

$$\text{Prob(Republican Vote)} = \Phi[\beta(\text{Better}) + \gamma(\text{Worse}) + \text{other terms}]$$

If we evaluate the above expression for a voter whose personal financial situation is unchanged (i.e., Better = Worse = 0) and set the "other terms" equal to zero, then we have (approximately):

$$\text{Prob(Republican Vote)} \cong 0.5 + \beta(0.4)(\text{Better}) + \gamma(0.4)(\text{Worse})$$

using an approximation suggested by Amemiya (1981). Using the regression estimates reported in the text, the change in the Republican vote share resulting from a 1% increase in the real income growth rate can be estimated by:

$$\Delta \text{ Prob (Republican Vote)} = \text{Prob (Republican Vote} \mid \text{Better)} \, \Delta \text{ Prob (Better)}$$
$$+ \text{Prob (Republican Vote} \mid \text{Same)} \, \Delta \text{ Prob (Same)}$$
$$+ \text{Prob (Republican Vote} \mid \text{Worse)} \, \Delta \text{ Prob (Worse)}$$

$$= (0.4) \, (0.013B - 0.018_\gamma)$$

The approximate change in the incumbent party (rather than Republican) vote share is reported in the text.

5. This suggests using the state unemployment rate as another indicator for the business conditions item in an errors-in-variables model.

6. The distinction between incumbent-oriented and policy-oriented voting is discussed in Kiewiet (1981). Instead of blaming the incumbents for all forms of economic difficulties, policy-oriented voters support the party that places a higher priority on attacking the problems they find most worrisome. Assuming Democrats place higher priority on full employment and Republicans on price stability (Hibbs, 1977), policy-oriented voting in response to inflation would result in more support for the Republicans, while concern over unemployment would help Democratic candidates, regardless of who the incumbents happened to be.

7. For static models without unobservable individual effects, repeated independent cross sections are equivalent to a panel.

8. Gerald Kramer has suggested that preferences over tax schedules would be a situation where sociotropic behavior can be easily distinguished from narrowly self-interested behavior.

REFERENCES

Ben-Gera, Mikal (1977). "Short-Term Economic Changes and Individual Voting Behavior." Unpublished manuscript, Yale University.

Bloom, Howard S., and H. Douglas Price (1975). "Voter Response to Short-run Economic Conditions: The Asymmetric Effect of Prosperity and Recession." *American Political Science Review* 69:1240–1254.

Brody, Richard A., and Paul M. Sniderman (1977). "From Life Space to Polling Place: The Relevance of Personal Concerns for Voting Behavior." *British Journal of Political Science* 7:337–360.

Butler, David, and Donald Stokes (1969). *Political Change in Britain.* New York: St. Martin's Press.

Campbell, Angus (1966). "Surge and Decline: A Study of Electoral Change." In Angus Campbell et al. (eds.), *Elections and the Political Order.* New York: John Wiley and Sons.

Doyle, William (1980). *Origins of the French Revolution.* New York: Oxford University Press.

Fair, Ray C. (1978). "The Effect of Economic Events on Votes for President." *The Review of Economics and Statistics* 60:159–173.

Feldman, Stanley (1982). "Economic Self-Interest and Political Behavior." *American Journal of Political Science* 26:446–466.

Fiorina, Morris P. (1978). "Economic Retrospective Voting in American National

Elections: A Micro-Analysis." *American Journal of Political Science* 22:426–443.

Fiorina, Morris P. (1981). "Short and Long-term Effects of Economic Conditions on Individual Voting Decisions." In Douglas Hibbs, Heimo Fassbender, and Douglas Rivers (eds.), *Contemporary Political Economy.* Amsterdam: North-Holland.

Fiorina, Morris P. (1981). *Retrospective Voting in American National Elections.* New Haven: Yale University Press, p. 5.

Hausman, Jerry A., and William E. Taylor (1981). "Panel Data and Unobservable Individual Effects." *Econometrica* 49:1377–1398.

Hibbs, Douglas A. (1979). "The Mass Public and Macroeconomic Policy: The Dynamics of Public Opinion Toward Unemployment and Inflation." *American Journal of Political Science* 23:705–731.

Hibbs, Douglas A., and Nicholas Vasilatos (1982). "Economic Outcomes and Political Support for British Governments among Occupational Classes: A Dynamic Analysis." *American Political Science Review* 76:259–279.

Hibbs, Douglas A., Douglas Rivers, and Nicholas Vasilatos (1982). "On the Demand for Economic Outcomes: Macroeconomic Performance and Mass Political Support in the United States, Great Britain, and Germany. *Journal of Politics* 43: 426–462.

Kernell, Sam (1978). "Explaining Presidential Popularity." *American Political Science Review* 72:506–522.

Kiewiet, D. Roderick (1983). *Macroeconomics and Micropolitics.* Chicago: University of Chicago Press.

Kinder, Donald R. (1981). "Presidents, Popularity, and Public Opinion." *Public Opinion Quarterly* 45:1–21.

Kinder, Donald R., and D. Roderick Kiewiet (1979). "Economic Discontent and Political Behavior: The Role of Personal Grievances and Collective Economic Judgements in Congressional Voting." *American Journal of Political Science* 23: 495–517.

Kinder, Donald R., and D. Roderick Kiewiet (1981). "Sociotropic Politics: The American Case." *British Journal of Political Science* 11:129–161.

Kinder, Donald R., and Walter Mebane (1983). "Politics and Economics in Everyday Life." In Kristen Monroe (ed.), *The Political Process and Economic Change.* New York: Agathon Press.

Klorman, Ricardo (1978). "Trend in Personal Finances and the Vote." *Public Opinion Quarterly* 42:31–48.

Kramer, Gerald H. (1977). "Short-Term Fluctuations in U.S. Voting Behavior, 1896–1964." *American Political Science Review* 65:131–143.

Kramer, Gerald H. (1983). "The Ecological Fallacy Revisited: Aggregate- Versus Individual-Level Findings on Economics and Elections and Sociotropic Voting." *American Political Science Review* 77:92–111.

Markus, Gregory B. (1984, February). "The Impact of Personal and National Economic Conditions on the Vote: Results from a Pooled Cross-Sectional Analysis." Paper presented at the Weingart Conference on the Institutional Context of Elections, California Institute of Technology, Pasadena, Calif.

Meltzer, Allan H., and Marc Vellrath (1975). "The Effects of Economic Policies on Votes for the Presidency: Some Evidence from Recent Elections." *Journal of Law and Economics* 18:781-798.

Monroe, Kristen (1979). "Economic Analyses of Electoral Behavior: A Critical Review." *Political Behavior* 1:137-173.

Nerlove, Marc (1972). "Lags in Economic Behavior." *Econometrica* 40:221-258.

Norpoth, Helmut (1984). "Economics, Politics, and the Cycle of Presidential Popularity." *Political Behavior* 6 (3):253-274.

Nossiter, T. J. (1974). *Influence, Opinion, and Political Idioms in Reformed England: Case Studies from the North-east, 1832-74*. New York: Harper and Row.

Olney, R. J. (1973). *Lincolnshire Politics, 1832-1885*. Oxford, U.K.: Oxford University Press.

Owens, John R., and Edward C. Olson (1980). "Economic Fluctuations and Congressional Elections." *American Journal of Political Science* 24:469-493.

Rivers, Douglas (1980, August). "The Dynamics of Party Support in the American Electorate, 1952-1976." Paper presented at the annual meeting of the American Political Science Association, Washington, D.C.

Rivers, Douglas (1983, September). "Policy versus Performance in Formal Voting Models." Paper presented at the annual meeting of the American Political Science Association, Chicago, Ill.

Rivers, Douglas (1984, February). "Seats, Votes, and the Electoral Connection." Paper presented at the Weingart Conference on the Institutional Context of Elections, California Institute of Technology, Pasadena, Calif.

Rosenstone, Steven (1983). *Forecasting Presidential Elections*. New Haven: Yale University Press.

Rosenstone, Steven, John Mark Hansen and Donald R. Kinder (1984). "Measuring Personal Economic Well-Being." Report submitted to the Board of Overseers, National Election Study, and the 1984 National Election Study Planning Committee.

Schlozman, Kay, and Sidney Verba (1979). *Injury to Insult*. Cambridge, Mass.: Harvard University Press, pp. 204-205.

Sniderman, Paul M., and Richard A. Brody (1977). "Coping: The Ethic of Self-Reliance." *American Journal of Political Science* 21:501-521.

Stigler, George J. (1973). "General Economic Conditions and National Elections." *American Economic Review* 63:160-167.

Tufte, Edward R. (1975). "Determinants of the Outcomes of Midterm Congressional Elections." *American Political Science Review* 69:812-826.

Tufte, Edward R. (1978). *Political Control of the Economy*. Princeton: Princeton University Press.

Weatherford, M. Stephen (1978). "Economic Conditions and Electoral Outcomes: Class Differences in the Political Response to Recession." *American Journal of Political Science* 22:917-938.

White, Halbert (1982). "Maximum Likelihood Estimation of Misspecified Models." *Econometrics* 50:1-26.

APPENDIX

Let $i=1,...,N$ index the observations in samples $t=1,...,T$ so that (x_t, y_t) composes the data from sample t with $x_t = (x_{1t},...,x_{Nt})'$ and $y_t = (y_{1t},...,y_{Nt})'$. (The restriction that the samples be of the same size is unnecessary and can easily be eliminated.) Let $x = (x_1',...,x_T')'$ and $y = (y_1',...,y_T')'$ and define the orthogonal projection operators:

$$P_N = \frac{1}{N} 1_N 1_N \qquad Q_N = I_N - P_N$$

where 1_N denotes an $N \times 1$ vector of ones. Note that $P_N y_t = \bar{y}_t 1_N$ where $\bar{y}_t = (1/N) \sum_{i=1}^{N} y_{it}$ and similarly for x_t. With this notation established, consider the following three regressions:

1. *Cross section*
   $b_t = x_t Q_N y_t / x_t Q_N x_t \quad (t = 1,...,T)$

2. *Average time series*
   $b = x'(I_T \otimes P_N) Q_{NT} (I_T \otimes P_N) y / x'(I_T \otimes P_N) Q_{NT} (N_T \otimes P_N) x$

3. *Pooled cross section*
   $b = x' Q_{NT} y / x' Q_{NT} x$

That is, for each cross section $t=1,...,T$, y_t can be regressed on x_t yielding an estimate b_t. Alternatively, $\bar{y}_t$ can be regressed on $\bar{x}_t$ yielding the average time series estimate b. Instead of averaging, the cross sections could be pooled and the NT observations used to produce the pooled cross-sectional estimate b. ($\otimes$ denotes the Kronecker product.) It is easily verified that:

$$Q_{NT} = (I_T \otimes Q_N) + (Q_T \otimes P_N)$$

Using $Q_N P_N = 0$ gives:

$$(I_T \otimes P_N) Q_{NT} (N_T \otimes P_N) = Q_T \otimes P_N$$

so that

$$b = x'(Q_T \otimes P_N) y / x'(Q_T \otimes P_N) x$$

With some rearrangement and substitution we find:

$$b = [bx'(Q_T \otimes P_N)x + \sum_{t=1}^{T} b_t(x_t' Q_N x_t)] / [x'(Q_T \otimes P_N)x + \sum_{t=1}^{T} x_t Q_N x_t]$$

We have shown that the pooled cross-sectional estimator b is a weighted average of the average time series estimator b and the T cross-sectional estimates $b_1,...,b_T$:

$$b = w_0 b + \sum_{t=1}^{T} w_t b_t \qquad (\sum_{t=0}^{T} w_t = 1, \ w_t \geq 0 \text{ for all } t)$$

where

$$w_0 = Ts^2 / (\sum_{t=1}^{T} s_t^2 + Ts^2)$$

$$w_t = s_t^2 / (\sum_{t=1}^{T} s_t^2 + Ts^2) \qquad (t=1,...,T)$$

Here s_t^2 is the variance of x in sample t and s^{-2} is the variance of x, i.e.,

$$s^{-2} = \frac{1}{T} \sum_{t=1}^{T} (x_t - x)^2 \qquad x = \frac{1}{T} \sum_{t=1}^{T} x_t$$

CHAPTER **12**

Economic Determinants and Electoral Outcomes: Some Personal Observations

Marie France Toinet
Fondation Nationale des Sciences Politiques, Paris

Have political scientists proven much in demonstrating that there is some kind of relationship between the state of the economy and electoral fortune at the polls? After all, the *vox populi* has always said as much. In the United States, it is often pointed out that "Americans vote their pocketbooks"; in France, the saying goes that "Frenchmen have their hearts on the left and their pocketbooks on the right." Furthermore, politicians are quite aware of that phenomenon, as Richard Nixon (1962, p. 309) stated very clearly: "I knew from bitter experience how, in both 1954 and 1958, slumps which hit bottom early in October contributed to substantial losses in the House and the Senate. The power of the "pocketbook" issue was shown more clearly in 1958 than in any off-year election in history. On the international front, the Administration had had one of its best years . . . yet, the economic dip in October was obviously uppermost in the people's minds when they went to the polls. They completely rejected the President's appeal for the election of Republicans to the House and Senate."

It would be well enough if political scientists had scientifically demonstrated the soundness of common sense: science, to affirm itself, does not have to disprove commonly held beliefs. But it is even more interesting to consider that, for a long time, political scientists did not see such a relationship, at least for midterm congressional elections; as Key (1964, p. 567) put it: "No such logical explanation can completely describe what the electorate does at midterm elections." Political scientists have now demonstrated that there is some tie between the economic state of the nation and political judgment about the incumbent party. It is quite an achievement. How much is thus proven remains to be taken into account.

That there is a relationship between the economic situation and electoral outcomes fails to insure that it is either regular or predictive. Let me speak first to the point about regularity. Economics probably always plays some role. But, its influence may peak some years or bottom out in other elections, if only because one economic determinant might become more or less visible in the public mind according to the following: (1) the period (inflation, in France, did not have the same influence before World War I, where it simply did not exist as a reality—and after); (2) the economic cycle (the same rate of unemployment will be considered more dramatic when the economy is entering a recession than when it is booming); or (3) the type of voter (inflation is good for borrowers, bad for lenders).

Now to the point about prediction. As Crewe (1984) has written:

Until recently, election specialists assumed that public opinion moved in a regular cycle which could be statistically "modelled" as a function of (a) time since the previous election and (b) changes in the inflation and unemployment rates . . . blown sky-high by the 1979–83 Parliament, that approach has been replaced by the more fruitful "shock-inertia" model. Roughly translated, this assumes that public opinion is stationary until moved by a dramatic event such as the Falklands, or the SDP breakaway, after which it remains stationary until the next "shock." Economic determinants may be a permanent underpinning of elections, or a dramatic shock, or both. It is doubtful they have a reliable (year to year) predictive value. The relationship may be constant. It is not necessarily linear.

It is very surprising for an outsider to realize that, at least in the studies considered, there seems to be little attempt to compare the impact of economic determinants with that of other determinants such as foreign policy matters or "social factors" (race relations, fear of crime, or abortion, for instance). Certainly, the problem tackled is "economic determinants," but are electoral reactions to economic growth or recession going to be the same when the country is primarily concerned with a foreign war or when peace and war are not uppermost? In the last 48 years, problems of peace or war were uppermost in the minds of the American people half the time, according to the Gallup Poll. This issue was mentioned along with another "non-foreign policy issue" another 7 times. Unemployment and/or high cost of living were considered the most important problems only 11 times, and in conjunction with other issues, another 8 times. Furthermore, even when, as in 1980, the high cost of living and unemployment appear as the most pressing concerns, all analysts agree that, if the hostages in Iran had been freed before the election, say in August, Reagan would probably have lost the election. Along the same lines, Thatcher would have lost the 1983 parliamentary elections in Britain on the face of her economic record: the Falklands saved her majority.

The point is that the relationship between economic determinants and electoral outcomes is not a one-way street; there may be intermediate variables disturbing the direct relationship. It is not that political scientists are unaware of the problem: Kramer (1971), Mueller (1973), Kernell (1978), and Lewis-Beck (1980) have considered it. Kramer (1971, p. 137) stated that he eliminated the "wartime elections of 1918; 1942 and 1944 have also been dropped, since wartime conditions and controls would substantially distort the meanings of our price and income series." Later on (p. 140), he wrote: "With respect to other years, there are substantial residuals in 1898, 1932, 1950 and 1964. In 1898 and in 1950, U.S. troops were involved in hostilities abroad and in both years the vote for the incumbent was appreciably less than predicted, *which is suggestive*. (The residuals in the immediate post-war elections of 1920 and 1946, though smaller in magnitude, also follow the same pattern.) The model underestimated the magnitudes of the Democratic landslides of 1932 and 1964, which is not surprising in view of *the special circumstances of those elections*." In other words, some of the most critical, important, and watershed elections in the United States do not fit the model. Lewis-Beck (1980, p. 313), who took into account the Algerian war, recognized that "it is quite possible that a significant Algerian war effect would have emerged if the series could have been extended back prior to 1960." And he concluded, after building and using a dummy variable on the war: "In any case, with or without the Algerian variable in the equation, the coefficients of the economic variables, which are my main concern, remain quite stable." Thus, Lewis-Beck demonstrated — at least after 1960 — that the war-peace issue does not constitute an *essentially* disturbing factor in the relationship between economic determination and presidential popularity — economic factors have constantly the same effect — but we still do not know if they are at all times the dominant explanatory factor. Certainly, economic determinants are a good permanent indicator. But are they the only one? Michelat and Simon (1977) have convincingly argued that, in France at least, religious behavior is one of the determinants of electoral behavior, if not the best.

Very conspicuously absent from the studies — except in Arcelus and Meltzer (1975) and Rosenstone (1983) — is nonvoting, which, in my view, is as much an electoral outcome as partisan alignment. Arcelus and Meltzer (1975,

p. 1232) stated very convincingly that "a voter's opportunity set includes more than a choice between rival candidates. He can—and many voters do— choose not to vote. Even casual examination of voting statistics suggests that changes in the participation rate of eligible voters often are larger than changes in the share of votes received by the major parties." I would quarrel with "often" and state that at least for the variance between off-year congressional elections and presidential elections (a situation very much studied on the American side) it is "always" the case. Unfortunately, the Arcelus and Meltzer study bogs down because they were obsessed with proving "rationality" instead of looking at the "political significance" of voting-nonvoting (Subileau and Toinet, 1984). I submit, particularly in the French case, that there is a relationship that would be worth looking into between economic determinants and electoral participation. Furthermore, there is no doubt that there is a direct relationship (once more, at least in the French case) between electoral turnout and partisan alignment (Subileau and Toinet, 1983). In the evaluation of the importance of economic variables, it might be interesting to consider turnout (and variance in turnout) both as an intermediate variable (with an eye on the effect on partisan alignment) and as a dependent variable.

Incumbency is one of the themes that has been thoroughly examined in the American studies. But *incumbency* has been defined as *party* incumbency. As Kramer (1971, p. 135) pointed out "the definition of the 'incumbent' party also requires some care since because of the division of power it is possible for one party to control either or both houses of Congress, while the other controls the presidency." Kramer (1971, p. 136) therefore decided: "we will take the party which controls the presidency as the incumbent party." The problem is that there is another *incumbency* factor that seems even more important in the American case: the *incumbency* of congressional candidates. This seems to be perhaps the most powerful explanatory factor in electoral outcomes if we consider that, since World War II, at least 90% of incumbents on average have been reelected. It is interesting to compare this with the French case where (under the Fifth Republic, at least) less than two-thirds of the incumbents are reelected. In the American case, election results are much closer when there is no incumbent. A differential effect of economic determinants on electoral outcomes might be uncovered if incumbent and nonincumbent districts were compared.

If we look at *party incumbency,* we have to wonder if the situation is going to be similar if we have *parties* incumbency. Who, for instance, among the Socialists and the Communists (or the Giscardians and Chiraquians) will benefit from or be harmed by the economic situation at the polls? Most probably, it is not going to be similar for both partners in the coalition. Along those lines, party incumbency may play a different role when there are two fairly similar parties (as in the American case) or two more strongly opposed coalitions (as in France, the Left or Right). French supporters may be dissatisfied; but, are they willing to go to the extreme and switch to the other side, as they easily do in the American case?

Another factor that might be expected to influence the impact of economic conditions would be the amount of electoral competition. Compare the United States and France: in no case since World War II has there been a one-candidate first ballot legislative election in France. But this occurs in about 10% of American congressional elections. I have suggested (Toinet, 1976) the strong impact this has on American participation. In 1974, average participation was 36%; however, there was just a 21% turnout when there was only one candidate, 28% turnout when there was a third party candidate, 38% when there were two major party candidates (one weak and one strong), and 50% when the difference of votes between Republicans and Democrats was less than 5 percentage points. In other words, the stronger the alternative, the greater the turnout. Do economic determinants weigh differently in those cases?

Still, in the incumbency-competition realm, many American specialists have shown the importance of former political experience in capturing either an incumbent's seat or a seat open through retirement or redistricting. As Jacobson and Kernell (quoted in Lipset, 1983, p. 89) have demonstrated: "Seventeen of the 23 incumbents who lost in 1982 were defeated by candidates who had previously held elective office. A majority of the 80 House freshmen in the class of '82, most of whom captured open seats, had served in state legislatures." In other words, is it political experience *and* incumbency that count in turnover (which actually occurs mainly in open seats), or is it economic determinants? As a matter of fact, if one considers the elections of 1982, one realizes that (1) the models used for predicting the number of seats each party would win in the House of Representatives were certainly more off-target in predictive use than they had been in retrospective use (Witt, 1983); and (2) a great part of the turnover happened in open-seat districts (through retirement or redistricting). Thus, did economic determinants play an equal role in incumbent districts and in open-seat districts? If the answer is positive, it seems to indicate that economic determinants are not essential in determining the outcome, granted this outcome was quite different in incumbent and open-seat districts. Some analysts of economic determinants seem ready to say as much. As Jacobson (who was off-target in 1982, predicting a loss of 45 to 55 for the GOP, which limited its actual defeat to 26 seats, but who was quick to say that campaign financing, strategic decisions by politicians, and candidate quality suggested smaller GOP losses) stated (see Broder, 1983) at the 1983 APSA convention: "Economic issues exercise no simple mechanical influence over voting decisions." His analysis was that, in being able to operate as a party, Republicans succeeded in minimizing Democratic gains. Fiorina (1978, p. 440) came to a similar conclusion about the 1974 congressional election: "Perhaps election returns vary not with objective economic conditions but with self-fulfilling expectations about those conditions held by the candidates and parties." But, then, are we still thinking there is a relationship between economic determinants and electoral outcomes? Voters and candidates are not interchangeable; voters' decisions are not candidates' decisions.

Just considering the aggregate data, it is interesting to note that most studies — not to say all — work on time series taking into account *global* results. Before World War II, some studies (Gosnell and Coleman, 1940; Ogburn and Coombs, 1940) were cross-sectional, but Kramer (1971, pp. 132–133) rejected them for the reason that "the correlations are small and account for only around 6% of the variance of the dependent variable" or, that the findings "create the overall impression of no systematic relationship between changes in prosperity and the Roosevelt vote." But with better data nowadays — at least on a state basis — and more sophisticated statistical tools, it seems tempting to check whether the models, offered on a national and long-range basis, work. They could be applied, for instance, across high-unemployment and low-unemployment states or districts or (if the data exist) between incumbent and open-seats districts. We have used precinct analysis on nonvoting in France, and it works quite well (Subileau and Toinet, 1983). Once more, I do not think we should give up one type of unit analysis for another but rather try to complement the global analysis with smaller unit analysis. I submit that the smaller the unit, the better our understanding of the rationale for a causal relationship detected at the global level, if only because the global level enables us to establish the actuality of the phenomenon but washes out the explanatory differentials.

Some analysts do consider that aggregate data are not the best way to get at the heart of the problem. For instance, Lewis-Beck (1983, p. 347) commenting on American findings, stated: "These macrolevel findings were rather confusing. While most showed an economic effect, a few did not. Further, among those which did, there was little agreement on the nature of the effect. That is, was it unemployment, income, or inflation which influenced the voter? And, what form did this influence take? Such perplexing questions could not be resolved at the aggregate level. . . ." What tactics to adopt then? "Analysis of the impact of economics on the vote had to descend to individual level survey data." And Lewis-Beck (1983, p. 34) concluded in the French case, "I find that economic conditions, both personal and collective, exert a significant influence on party choice in French legislative elections." The problem here is that Lewis-Beck mentioned "the vote" and "party choice in French legislative elections." The studies demonstrate, in my opinion, that people in successive *samples* associate, with a rather high level of cohesion, economic conditions and presidential *popularity* or how they *intend* to vote.

But, whatever the merits of recent articles on the problem (Lafay, 1978; Sigelman, 1979; and Lewis-Beck and Rice, 1982), I remain unconvinced that presidential popularity and/or vote intentions translate directly into *actual* votes 1 year or 6 months later. Kramer (1983) wrote as much: ". . . individual-level survey data, at least when analyzed with the usual methods, are not really very useful for studying the effects of short-term economic fluctuations on individual voting decisions" (p. 94). As a matter of fact, in France, the index of satisfaction with the Socialist party was at its highest (51%) in 1974, when it lost the presidential election and lower in 1981 (47%) when it won (Parodi and Duhamel, 1981, p. 158). And the vote intentions were quite different and much higher, to the very end, than the index of popularity in favor of President Giscard d'Estaing. Even more interesting for distinguishing popularity and vote intentions: in December 1983, a survey published in *VSD* showed that, while the popularity of the French government was way down, more people *intended* to vote for the Left than for the Right if "the presidential election were held today." But would it happen? In other words, if there is a strong relation between economic conditions and government popularity, it may not—or it may—translate into actual voting. Furthermore, as the French case seems to show, there may be a sharp difference between types of elections—even between the two ballots. In 1977, the voters gave a harsh lesson to the Giscardian government in the municipal elections but gave it a majority in the 1978 legislative elections. In the 1983 municipal elections, the pattern was even more interesting; the voters also gave a very harsh lesson on the first ballot to the Socialist government but did not seem to want to go all the way and somewhat rallied in its favor on the second ballot.

Whatever the respective merits of aggregate data and survey data, I have a feeling, from my own work on nonvoting, that they are *complementary*; each type brings some information we cannot get through the other type. But, we cannot hope to get at the heart of the matter by using ever more sophisticated, statistical methods which might enable us to get better predictive models but do not help us to understand better the phenomenon itself. Let me clarify this point, which seems fundamental. I hope that, given the very limited statistician I am, I will be pardoned for going out on a limb.

Individual studies seem to prove, in a very detailed and convincing way, the connection between economic determinants and electoral outcomes—to the point of predicting how many extra points in inflation or in unemployment are needed in order to subtract so many points from presidential popularity or incumbent-party vote totals. But when one looks at these case studies in a global way, there is, in fact, very little agreement. Which economic determinant is more important? Are voters more sensitive to their own economic experience or to what they perceive as a national problem? Are their choices more incumbency-oriented or policy-oriented? Do economic determinants have a more direct influence on popularity ratings or on electoral outcomes? In presidential elections or in congressional elections? Are aggregate data or survey data more adequate? There is no study that does not contradict, at least in part, some preceding study. As Kiewiet (1983, p. 125) put it: "For someone looking for simple yes–no answers, the results of this intensive examination of these questions are probably not very satisfying; indeed, the voting analysts have generated at least some evidence in support of both the personal experiences and national assessments versions of both the incumbency-oriented and policy-oriented hypotheses." Indeed, this somewhat pessimistic evaluation of the research literature might be extended to the whole range of questions just enumerated. And the problem seems to be, granted the state of the art, whether one can go further than the "broad patterns" that, Kiewiet felt, "have repeatedly emerged."

We now know there is some kind of relationship between some kinds of economic determinants and some kind of electoral outcomes — an achievement that should be neither ignored nor downgraded. But we still know very little about which economic factor influences which category of voters, how and with which effect on which electoral outcome. Analysts in the field seem to look for ever more sophisticated statistical methods, ever better model specification, ever more convincing corrections for autocorrelation, collinearity, or the time lag, and ever firmer statistical significance. But that methodological rigor seems to be less interested in the explanatory value of models than in their predictive value. It is, of course, a question of priority. Mine is to understand the nature and the rationality of the established relationship. I have a feeling that, at the present stage, too much intellectual energy is devoted to the bettering of the statistical tools, at the expense of understanding the phenomenon.

The basic problem is this: Are we first and foremost statisticians or political scientists? Some electoral studies are much more "open" than others both in their methodology and in their use of available data. In the United States, the Chicago school, for instance, borrowed from the historical and sociological disciplines, looked at different levels of aggregate data, used cartography, charts and graphs, and was particularly strong in using comparative methods. In my opinion, Gosnell's *Why Europe Votes* (1930) and Key's *Southern Politics* (1949) remain superb and unparalleled pieces of research because they did not lose themselves in too narrow an outlook (methodologically, but also in looking at the broader picture). In the same way, Siegfried's *Tableau de la France de l'Ouest* (1913) and Bois's *Les Paysans de l'Ouest* (1960) remain among the best explanations of French electoral behavior.

At present there are, of course, students of American elections who maintain this tradition. I would like to show why, in my opinion, they have been able to go further in the analysis of the phenomenon they were tackling, and I will borrow an example from Page and Brody (1972). In 1968, nearly half the Americans questioned in a survey spontaneously mentioned Vietnam as the most important problem confronting the nation (Page and Brody, 1972, p. 382). Most of those who cited Vietnam said they were "extremely" concerned about the problem. Yet, the voters did not use the 1968 elections as a referendum on Vietnam. The problem Page and Brody (1972, p. 382) tried to tackle is as follows: Why did such a potent issue have so little effect on voting? In the tradition of the "responsible electorate," they were not satisfied with this "illogical electorate." They proceeded to demonstrate through a study both of the electorate's opinions (in a survey) and the candidates' positions (in statements) that there was a voter rationality. That conclusion shows the following:

> In 1968, the conventional wisdom about American electoral politics remained true; policy preferences had little effect on the major-party vote. The reason for this slight impact of a great issue lay in voters' perceptions of where the candidates stood on Vietnam. Most people saw little or no difference between Nixon's position and Humphrey's. Further, those who saw a difference did not have firmly grounded perceptions, but tended to imagine the candidates as standing wherever they wanted them to stand.
>
> The widespread failure to see any difference between the candidates, and general confusion over where they stood, did not result from inability of the public to perceive correctly. . . .
>
> In fact, those who saw little difference between Nixon and Humphrey on Vietnam were responding to reality. There was only a slight difference between them, as evidenced by their campaign speeches. Those who misperceived the candidates' positions were given ample opportunity by the candidates' ambiguity. . . .
>
> In this case, at least, the behavior of candidates seems to have inhibited the occurrence of policy voting. . . . Our picture of the ignorant voter may be, as V. O. Key Jr. has suggested, largely a reflection of the choices which he is offered. (Page and Brody, 1972, pp. 994–995).

It may be that it is impossible to proceed along those lines in our subject matter. Yet, there are possibilities if we look a little beyond the tool to the reality. I completely agree with Lewis-Beck (1983) that one has to go to the individual level to understand the impact of economics on the vote. But why stop with these survey data? There is a solid tradition, both in this country (Lane, 1962) and in France (in English, Michelat, and Simon, 1977), that in-depth nondirective interviews, along with survey data and aggregate data, enable us to probe deeper and understand better voters' attitudes. Why not use them on our subject matter? The "cultural" explanation—of which I am far from convinced—might thus be much better evaluated (see Feldman, 1982; Kinder and Kiewiet, 1979; Kinder and Mebane, 1983; Lewis-Beck, 1983).

Some more systematic analysis of the meaning of the variables, whether dependent or independent, seems warranted. Sociologist Schnapper (1982), for instance, has most usefully deciphered what that simple word *unemployment* means, emphasizing the differences both in time and in national perspective. It is as a socially determined experience that she tries to elucidate the relationship between unemployment and politics. We badly need to have the same type of analysis done on other independent variables. Just to give an example, most analysts agree that the most important predictive indicator is real disposable income (RDI) per capita in the year before the election. But I wonder if we get very far in understanding our favored relationship in looking at global figures. After all, the variations in RDI vary considerably among different categories of the population. The *Wall Street Journal* has recently (January 30, 1984) reported that "average pay raises fell to a record low 2.6% for the first year of major labor contracts settled last year." But of the more than 3 million workers concerned, 62% received a pay boost and 38% a pay cut or freeze. Are their reactions to the "good economic news" going to be the same? Are they going to trust the president to the same extent?

A more systematic and differentiated analysis of the dependent variables is just as needed. For instance, what is the exact meaning, for the voter, of the two main parties in the United States? It is already difficult to reconcile that Presidents Eisenhower and Reagan belong to the same party or, for that matter, that Presidents Roosevelt and Carter did also. The reconciliation is even more difficult at the congressional level; what else do Morris Udall (D., Ariz.) and Bill Nichols (D., Ala.) have in common besides a party tag? Their votes show a very liberal Udall closer to his liberal Republican colleague, Edward Boland (R., Mass.) than to conservative Nichols, himself closer to conservative Republican Edwards (R., Ala.). Once more, globalism seems a problem—just as it is one in France when we lump together Communists and Socialists as "the Left". Each time the distinction has been made (Rosa and Amson, 1976; Lafay, 1982), strange things have happened. Counter to Tufte's (1978) hypothesis that a declining economy produces an increase in the votes for opposition parties (a "throw the rascals out" effect), this rationale does not work in Cartesian France. The Communists (Lafay, 1982, p. 699) seemed to be less popular when there was higher unemployment between 1977 and 1981. The logical conclusion is, of course, that Giscard and

Barre should have vastly increased unemployment if they had wanted to destroy once and for all the attractiveness of the PCF!

It is very easy to recommend what should be attempted when one is an outside observer. Yet, concerning the independent variables, one would like to see work done on the variations in political outlook induced by other factors; value of the national currency, budget deficit, trade balance, Dow Jones Industrial Average. The study would be most interesting on a comparative basis. It is striking that the deficit in the United States was not supposed to interest the voters. But the issue has been creeping up in surveys since the beginning of 1984. Is that going to skew the economic-political relationship? Is there a difference in time? Who is to be held responsible? President or Congress? Liberals or conservatives? Republicans or Democrats? Different social classes? That there is class-based voting has been demonstrated by Hibbs and Vasilatos (1982) for Britain: "The regression analyses indicate that variations in the relative sensitivity of occupational classes to macroeconomic configurations are sizeable" (p. 263). Is it similar in France and the United States? Are certain issues typical of one country? Are the French more obsessed with the value of their currency than are Americans? Or does the obsession appear when there is a decline in the currency — in the United States during 1979 through 1980 and in France since the summer of 1982?

Is there also a change in time, a differentiation in expectations with time? For example, the unemployment level passing the 1 million mark was supposed to be unacceptable in France, which at present has 2.5 million unemployed people; Americans today consider remarkably good an inflation rate that would have been outrageous in Eisenhower's years. Thus, do the terms of the equation, perfect for yesterday, work for tomorrow? Of course, a time-lag factor has been introduced in the equations. But is it frozen forever? Is the perception not as important as reality? For instance, in France, before the elections of 1981, the French were convinced that their standard of living was getting lower — even though all the figures showed otherwise. In the United States, the economic recovery started in November 1982. But in early April 1983, it seemed as if the country was still in a recession. By the end of April, this perception had visibly and completely changed. This leads us, of course, to the problem of information on economic matters: how and how well are citizens informed? How do they reach and integrate the information? When does it sink in, both in journalists' heads and their own? Last but not least, there are intermediaries between government and citizens, who aggregate, select, inform, present demands: pressure groups, political parties, the press, etc. How do they influence, weigh on, skew, orient the relationship under study?

Our subject matter seems to have been analyzed and evaluated in purely statistical terms. May a nonstatistical Thomas be allowed to suggest that a wider spectrum of methods and tools buttressed by simpler statistics would allow progress on interpretations—which do not seem the most noticeable strength of the field. I know it well in nonvoting studies. A parallel case might be made for economic determinants. Some kind of relationship has been established. Its effects have been measured. But what it means in political and ideological terms remains very much in limbo.

There remains the basic question, whatever our speciality: How do we perceive ourselves as political scientists? We are all obsessed with political science being as "hard" a science as physics—or at least as economics. As our data are much less flexible, less reproducible, and plainly not as good as in these sciences, we tend to rely on our statistical tools in order to be scientific. I submit those tools are individually much too sophisticated for the quality of our data. At the same time, we do not use the full panoply as completely as our predecessors. Would we not be better off in reversing the trend? Furthermore, some of us believe that to be considered a hard science, political science should emphasize its predictive value rather than its explanatory value. We are entranced by the idea of being as good at prediction as economists; our dream is to be able to say that for each rise of 1.3589% in RDI 3 months before the election, the incumbent party will get 0.5670 extra seats. The track record, though, has not been particularly impressive, either in political science or in economics. Further, and more important, I think it is a misunderstanding of what science is all about. Science is *understanding* phenomena: we prove understanding through reproduction but reproduction-prediction is not the goal. If we select predictive value over explanatory value, we may become the prince's advisor—or his recipe maker, which is fine, but this is not a scientific endeavor. And science will thus be poorer, scientific progress hampered.

REFERENCES

Arcelus, F., and Meltzer, A. H. (1975). The effects of aggregate economic variables on congressional elections. *American Political Science Review* 69: 1232-1239.

Bois, P. (1960). *Paysans de l'Ouest*. Le Mans: Vilaire.

Broder, D. S. (1983). Economy downplayed as factor in U.S. voting. *International Herald Tribune,* Sept. 12, 1983.

Crewe, I. (1984). The shocks that could shake our certainties. *Manchester Guardian,* Jan. 13, 1984.

Feldman, S. (1982). Economic self-interest and political behavior, *American Journal of Political Science* 26: 446-466.

Fiorina, M. P. (1978). Economic retrospective voting in American national elections: a micro-analysis. *American Journal of Political Science* 22: 426-443.

Gosnell, H. F. (1930). *Why Europe Votes*. Chicago: Chicago University Press.

Gosnell, H. F., and Coleman, W. G. (1940). Political trends in industrial America: Pennsylvania as an example. *Public Opinion Quarterly* 3: 473–484.

Hibbs, D. A., Jr., and Vasilatos, N. (1982). Economic outcomes and political support for British governments among occupational classes: a dynamic analysis. *American Political Science Review* 76: 259–279.

Kernell, S. (1978). Explaining presidential popularity. *American Political Science Review* 72: 506–522.

Key. V. O., Jr. (1949). *Southern Politics*. New York: Random House.

Key, V. O., Jr. (1964). *Politics, Parties, and Pressure Groups*. New York: Thomas Y. Crowell.

Kiewiet, D. R. (1983). *Macro-Economics and Micro-Politics: the Electoral Effects of Economic Issues*. Chicago and London: University of Chicago Press.

Kinder, D. R., and Kiewiet, D. R. (1979). Economic discontent and political behavior: the role of personal grievances and collective economic judgments in congressional voting. *American Journal of Political Science* 23: 495–527.

Kinder, D. R., and Mebane, W. R. (1983). Politics and economics in everyday life. In K. Monroe (ed.), *The Political Process and Economic Change*. New York: Agathon Press.

Kramer, G. H. (1971). Short-term fluctuations in U.S. voting behavior, 1896–1964. *American Political Science Review* 65: 131–143.

Kramer, G. H. (1983). The ecological fallacy revisited: aggregate – versus individual – level findings on economics and elections, and sociotropic voting. *American Political Science Review* 77: 92–111.

Lafay, J. D. (1978). Une lecture économique de la victoire de la majorité en mars 1978. *Vie et Sciences Economiques,* 51–54.

Lafay, J. D. (1982). Chômage et comportements politiques: Bilan des analyses économiques. *Revue Française de Science Politique,* 692–702.

Lane, R. E. (1962). *Political Ideology*. New York: Free Press.

Lewis-Beck, M. S. (1980). Economic conditions and executive popularity: the French experience. *American Journal of Political Science* 24: 306–323.

Lewis-Beck, M. S. (1983). Economics and the French voter: a micro-analysis. *Public Opinion Quarterly* 47: 347–360.

Lewis-Beck, M. S., and Rice, T. W. (1982). Presidential popularity and presidential vote. *Public Opinion Quarterly* 46: 534–537.

Lipset, S. M. (1983). The congressional candidate. *Journal of Contemporary Studies,* 85–105.

Michelat, G., and Simon, M. (1977). Religion, class, and politics. *Comparative Politics* 9: 159–186.

Mueller, J. E. (1973). *War, Presidents, and Public Opinion*. New York: Wiley.

Nixon, R. M. (1962). *Six Crises*. Garden City, N.Y.: Doubleday.

Ogburn, W. F., and Coombs, L. C. (1940). The economic factor in the Roosevelt elections. *American Political Science Review* 34: 719–736.

Page, B. I., and Brody, R. A. (1972). Policy voting and the electoral process: the Vietnam war issue. *American Political Science Review* 66: 979–995.

Parodi, J. L., and Duhamel, O. (1981). Chronique de l'opinion publique: profil de l'année politique. *Pouvoirs* no. 19: 153–162.

Rosa, J. J., and Amson, D. (1976). Conditions économiques et élections. *Revue Française de Science Politique* 26: 1101–1124.

Rosenstone, S. J. (1983). *Forecasting Presidential Elections.* New Haven: Yale University Press.

Schnapper, D. (1982). Chômage et politique. *Revue Française de Science Politique,* 670–691.

Sigelman, L. (1979). Presidential popularity and presidential elections. *Public Opinion Quarterly* 43: 532–534.

Siegfried, A. (1913). *Tableau Politique de la France de l'Ouest sous la Troisième République.* Paris: A. Colin.

Subileau, F., and Toinet, M. F. (1983). Paris singulier? Les enjeux de la participation. Publication forthcoming.

Subileau, F., and Toinet, M. F. (1984) L'abstentionnisme en France et aux Etats-Unis. Paper presented at the AFSP convention, January, 1984.

Toinet, M. F. (1976). La concurrence électorale imparfaite aux Etats-Unis. *Revue Française de Science Politique* 899–928.

Tufte, E. R. (1978). *Political Control of the Economy.* Princeton: Princeton University Press.

Witt, E. (1983). A model election? *Public Opinion* 5: 46–49.

Author Index

*Names in parentheses are senior authors in "et al." references.